Home Decorating For Dummies®

Cheat Sheet

BUSINESS AND GENERAL REFERENCE BOOK SERIES FROM IDG

Handy Measurements

- Find the overall square footage of your room by multiplying the room's length by its width and squaring it (this is the *area*). You need this handy number for determining if a piece of furniture will fit in the room and for estimating quantities and prices.

- Figure the amount of tile you need by dividing the width of the floor by the width of the tile (horizontal row) and the length of the floor by the height of the tile (vertical row). Buy up to 10 percent more tiles than you need, to allow for breakage and error.

- Determine how many gallons of paint you need in order to paint a ceiling by measuring your floor's length and width, multiplying them, and then squaring the numbers. Divide this number by the spreading rate (see the paint can for this figure).

- Establish how many gallons of paint you need for walls by adding the areas of the ceiling and walls. Divide this figure by the spreading rate (located on the can). If you're going from light to dark, double the amount (for a second coat). If the surface is porous, you may need an additional 25 to 50 percent more paint — ask your store's paint pro for advice.

- Measure the wall from floor to ceiling to determine wall space.

- Average ceilings are about 8 feet high. Tall ceilings range from 10 to 12 feet or more. Low ceilings are anything under 8 feet. Use corrective decorating techniques by using the right color, texture, or pattern to make the most of space.

- Be sure to add walk-around and breathing space between pieces of furniture to avoid clutter. Between chairs and sofas in seating groups, allow about 2 to 5 feet. Add up to a foot around your bed for bed-dressing and sheet changing. Leave 4 to 5 feet of clear walking space for traffic flow through rooms.

Playing with Pattern

- Mix patterns such as checks with florals or large-scaled patterns with small-scaled patterns.

- Not sure when enough is enough? Play it safe! Use three different patterns that contrast in scale but relate in color.

- More is more when you confidently mix up to five patterns. Here's how: Let one large-scaled pattern dominate over one medium-scaled floral and another geometric, and toss in two small-scaled accent patterns (your choice of floral or geometric). Make sure the colors in the large-scaled pattern are repeated in all the others.

- Place pattern everywhere! Put the same pattern on the walls, windows, and furnishings.

Toying with Texture

- Traditional rooms look best in refined, smooth textures.

- Contemporary spaces need more textural interest.

- Feminine rooms need elegant and subtle textures.

- Masculine décor calls for nubby, tweedy, and rugged texture.

- The more neutrally-colored the room, the more important texture becomes.

- Heavy textures "eat" space, so use them only in large or cozy rooms.

Creating with Color

- Paint small spaces in whispers of a cool, light color.

- Cover big spaces in a cozy, warm, confident color.

- Light, cool colors make walls seem to fade away into the distance, making rooms seem spacious.

- Dark, warm colors make walls seem to come closer.

- For the best color schemes, pick neutral or neutralized colors that you'll never grow tired of.

- Distribute colors naturally, with dark colors on the floor, medium colors on the walls, and light colors on the ceiling. Use the law of chromatic distribution:

  - Put neutral colors on large surfaces or objects, such as the floor and sofa.

  - Use stronger shades in a smaller amount on smaller spaces or items, such as a short wall or a chair.

  - Employ the strongest accent color in the smallest spaces and places.

  - Scatter accent color around the room to make an impact.

IDG BOOKS WORLDWIDE

Copyright © 1998 IDG Books Worldwide, Inc. All rights reserved.

Cheat Sheet $2.95 value. Item 5107-8.

For more information about IDG Books, call 1-800-762-2974.

W9-CED-815

...For Dummies: Bestselling Book Series for Beginners

Home Decorating For Dummies®

Cheat Sheet

Decorator's Bag of Tricks

Decorating magic to go! Pack a portable carry-all filled with all the must-haves of a professional decorator:

- **Tool kit, tackle box, bucket, or basket:** Use this for storing your gear. Keep it handy for quick fix-its and instant decorating.

- **Measuring tape:** A 25-foot retractable steel tape works best.

- **Hammer:** Choose one that lets you hammer in nails and pry them up, too. Pick a size that fits comfortably in your hand.

- **Nail kit:** Look for a set that includes a variety of sizes for various jobs. Or assemble your own, including fine nails, long nails, short nails, and finishing nails.

- **Screwdriver set:** Pick a pack that includes several sizes of both standard and Phillips head (cross-shaped head) screwdrivers. Don't use the wrong size or style driver — you'll destroy the screw.

- **Screws:** Choose a variety pack of styles and sizes.

- **Magic Hem:** Iron-on Magic Hem creates seams without sewing. It's available at grocery stores and craft or sewing shops.

- **Pins:** Keep straight pins and safety pins for draping and shaping.

- **Velcro:** This comes in handy for making items such as easy-to-remove slipcovers.

- **Glue gun:** Use this for a variety of decorating and crafts projects.

- **Wire:** Use wire for hanging, fixing, and holding things.

- **Picture hangers:** Use these to make hanging art easier.

- **Plate hangers:** Look for these in different sizes for both small and large plates.

- **Notebook:** Pick one that has unlined sheets (for sketching and note-taking) and is small enough to fit inside your kit.

Quick-Start Decorating

- **Fix your budget!** Spend no more than what you have.

- **Formulate an action plan.** Establish goals. Set priorities. Decide what room or rooms you want finished and in what order. Decorating goes faster when you have a plan.

- **Scope out the job.** Create a floor plan using a computer-aided program or draw one by hand on graph paper.

- **Discover your personal style.** Are you Contemporary or Traditional? Knowing your style eliminates confusion (and wasted time) by steering you toward the best choices.

- **Shop!** Pick stores that stock a large selection for quick delivery or carrying home. Shop by mail. Surf the Internet for information on prices and products from the comfort of your home.

- **Do first things first!** Have all carpentry and wiring performed before you cover your walls and floors. Decorate the ceiling, walls, and floor before you bring in furniture.

- **Buy major pieces of furniture first and accessories last.**

- **Spice up your décor with accessories galore!** Pick pieces with personal meaning.

Furniture Facts

- Furniture is marketed in three distinct price ranges: budget (affordable), moderate, and expensive.

- *To the trade* means that only a decorator or designer can purchase these exclusive home furnishing products.

- *Fully-assembled* (or *pre-assembled*) furniture is ready to use right out of the crate.

- *RTA* (ready-to-assemble) and *KD* (knock down) *furniture* come unassembled in flat boxes and must be put together by the buyer. RTA and KD items cost less than fully-assembled furniture.

- *Case goods* are cabinets, tables, or any piece of furniture that has no upholstery.

- *Upholstered furniture* is any furniture that is covered with upholstery, such as sofas and lounge chairs.

- The manufacturer's brochures and hang-tags provide information on whether furniture is fireproof or fire-retardant.

- Quality furniture features good materials, careful construction techniques, and durable finishes.

Praise For ~~Home Decorating~~ *For Dummies*

"If even thinking about reupholstering a chair or repainting the dining room makes you break out in a cold sweat, *Home Decorating For Dummies* is for you. Pat and Kaye McMillan's smart, sassy book breaks down the barrier of elitism that surrounds most interior-design writing. The coauthors demystify the entire process — from setting a budget to arranging furniture, from establishing a color scheme to picking artwork — to help you achieve professional results without the stress that often plagues decorating projects."

> — Olivia Bell Buehl, author of *Tiles: Choosing, Designing and Living with Ceramic Tile*

"Our homes should be a retreat from the pressures of the outside world, but often we give up because we think good design requires a Ph.D. Thanks to the easy, understandable approach of *Home Decorating For Dummies,* even a novice can learn to achieve comfort with style."

> — Charlyne Varkonyi Schaub, Home & Garden Editor, *Sun Sentinel,* Fort Lauderdale, FL

"Everyone decorates . . . but do you want to do it badly or beautifully? This book gives you a roadmap to a beautiful home so you can develop concepts, understand space and scale, and budget realistically. It then gets to specifics on walls, ceilings, and artwork. Just when you've encountered a huge problem, authors Pat and Kaye McMillan lend you their years of successful experience to demystify the process. A must-have resource for the novice and professional alike."

> — Jane Cornell, author of *Lighting Your Home*

"*Home Decorating For Dummies* will help you design your own magical environment!"

> — Oleg Cassini, Designer

"In *Home Decorating For Dummies,* Pat and Kaye McMillan have produced a work which is well-written and intensely practical. Although their subject can cause anxiety in most of us, this book takes the fear out of producing a pleasingly decorated room without devastating one's budget."

> — Dr. Daniel Ariail, author of *The Carpenter's Apprentice*

TM

References for the Rest of Us!™

BESTSELLING BOOK SERIES FROM IDG

Do you find that traditional reference books are overloaded with technical details and advice you'll never use? Do you postpone important life decisions because you just don't want to deal with them? Then our ...*For Dummies*® business and general reference book series is for you.

...*For Dummies* business and general reference books are written for those frustrated and hard-working souls who know they aren't dumb, but find that the myriad of personal and business issues and the accompanying horror stories make them feel helpless. ...*For Dummies* books use a lighthearted approach, a down-to-earth style, and even cartoons and humorous icons to diffuse fears and build confidence. Lighthearted but not lightweight, these books are perfect survival guides to solve your everyday personal and business problems.

Already, millions of satisfied readers agree. They have made ...*For Dummies* the #1 introductory level computer book series and a best-selling business book series. They have written asking for more. So, if you're looking for the best and easiest way to learn about business and other general reference topics, look to ...*For Dummies* to give you a helping hand.

TM

IDG BOOKS WORLDWIDE

HOME DECORATING FOR DUMMIES®

by Patricia Hart McMillan
and Katharine Kaye McMillan

IDG Books Worldwide, Inc.
An International Data Group Company

Foster City, CA ♦ Chicago, IL ♦ Indianapolis, IN ♦ New York, NY

Home Decorating For Dummies®

Published by
IDG Books Worldwide, Inc.
An International Data Group Company
919 E. Hillsdale Blvd.
Suite 400
Foster City, CA 94404
www.idgbooks.com (IDG Books Worldwide Web site)
www.dummies.com (Dummies Press Web site)

Library of Congress Catalog Card No.: 98-86179

ISBN: 0-7645-5107-8

Printed in the United States of America

10 9 8 7 6 5 4 3 2 1

1E/RU/QY/ZY/IN

Distributed in the United States by IDG Books Worldwide, Inc.

Distributed by Macmillan Canada for Canada; by Transworld Publishers Limited in the United Kingdom; by IDG Norge Books for Norway; by IDG Sweden Books for Sweden; by Woodslane Pty. Ltd. for Australia; by Woodslane (NZ) Ltd. for New Zealand; by Addison Wesley Longman Singapore Pte Ltd. for Singapore, Malaysia, Thailand, Indonesia and Korea; by Norma Comunicaciones S.A. for Colombia; by Intersoft for South Africa; by International Thomson Publishing for Germany, Austria and Switzerland; by Toppan Company Ltd. for Japan; by Distribuidora Cuspide for Argentina; by Livraria Cultura for Brazil; by Ediciencia S.A. for Ecuador; by Ediciones ZETA S.C.R. Ltda. for Peru; by WS Computer Publishing Corporation, Inc., for the Philippines; by Unalis Corporation for Taiwan; by Contemporanea de Ediciones for Venezuela; by Computer Book & Magazine Store for Puerto Rico; by Express Computer Distributors for the Caribbean and West Indies. Authorized Sales Agent: Anthony Rudkin Associates for the Middle East and North Africa.

For general information on IDG Books Worldwide's books in the U.S., please call our Consumer Customer Service department at 800-762-2974. For reseller information, including discounts and premium sales, please call our Reseller Customer Service department at 800-434-3422.

For information on where to purchase IDG Books Worldwide's books outside the U.S., please contact our International Sales department at 650-655-3200 or fax 650-655-3297.

For information on foreign language translations, please contact our Foreign & Subsidiary Rights department at 650-655-3021 or fax 650-655-3281.

For sales inquiries and special prices for bulk quantities, please contact our Sales department at 650-655-3200 or write to the address above.

For information on using IDG Books Worldwide's books in the classroom or for ordering examination copies, please contact our Educational Sales department at 800-434-2086 or fax 317-596-5499.

For press review copies, author interviews, or other publicity information, please contact our Public Relations department at 650-655-3000 or fax 650-655-3299.

For authorization to photocopy items for corporate, personal, or educational use, please contact Copyright Clearance Center, 222 Rosewood Drive, Danvers, MA 01923, or fax 978-750-4470.

is a trademark under exclusive license to IDG Books Worldwide, Inc., from International Data Group, Inc.

IDG
BOOKS
WORLDWIDE

About the Authors

Patricia Hart McMillan is a nationally recognized interior designer, writer, and magazine editor. She has co-authored three definitive books on interior design and taught dozens of college courses and seminars on interior design. Her design work for private clients, designer showcase houses, and corporations has appeared in magazines and books worldwide. She currently contributes feature articles and interior design projects to numerous magazines. Previously, she has held editorial posts at remodeling magazines, newspapers, and other decorating publications, and has been director of a home furnishings public relations firm. She holds a Bachelor of Arts degree in English, with a minor in art history (with an emphasis in architecture), from the State University of New York (New Paltz) and a certificate of interior design from The New York School of Interior Design.

Katharine Kaye McMillan is a writer who contributes to numerous design and decorating magazines and other publications and is co-author with her mother, Patricia Hart McMillan, of other decorating books. She is contributing editor to *Florida Design* and *Design: The Magazine of Luxurious Living*. A graduate of the University of Texas (Austin), she is president of McMillan Associates Public Relations and a novelist.

ABOUT IDG BOOKS WORLDWIDE

Welcome to the world of IDG Books Worldwide.

IDG Books Worldwide, Inc., is a subsidiary of International Data Group, the world's largest publisher of computer-related information and the leading global provider of information services on information technology. IDG was founded more than 25 years ago and now employs more than 8,500 people worldwide. IDG publishes more than 275 computer publications in over 75 countries (see listing below). More than 90 million people read one or more IDG publications each month.

Launched in 1990, IDG Books Worldwide is today the #1 publisher of best-selling computer books in the United States. We are proud to have received eight awards from the Computer Press Association in recognition of editorial excellence and three from *Computer Currents'* First Annual Readers' Choice Awards. Our best-selling *...For Dummies*® series has more than 50 million copies in print with translations in 38 languages. IDG Books Worldwide, through a joint venture with IDG's Hi-Tech Beijing, became the first U.S. publisher to publish a computer book in the People's Republic of China. In record time, IDG Books Worldwide has become the first choice for millions of readers around the world who want to learn how to better manage their businesses.

Our mission is simple: Every one of our books is designed to bring extra value and skill-building instructions to the reader. Our books are written by experts who understand and care about our readers. The knowledge base of our editorial staff comes from years of experience in publishing, education, and journalism — experience we use to produce books for the '90s. In short, we care about books, so we attract the best people. We devote special attention to details such as audience, interior design, use of icons, and illustrations. And because we use an efficient process of authoring, editing, and desktop publishing our books electronically, we can spend more time ensuring superior content and spend less time on the technicalities of making books.

You can count on our commitment to deliver high-quality books at competitive prices on topics you want to read about. At IDG Books Worldwide, we continue in the IDG tradition of delivering quality for more than 25 years. You'll find no better book on a subject than one from IDG Books Worldwide.

John Kilcullen
CEO
IDG Books Worldwide, Inc.

Steven Berkowitz
President and Publisher
IDG Books Worldwide, Inc.

**Eighth Annual
Computer Press
Awards ≥1992**

**Ninth Annual
Computer Press
Awards ≥1993**

**Tenth Annual
Computer Press
Awards ≥1994**

**Eleventh Annual
Computer Press
Awards ≥1995**

IDG Books Worldwide, Inc., is a subsidiary of International Data Group, the world's largest publisher of computer-related information and the leading global provider of information services on information technology. International Data Group publishes over 275 computer publications in over 75 countries. More than 90 million people read one or more International Data Group publications each month. International Data Group's publications include: **ARGENTINA:** Buyer's Guide, Computerworld Argentina, PC World Argentina; **AUSTRALIA:** Australian Macworld, Australian PC World, Australian Reseller News, Computerworld, IT Casebook, Network World, Publish, Webmaster; **AUSTRIA:** Computerwelt Osterreich, Networks Austria, PC Tip Austria; **BANGLADESH:** PC World Bangladesh; **BELARUS:** PC World Belarus; **BELGIUM:** Data News; **BRAZIL:** Annuário de Informática, Computerworld, Connections, Macworld, PC Player, PC World, Publish, Reseller News, Supergamepower; **BULGARIA:** Computerworld Bulgaria, Network World Bulgaria, PC & MacWorld Bulgaria; **CANADA:** CIO Canada, Client/Server World, ComputerWorld Canada, InfoWorld Canada, NetworkWorld Canada, WebWorld; **CHILE:** Computerworld Chile, PC World Chile; **COLOMBIA:** Computerworld Colombia, PC World Colombia; **COSTA RICA:** PC World Centro America; **THE CZECH AND SLOVAK REPUBLICS:** Computerworld Czechoslovakia, Macworld Czech Republic, PC World Czechoslovakia; **DENMARK:** Communications World Danmark, Computerworld Danmark, Macworld Danmark, PC World Danmark, Techworld Danmark; **DOMINICAN REPUBLIC:** PC World Republica Dominicana; **ECUADOR:** PC World Ecuador; **EGYPT:** Computerworld Middle East, PC World Middle East; **EL SALVADOR:** PC World Centro America; **FINLAND:** MikroPC, Tietoverkko, Tietoviikko; **FRANCE:** Distributique, Hebdo, Info PC, Le Monde Informatique, Macworld, Reseaux & Telecoms, WebMaster France; **GERMANY:** Computer Partner, Computerwoche, Computerwoche Extra, Computerwoche FOCUS, Global Online, Macwelt, PC Welt; **GREECE:** Amiga Computing, GamePro Greece, Multimedia World; **GUATEMALA:** PC World Centro America; **HONDURAS:** PC World Centro America; **HONG KONG:** Computerworld Hong Kong, PC World Hong Kong, Publish in Asia; **HUNGARY:** ABCD CD-ROM, Computerworld Szamitastechnika, Internetto online Magazine, PC World Hungary, PC-X Magazin Hungary; **ICELAND:** Tolvuheimur PC World Island; **INDIA:** Information Communications World, Information Systems Computerworld, PC World India, Publish in Asia; **INDONESIA:** InfoKomputer PC World, Komputek Computerworld, Publish in Asia; **IRELAND:** ComputerScope, PC Live!; **ISRAEL:** Macworld Israel, People & Computers/Computerworld; **ITALY:** Computerworld Italia, Macworld Italia, Networking Italia, PC World Italia; **JAPAN:** DTP World, Macworld Japan, Nikkei Personal Computing, OS/2 World Japan, SunWorld Japan, Windows NT World, Windows World Japan; **KENYA:** PC World East African; **KOREA:** Hi-Tech Information, Macworld Korea, PC World Korea; **MACEDONIA:** PC World Macedonia; **MALAYSIA:** Computerworld Malaysia, PC World Malaysia, Publish in Asia; **MALTA:** PC World Malta; **MEXICO:** Computerworld Mexico, PC World Mexico; **MYANMAR:** PC World Myanmar; **NETHERLANDS:** Computer! Totaal, LAN Internetworking Magazine, LAN World Buyers Guide, Macworld Netherlands, Net, WebWereld; **NEW ZEALAND:** Absolute Beginners Guide and Plain & Simple Series, Computer Buyer, Computer Industry Directory, Computerworld New Zealand, MTB, Network World, PC World New Zealand; **NICARAGUA:** PC World Centro America; **NORWAY:** Computerworld Norge, CW Rapport, Datamagasinet, Financial Rapport, Kursguide Norge, Macworld Norge, Multimediaworld Norge, PC World Ekspress Norge, PC World Nettverk, PC World Norge, PC World ProduktGuide Norge; **PAKISTAN:** Computerworld Pakistan; **PANAMA:** PC World Panama; **PEOPLE'S REPUBLIC OF CHINA:** China Computer Users, China Computerworld, China InfoWorld, China Telecom World Weekly, Computer & Communication, Electronic Design China, Electronics Today, Electronics Weekly, Game Software, PC World China, Popular Computer Week, Software Weekly, Software World, Telecom World; **PERU:** Computerworld Peru, PC World Profesional Peru, PC World SoHo Peru; **PHILIPPINES:** Click!, Computerworld Philippines, PC World Philippines, Publish in Asia; **POLAND:** Computerworld Poland, Computerworld Special Report Poland, Cyber, Macworld Poland, Networld Poland, PC World Komputer; **PORTUGAL:** Cerebro/PC World, Computerworld/Correio Informático, Dealer World Portugal, Mac*In/PC*In Portugal, Multimedia World; **PUERTO RICO:** PC World Puerto Rico; **ROMANIA:** Computerworld Romania, PC World Romania, Telecom Romania; **RUSSIA:** Computerworld Russia, Mir PK, Publish, Seti; **SINGAPORE:** Computerworld Singapore, PC World Singapore, Publish in Asia; **SLOVENIA:** Monitor; **SOUTH AFRICA:** Computing SA, Network World SA, Software World SA; **SPAIN:** Communicaciones World España, Computerworld España, Dealer World España, Macworld España, PC World España; **SRI LANKA:** Infolink PC World; **SWEDEN:** CAP&Design, Computer Sweden, Corporate Computing Sweden, Internetworld Sweden, it branschen, Macworld Sweden, MaxiData Sweden, MikroDatorn, Nätverk & Kommunikation, PC World Sweden, PCaktiv, Windows World Sweden; **SWITZERLAND:** Computerworld Schweiz, Macworld Schweiz, PCtip; **TAIWAN:** Computerworld Taiwan, Macworld Taiwan, NEW ViSiON/Publish, PC World Taiwan, Windows World Taiwan; **THAILAND:** Publish in Asia, Thai Computerworld; **TURKEY:** Computerworld Turkiye, Macworld Turkiye, Network World Turkiye, PC World Turkiye; **UKRAINE:** Computerworld Kiev, Multimedia World Ukraine, PC World Ukraine; **UNITED KINGDOM:** Acorn User UK, Amiga Action UK, Amiga Computing UK, Apple Talk UK, Computing, Macworld, Parents and Computers UK, PC Advisor, PC Home, PSX Pro, The WEB; **UNITED STATES:** Cable in the Classroom, CIO Magazine, Computerworld, DOS World, Federal Computer Week, GamePro Magazine, InfoWorld, I-Way, Macworld, Network World, PC Games, PC World, Publish, Video Event, THE WEB Magazine, and WebMaster; online webzines: JavaWorld, NetscapeWorld, and SunWorld Online; **URUGUAY:** InfoWorld Uruguay; **VENEZUELA:** Computerworld Venezuela, PC World Venezuela; and **VIETNAM:** PC World Vietnam. 5/7/98

Dedication

Dedicated with love to:

My aunt, Mayme Ephlin Jones, who, by passing along her *Ladies Home Journal* magazines, encouraged a career; and, to Marie Bianco, a gracious hostess, who gave so lovingly to our wonderful granddaughters, Pippa and Syrie Bianco.

— Patricia Hart McMillan

For the next generation, my nieces and nephew, Pippa, Syrie, and James McMillan Bianco, whose greatest gift to the world is their extraordinary love for everything beautiful.

— Katharine Kaye McMillan

Author's Acknowledgments

Books are not made by authors alone. We wrote the text, but a team — in fact, a small army — created *Home Decorating For Dummies*. We are delighted to be a part of that team. And, while we're proud that our names are on the cover, we're also happy to acknowledge those wonderful people who did their part to create what we all hope is a helpful, useful guide to the art and science of interior decorating.

First, of course, we thank and express our admiration for Holly McGuire, Acquisitons Editor, IDG Books. We are grateful for her faith in us and the book, and for her ability to set the project in motion so adroitly. We appreciate Senior Project Editor Jennifer Ehrlich's rich combination of professionalism and personal warmth. We also enjoyed the generous contributions of Copy Editor Elizabeth Kuball. To all the folks who worked behind the scenes to help ensure this book's existence, thank you.

Liz Kurtzman, whose illustrations enliven and enlighten even the dullest prose, must know that we laughed at and love her drawings!

No decorating book is a success without interesting pictures and our heartfelt thanks goes to the companies and their representatives who supplied so many truly wonderful photographs for this book. Chief among them is Lis King, the talented and dedicated public relations representative for the American and International Designers Network, Blonder, The Hammer & Nail, Rutt Custom Kitchen, and Summitville Tile. Laura Kohler, Carrie Draves, and others in the communications and public relations department of Kohler Interiors Group were most helpful.

Francis L. Giknis, manager of Marketing & Services for Georgia-Pacific Building Products sent us great photographs in record time! Rose Bennett Gilbert, public relations representative of Crossville Tile supplied a perfect photograph and great good humor. Susan Fletcher of the Lou Hammond Company, representatives of Hunter-Douglas; Kay Degenhardt and Kristi King, who represent Imperial Wallcoverings; Sandra Spinatsch of Plasti-Kote; Connie Edwards, CKD, Director of Design for American Woodmark; Denise Ladree of American Olean; Bernhardt's Sandra White, Kasumi of Urbana, with whom we've worked on trends stories from High Point to Paris; Robert Viol of Herman Miller; Lori Krengel and Jim Krengel, ASID, CKD, CBD, of Kitchens by Krengel; Walter Anderson of the Resilient Floor Covering Institute; Donna Luzzo and Rhonda Moritz of the National Kitchen & Bath Association (NKBA); Rudy Santos, CKD, RoSan Custom Kitchens & Baths and RoSan Imports; Ilene Miller of Robern; Lynne Forrest of Century Furniture; Michelle Riekens, Terri Brunson, and Chris O'Neill of Focal Point Products; Harriet Schoenthal, public relations counsel to The Hardwood Association and Swain Furniture; Jane Bender, Henredon; Karen McNeill Harris for This End Up and Kingsdown; Lee Cubell of Kingdown; Anne Martin of West Point Stevens; Larissa Myles of L.C. Williams for La-Z-Boy; Cathy Kauffman of Armstrong World Industries; Debra Iannaci of Expert Software; Rudy Porchivina, Porchivina & Assoc. for Brøderbund Software; Frederick Bernard, ITN International for Salon Du Meuble De Paris; and Sonia Schoenstedt, la Compagnie d' Organisation des Salons des Professionals (COSP), for Salon Du Meuble and Tapis De Paris — thanks to all of you for responding so quickly and so kindly!

We are especially grateful to all the photographers who allowed their photographs for manufacturers' publicity efforts to be shown. We credited you when we knew your names; when we did not, please forgive us.

We hope you all share our pride in *Home Decorating For Dummies!*

Publisher's Acknowledgments

We're proud of this book; please register your comments through our IDG Books Worldwide Online Registration Form located at http://my2cents.dummies.com.

Some of the people who helped bring this book to market include the following:

Acquisitions, Development, and Editorial

Senior Project Editor: Jennifer Ehrlich

Acquisitions Editor: Holly McGuire

Copy Editor: Elizabeth Netedu Kuball

Technical Editor: Elaine Petrowski

Editorial Manager: Mary C. Corder

Editorial Assistant: Donna Love

Production

Project Coordinator: Valery Bourke

Layout and Graphics: Lou Boudreau, Linda M. Boyer, J. Tyler Connor, Maridee V. Ennis, Angela F. Hunckler, Brent Savage, Janet Seib, Deirdre Smith

Proofreaders: Christine Berman, Kelli Botta, Michelle Croninger, Nancy Price, Rebecca Senninger, Kathleen Sparrow, Janet M. Withers

Indexer: Sherry Massey

Special Help

Christine Meloy Beck; Colleen Rainsberger

General and Administrative

IDG Books Worldwide, Inc.: John Kilcullen, CEO; Steven Berkowitz, President and Publisher

IDG Books Technology Publishing: Brenda McLaughlin, Senior Vice President and Group Publisher

Dummies Technology Press and Dummies Editorial: Diane Graves Steele, Vice President and Associate Publisher; Mary Bednarek, Director of Acquisitions and Product Development; Kristin A. Cocks, Editorial Director

Dummies Trade Press: Kathleen A. Welton, Vice President and Publisher; Kevin Thornton, Acquisitions Manager

IDG Books Production for Dummies Press: Michael R. Britton, Vice President of Production and Creative Services; Beth Jenkins Roberts, Production Director; Cindy L. Phipps, Manager of Project Coordination, Production Proofreading, and Indexing; Kathie S. Schutte, Supervisor of Page Layout; Shelley Lea, Supervisor of Graphics and Design; Debbie J. Gates, Production Systems Specialist; Robert Springer, Supervisor of Proofreading; Debbie Stailey, Special Projects Coordinator; Tony Augsburger, Supervisor of Reprints and Bluelines

Dummies Packaging and Book Design: Robin Seaman, Creative Director; Jocelyn Kelaita, Product Packaging Coordinator; Kavish + Kavish, Cover Design

◆

The publisher would like to give special thanks to Patrick J. McGovern, without whom this book would not have been possible.

◆

Contents at a Glance

Cartoons at a Glance

By Rich Tennant

page 7

page 41

page 217

page 117

page 263

page 179

page 297

page 81

Fax: 978-546-7747 • E-mail: the5wave@tiac.net

Table of Contents

· ·

Part V: Tackling the Three Tough Rooms: Kitchen, Bath, and Home Office 179

Chapter 17: Creating Your Dream Kitchen 181

Introduction

● ●

Decorating demystified. That's the promise of *Home Decorating For Dummies*. No longer is decorating a task as complicated as brain surgery or as tricky as rocket science. Nor is it an art so intricate that it can only be practiced by a professional. With the help of this book, decorating can now virtually be mastered, or at least *managed,* by all those who dare to care how their homes look and function.

You've probably discovered — either by making expensive mistakes or by suffering from confusion and indecision — that decorating, if done improperly, can yield poor results. You know there is a better way than trial and error. Done properly, decorating can be a rewarding experience. And that's why you bought this book: to figure out how to decorate like a pro using tried-and-true techniques and creating your own decorating magic. Decorating is both a science and an art that can be taught to almost anyone. At your fingertips, right here in your hands, you have one of the best decorating teachers available today.

The scientific part of home decorating does have its rocket scientist moments — you have to know plenty of technical things — and some of this technical information may sound strange to you. For example, you may wonder why you need to know that the spacing between chairs is a minimum of two feet and a maximum of five feet. (Two to five feet is the most comfortable conversational distance.) Home decorating also has its brain surgery moments. Some tasks may be too difficult to perform without some expertise — expertise you can either hire someone else to do or learn more about and do yourself.

The artistic part of home decorating deals with style, taste, and personal convenience. What is your personal style? How do you achieve it? When should you consult a professional? When can you go it alone? Happily, you can rely on us and our combined years of teaching, training, and writing about design and decorating. *Home Decorating For Dummies* is the distillation of college courses, seminars, and years of actual design practice for corporate and private clients, including legendary fashion designer Oleg Cassini.

Who Needs to Read This Book?

Having trouble finding your own personal style? Finding it difficult to mix and match colors and patterns? Struggling to simply group your family photos? If you want a house that truly feels like a home but are unsure how to achieve it, *Home Decorating For Dummies* is for you! Face it: Comfort, convenience, and good looks matter. Attitude, advice, and encouragement is what we offer. In this book, we guide you in developing your attitude toward your house while teaching you valuable facts about home decorating that will encourage you to make beautiful decisions and spend money wisely. If you're reading this book, you're no dummy!

- **First-time home (or apartment) buyers (or renters).** You have a whole new place to decorate. Where do you start? How do you budget? How do you keep your sanity? This book has the answers.

- **Upgraders from college-dorm-room-dweller to Real World person.** You're on the cusp between Baby Boomer and Generation X, going from dorm-world to real world. Suddenly you realize, "Hey, I'm an adult! I don't want to sit on milk cartons the rest of my life!" You need information on buying furniture, knowing your style, and accessorizing with art and objects.

- **New home buyers.** You've moved from your starter home into a bigger home. Maybe you've even moved to a whole new region of the country. You need to know how to make your old furniture more appealing in a new setting, how to add additional needed furnishings, and how to make your style seem fresh and right for your new locale, especially if you've made a major move. Perhaps you've traded a large living room for a small one that you'd like to look larger or vice versa.

- **Newly blended families.** He has furniture, she has furniture. Can it all work together harmoniously? Meshing two personal styles into one calls for decorating magic. What clever color scheme can unite the two? What should be put where? What new pieces will make old pieces work better? Decorating can save this household from stylistic splits. First-time newlyweds and those marrying for the second time around sometimes face the fact that it's more difficult to merge furniture than families. The answers to these questions are all in this book.

- **And all the rest of us who simply have an interest in decorating.** This book is for anyone who wants to know how to make a small room look larger or an oddly shaped room appear less so, or turn an ugly room pretty through the power of decorating alchemy. Great decorating can not only result in a smart-looking residence but a smart-functioning one, too.

One more point: This book is for anyone who wants to develop his or her imagination. How do designers and decorators get wonderful ideas? From thin air? Not quite. The answer is, from their imaginations, which have been developed through education and experience. A surprise here and there makes a room uniquely yours. Don't forget: Imagination counts.

How to Use This Book

You don't need to read *Home Decorating For Dummies* thoroughly. Instead, we suggest that you flip through the book and find the topic that intrigues you most (or gives you the most headaches) and skim those sections first. If, on the other hand, you're on a mission to tackle a certain project, check out the Table of Contents or Index and go straight to the relevant section. Then put the book down until you need it again.

If you want to glean every bit of information that you can about the topic of home decorating, feel free to read the book from cover to cover. It's laid out in a series of logical steps and filled with fun tips designed to give you a basic foundation of understanding. Feel free to take your time exploring, reflecting, and educating yourself about a vitally important subject — your personal taste.

However you decide to use this book, read actively, using a highlighter and pen or pencil to take notes in the margins. Dog-ear the pages. Write down information, ideas, and questions. (You may have so many brainwaves that you'll need to start a file folder and notebook.) Your copy of *Home Decorating For Dummies* is your personal reference to your home, filled with invaluable tidbits of information. Take the book (and your files) with you when you shop for home furnishing items. You'll find yourself referring to it frequently for measurements, concepts, and good advice.

How This Book Is Organized

Home Decorating For Dummies is divided into eight parts. The goal of this book is to get you up and decorating with confidence in record speed. The knowledge you gain along the way will enable you to make the best possible decorating decisions. If, like the average homeowner, you only decorate every 15 years or so, you may be living with what you buy today well into the 21st century.

Part I: Basic Planning

Before you develop your vision of a happy home, you need to come up with a budget. Chapter 1 contains all the methods of structuring a budget using the time-honored pencil and paper or your computer. We also include information on when and why it pays to hire a professional designer or decorator and how to work effectively with a professional. Chapter 2 covers scoping out the job, planning for function, analyzing space, balancing architectural features and furniture, drawing floor plans, creating graphs, using computer design software, and planning for physical or mental challenges. Chapter 3 deals with design concepts (including size, scale, and proportion), harmony and unity, variety and contrast, balance, rhythm, and ornamentation.

Part II: Creating Surface Interest

Surfaces are everywhere. What do you do with huge expanses of space? Or with little swaths of space? Chapter 4 covers color schemes, how color affects feelings, and how it affects a room visually. Chapter 5 deals with how pattern affects the way we see a room, how pattern provides interest and relief, the different kinds of patterns and the settings in which they should be used, and how to mix and match patterns for the best effect. Chapter 6 examines how texture adds mood to a room, how to add texture to walls, floors, and ceilings, and how to mix textures to maximize good looks and comfort. Chapter 7 provides information on how to solve common decorating problems.

Part III: Style and Substance

Understanding different decorating styles can help you develop your own personal style. Chapters 8 and 9 cover Historic and Contemporary styles. In Chapter 10 you figure out your own personal style. And Chapter 11 provides all the information you need on finding the right furniture to correspond with your style.

Part IV: Creating Backgrounds

Walls, floors, ceilings, and windows form the background of any room, and lighting makes it possible for the room to function and adds ambience. Just what do you do to make the most of these monolithic surfaces? Chapter 12 explains painting and decorative painting; the use of wallpaper, wall coverings, and fabrics; stenciling; molding; mirroring; and paneling — plus tricks with color that reshape walls. Chapter 13 has the lowdown on flooring and floor coverings from wall-to-wall carpeting to wood, stone, and ceramic, plus tricks with color and pattern that reshape floors. Chapter 14 shows you how to add zest to your ceilings with color, pattern, texture, and materials. Chapter 15 points you to methods that help you control light and add pizzazz to your windows. In Chapter 16, we give you advice on how to create mood and ambience with creative lighting that adds a special glow to any room.

Part V: Tackling the Three Tough Rooms: Kitchens, Baths, and Home Offices

Take the ball and run with it! You need lots of know-how to effectively create the three tough rooms: kitchen, bath, and home office. Chapter 17 includes information on how to put function first without sacrificing style in your kitchen. Chapter 18 includes planning for function, bath planning rules, and more. Chapter 19 takes the guesswork out of creating a workable home office. Here we provide the skinny on furnishings (choosing them and placing them), equipment, walls, floors, and other functional surfaces.

Part VI: Fixing Up the Four Easy Rooms: Bedrooms, Living Rooms, Dining Rooms, and Bonus Areas

This part tells you what you need to know to create the perfect easy living areas of the bedroom, living room, family room, and other lively places. Chapter 20 covers outfitting bedrooms for function, fun, and style for grown-ups, kids, and guests. Chapter 21 offers decorating advice for creating a liveable living room with style and personality. Chapter 22 reveals how to create the perfect dining room. Chapter 23 tells you what decorating tips will make your bonus places and spaces, such as entryways, attics, basements, porches, balconies, and lofts, functional and attractive. Each chapter includes tips on buying key pieces of furniture — beds, sofas, tables, and more.

Part VII: Embellishments: Accessorizing with Art and Other Stuff

Get in touch with your artsy side in this part on art and other stuff. In Chapter 24 we not only give you suggestions on what types of art to buy and use, but we also give tips on how and where to place it. Chapter 25 tells you more than you ever wanted to know about using (and not abusing) those all-important accessories.

Part VIII: The Part of Tens

Aahh . . . now comes the part of the book that includes power punches of quick ideas for decorating your home. The Part of Tens discusses the topics of updating an old lamp and finding ten great ways to make old furnishings work in a new setting.

Icons Used in This Book

As you work your way around this book, you'll notice little pictures in the margins. Lovingly referred to as *icons,* these little pictures tell you something about the paragraph that they sit next to. Pay special attention to the information next to these guys:

This icon flags decorating tips from designers and decorators — tips you don't want to overlook.

This nerdy guy alerts you to technological information that you may want to skip.

This symbol alerts you to any dangers or pitfalls that may blow your decorating scheme or budget.

When you see this icon, sit up and take note; this is important information you need to remember.

This icon marks very cool and tasteful ideas that you can use without taking out a second mortgage on your house. Your billfold will thank you for checking out these paragraphs.

Watch out for these guys; you find them next to ideas on how to create a little decorating sleight-of-hand. Baseboards a bit crooked? This icon may lead you to a decorating solution.

Don't bother reinventing the wheel. You can always rely on these sure-fire decorating solutions.

Why work harder than you have to? Take advantage of these shortcuts to success.

Where to Go from Here

What do you do after you're armed with *Home Decorating For Dummies?* Go shopping, of course! Pick up samples and swatches. Read decorating magazines if you want even more hot trends, tips, and information. Get on the Internet and chat about decorating! Pick up brochures, books, and other sources of information. The possibilities are endless. Still here? Go!

Part I
Basic Planning

The 5th Wave   By Rich Tennant

"Well, it _does_ make the room look larger."

In this part . . .

Before you can begin decorating — or redecorating — your home, you have to consider a few of the practicalities. How much money do you have to work with? How big are the rooms you want to focus on? And what exactly is "design"? The chapters in this part guide you through the preliminaries to home decorating and get you ready for the fun stuff!

Chapter 1

Budget Planning

• •

• •

*B*efore you can do any redecorating, you have to know how much money you can spend. In this chapter, we help you come up with a budget that will guide all of your decorating projects. We walk you through the process of listing your priorities — and help you figure out which projects can be put off until later. We also show you ways that you can achieve the look you want for less money by doing a little bit of research and comparing costs. Finally, we show you how you can find a professional designer to help you through the process — without spending your entire budget on her paycheck.

Go Figure!

When you start thinking about decorating a home — whether you're starting from scratch or are just updating what you already have — you may not be sure how much money you'll need. Some experts suggest that furnishing your very first home, from top to bottom, should cost no more than one-third the cost of the house. Another guideline says that you should budget about $10,000 per room, especially if you're buying major appliances, electronic equipment, and other big-ticket items. With every home you buy after your first, you'll probably need to budget less than a third of the cost of the house, because you'll already have a base of furnishings and accessories. These figures may sound high — and they are — but careful planning and savvy shopping can help you spend less than these accepted norms.

The budgeting process

Budgeting is a two-phase process. First, you have to figure out how much money you have to work with. No matter what figure the experts say is the bare minimum, only *you* can determine what you have — and what you can do with what you have. After you decide how much you can comfortably spend, consider that amount your *total* decorating budget. Plan accordingly, deciding how, when, where, and for what you will spend that money. Sounds simple enough, right?

Actually, planning a budget should be a simple cut-and-dried process. But, problems can easily arise. So, when you sit down with paper and pencil (or spreadsheet program and mouse!) to figure out your budget, keep the following suggestions in mind:

- ✔ **Be honest — with yourself and with your decorator (if you decide to use one) — about how much or how little you can spend.** Don't be embarrassed to tell a fancy drapery maker that you can't afford the layered look with elaborate padded valances. But even the truly wealthy have fixed budgets, and you're always better off spending within your means.

- ✔ **Be realistic about your goals.** Assess your decorating project as you would any business deal. If you can't make a silk purse out of what will always be a sow's ear, decorate modestly for short-term occupancy while you save for a house that's worthy of your investment of time and money. Even if your house is simply in need of refurbishing, consider redecorating in manageable phases so your budget isn't crunched.

- ✔ **Think about where and when you're going to spend the money you have.** You don't have to shop at the most expensive stores in town. Even top designers around the world scour flea markets. Flea market shopping isn't embarrassing — it's the "in" thing to do! Spend some time developing an eye for quality items — the ones that those leading designers are hoping to find before *you* do!

In order to come up with a realistic budget, you need to know what you want to accomplish. How extensive is your vision? The scope of your decorating scheme can range from a total renovation, to retrofitting and remodeling, to simply gilding the lily. If your decorating project calls for modifications, repairs, and replacements, be sure to figure in the cost of labor (unless, of course, you plan to do the work yourself), along with materials and home furnishings purchases, such as appliances, floor covering, or furniture.

This book deals with decorating, which includes embellishing existing surfaces and furnishing existing spaces — basically, working with the architecture that you already have. Some light remodeling projects — such as wallpapering walls — fall within the realm of decorating. But if your plan calls for knocking down old walls, building in new walls, reinventing spaces, or doing any other huge projects, you're actually planning to do what's called *remodeling*. And remodeling requires an entirely separate — and much bigger — budget. For great information on remodeling, be sure to check out *Home Remodeling For Dummies* by Morris and James Carey (IDG Books Worldwide, Inc.).

When you're coming up with your decorating budget, be sure to do the following things:

- **Decide how much you can spend.** This figure may be what you plan to spend all at one time, in one lump sum, or it may be the total costs of redecorating, spread out over time. (If you plan to spread the costs out over a period of time, be sure to note how long you will need to complete the project.) Write that sum on a copy of the Decorating Project Worksheet provided later in this chapter, and stick to it!

- **Research standard retail prices and options.** Don't forget flea markets, consignment shops, estate sales, auctions, Internet ads, and discount stores. Doing some research is the only way you'll discover how much things cost and recognize a bargain when you see it. You'll also see what options exist in your area. All of this information is a priceless reference when it comes time to decide the scope of your project and what you'll actually buy.

Have you ever seen decorating magazine features that show one room that costs tens of thousands of dollars to decorate and a second look-alike room that costs only peanuts, even though they look virtually the same? Keep in mind that you can get a fabulous look and stay within a real-life budget!

Basic considerations

When you begin to set a budget, ask yourself these key questions:

- **Do I own or rent my house?** If you own your house, you're free to make changes to walls and floors that you cannot make to rental properties. Also, when you're dealing with rental property, investing in improvements that you can't take with you when you move isn't wise, because you don't get any of that money back like you do when you sell a house.

If you rent, plan to buy only items you can take with you when you move. For example, buy rugs instead of wall-to-wall carpeting; bookshelves and armoires instead of built-in cabinets; stock window treatments instead of custom-made blinds and curtains. Time- and labor-intensive projects like professionally done faux-painted walls or floors may also be a waste of your resources. (Of course, if you enjoy doing the work yourself, you may find something like faux painting is worth it to you, whether or not the landlord repaints after you leave.)

✔ **How long will I live here?** Spending money for improvements that you'll enjoy over a long period of time makes sense. It usually does not make sense to invest your money in things that you will only use for a short time.

✔ **What's the house that I own worth on the local market?** Be sure not to spend more money on improvements than those improvements will bring in when you decide to sell your house. You can expect to recover about 80 percent of the cost of adding things like new fixtures and appliances, kitchen cabinets, thermal windows, or upgraded flooring (such as wood or ceramic tile), all of which keep your house in good operating condition and provide basic comforts.

✔ **How does my house compare in value to neighboring houses?** Ideally, realtors say, your house should compare favorably with other houses and look as though it belongs in your neighborhood. Your local real estate agency can help you determine which upgrades are a worthwhile, and even necessary, investment. If you own a home that's located in a very competitive area, you need to consider how much of your budget should go toward changes that will affect not only the liveability, but the saleability of your house, regardless of how long you plan to live there. If you think you'll live in the house for five years or more, certain changes like a new floor or wall coverings, improved lighting, and updated kitchens and baths, will make your home both more liveable and more saleable.

Just remember that decorating for resale affects many decorating decisions, especially your color scheme. If you think you'll be selling within a short time, decorate to sell, not to please yourself. If you're planning on putting your home on the market within the next year, the less personal you make your home, the better. A neutral color scheme, for example, is a good bet.

Setting Goals and Establishing Priorities

Setting goals and ordering your priorities speeds up your decision-making and decorating processes. Do your planning in writing. (Complete the Decorating Project Worksheet later in this chapter.) And follow these easy steps:

1. **Put the title of your project at the top of the page.**

   For example, you could write, "Decorate the Living Room in Time for Cindy's Birthday Party."

2. **On the first line, enter the amount of your budget at the far right.**

3. **In one column, make a list of the work that needs to be done (buying and laying new carpeting, selecting and hanging new wallpaper, installing track lighting), and in a second column, enter the estimated costs of these jobs (based on known retail prices).**

4. **Arrange the items you need to do in order of priority.**

   The priority of each item is influenced by two things: the logical sequence (painting the walls, and then recarpeting the floor) and affordability (saving for a big ticket item over time and buying it last).

5. **Review your priorities.**

   Would you be able to buy a less expensive item (such as a look-alike synthetic instead of costly, wool, wall-to-wall carpeting) sooner, in time to celebrate an important family event? If so, you may want to revise your choices and priorities and move forward.

6. **Add project start and finish dates to your Decorating Project Worksheet.**

Researching Costs

As you come up with your budget, first establish the basic needs of each room. List what you want. After you've made your shopping list, check out the prices. Look at catalogs and newspaper advertisements. Visit several retail stores to learn what is available and at what prices. Try to compare apples to apples, and oranges to oranges. In other words, ask questions about materials (wood or laminate) construction (handcrafted or machine-made), finishes (one- or ten-step finish), upholstery fabric grades (generally the more expensive, the better the construction), and other indicators of quality.

Don't neglect flea markets, consignment shops, garage sales, and junk shops. Just be prepared to buy what you find right then and there — if you wait, someone else will snatch it. Pre-owned furniture (even if you need to refinish or reupholster it) can also be a true bargain.

If you want to shop from the comfort of your home, browse Internet Web sites for prices. Many manufacturers and retailers have Web sites where you can not only see products and learn facts but also place orders when the time is right.

The most convenient way to research costs for budget planning is by maintaining a file of catalogs. Catalogs with full descriptions of specifications are invaluable resources, with information on everything from cost and size to materials and options. Great reference catalogs include the classics such as Spiegel, Sears Home Life, IKEA, This End Up Furniture Co., Home Depot, and Ballard's. Collect sales brochures from reputable stores, too. Keep all your materials in a file folder for quick and easy reference.

If you're a direct mail shopper, don't forget to add shipping and delivery costs to your budget! For large pieces of furniture, shipping costs can be significant. But shipping costs can also be reduced by arranging to have your items held and shipped with other orders destined for your city. It pays to investigate the possibility when placing your order!

Cost-Cutting Techniques

If you got a little nervous when we mentioned earlier in this chapter that some folks assume the guideline cost for decorating a room is $10,000, try to relax. You can cut your costs in many easy — and pain-free — ways. Take a look at the following suggestions:

- **Get professional help — free with your purchase, of course.** Professionals have a whole bag of cost-cutting tricks, and most are happy to share them. Most furniture stores have a bona fide interior designer on staff, whose services come free with your purchase. Naturally, the store expects to sell you some of its furniture, but if you've checked out your sources and found a professional who has met your requirements, the store where he or she works is as good a place as any to buy your furniture.

- **Consider leaving windows bare, and save a bundle.** If, however, privacy or light control is a must, choose minimal window treatments. Roller or slim-slat blinds fill the bill. Vinyl blinds cost less than aluminum, although aluminum blinds retain their shape longer.

- **Choose less expensive stock draperies over expensive custom-made ones.** You can always customize stock curtains with trim. Or make your own unlined, shirred-on-the-rod curtains, by creating rod pockets in the wide hems of sheets in appropriate patterns.

- **Don't follow that impulse for instant gratification.** Wait for the special sale, or shop for the right item at the price you can afford. Often the sale date is only a few days away, or you may be only one store away from finding the right piece at the right price!

- **Frame art in stock-size frames and mats.** Custom framing and matting can cost an arm and a leg.

- **Use one paint for walls throughout your house.** Switching paint colors and finishes is more costly. Stick to a good reliable paint brand, but do watch for and ask about special sales events. If using a variety of colors is important, choose stock colors, which in some cases are less than half the cost of custom colors.

- **Have all purchases from one store delivered together.** Stores generally charge for each separate trip.

- ✓ **Shop in unorthodox places for interesting, offbeat, inexpensive accessories.** Consider boating, hardware, farm supply, and other off-the-beaten-path stores — and expect the unexpected.

- ✓ **Allow yourself ample time for shopping over an extended period, which will allow you to take advantage of bargains**. Create your own "buying calendar." Call the stores where you plan to shop, and ask about scheduled sales, which some stores plan as annual special events. Consider buying at special pre-season and/or end-of-season sales.

Working with a Professional Designer

Rich or poor, design-wise or not, everyone works with a budget. Neither needing to work with a budget nor wanting to cut costs precludes working with a professional designer. *Remember:* Some retail stores have professional designers on staff whose creative talents are free with your purchase.

Professional designers work with clients in any number of ways, including the following:

- ✓ On a fee basis (per hour, per day, or per project)

- ✓ For a percentage markup on furnishings (less than the 100 percent markup by retailers), which they buy for you at *wholesale* (usually about one-half the retail price) from a *to-the-trade* (designers only) source

- ✓ In some combination of these two billing methods, negotiable before the project begins and stated in a written, binding contract.

Interior designers, like doctors and architects, most often receive business by word of mouth. You don't have to wait to *hear* about a great designer. You can find one quickly by consulting the telephone directory or call the 800 number provided in the sidebar below.

TIP

Design by committee

Many design-competent people hire an interior designer with the initials A.S.I.D. (American Society of Interior Designers) following the designer's name for several reasons. These professionals have a team of skilled mechanics and craftsmen ready to do demanding, exacting work. A.S.I.D. designers are also great sources of unique furnishings and materials not available to the public. They know how to make the most of very little, so the advice of design professionals saves their clients' time and makes the most of their clients' money. For the names of A.S.I.D. members in your area, call the A.S.I.D. World-Wide Referral at 800-610-2743.

In some cases, you can also contact designers in designer showrooms or design centers. For example, DCOTA (Design Center of The Americas) in Dania, Florida, is just one of many designer showroom centers in the U.S. with a "designer on call" program. This program gives the walk-in public access to designer showrooms, in the company of a professional designer who is authorized by law and prior arrangement to do business there. For many, the thrill of shopping in a "to the trade only" (to professional interior designers only) setting such as this is both entertaining and rewarding. And customers also have the joy of knowing that not everyone on the street will have the same furnishings. For this privilege, you won't need an appointment, but you may need a sizeable budget!

Decorating Project Worksheet

Project:

Start Date: _____ **Finish Date:** _____

ALLOCATED BUDGET (how much money you have to spend) $ _____

Estimated Costs:

Item	*Amount*
Walls	$
Floors	$
Ceilings	$
Windows	$
Lighting	$
Furniture*	$
Accessories*	$
Carpenter	$
Painter	$
Plumber	$
Electrician	$
Paper Hanger	$
Floor Layer	$
Miscellaneous	$

TOTAL ESTIMATED COST (how much it will cost) $ _____

*Make itemized lists of these items on separate pages.

Chapter 2
Space Planning

In This Chapter
▶ Assembling the tools you need to make a floor plan
▶ Measuring your room
▶ Drawing a floor plan
▶ Arranging your furniture on paper
▶ Using a computer to create a floor plan

*W*henever you undertake a decorating job, you need to think about how much space you have to work with. In this chapter, we provide you with the tools that can make creating a floor plan easier. You'll also take measurements and draw the plan. We show you how to arrange furniture on paper, testing out the many different ways you can arrange a room. Finally, we show you how you can use CD-ROMs on your computer to create floor plans. What are you waiting for? Read on!

Preparing a Floor Plan

Before you can begin any decorating job, you need to know how much space you have and what that space can do for you. Drawing a floor plan of the room gives you something concrete to work with — and it lets you experiment with different options before you spend the time and money to actually make those changes. Finally, a floor plan helps you map out how much material — paint or carpeting, for example — you'll need to get the job done.

Poor planning almost always results in poor decorating. For your design to be successful, take the time to plan! Then take your floor plan with you when you shop.

Finding the right tools for creating your plan

Drawing a floor plan, requires the right tools. Before you begin, be sure you have on hand the following items:

- **Binder (or folder):** Use this to hold notes, sketches, and floor plans.

- **Notebook:** A notebook comes in handy for recording measurements and comments.

  Make plenty of notes, because, as you already know, memory isn't always reliable.

- **Sketch pad:** Use this for roughing out ideas or sketching interesting things.

- **Graph paper (with $1/4$-inch markings):** Graph paper comes in handy when you're actually drawing the plan. Be sure to get paper that is the standard $8^1/_2$ x 11 inches or larger.

- **Writing instruments:** Have on hand pencils, erasers, pens and markers (in various colors and widths), and chalk.

  Use chalk to make temporary marks on floors or walls when you're measuring distances longer than your measuring tape.

- **Standard 25-foot retractable steel measuring tape:** Pick a sturdy model with a one-inch-wide blade, like those used by carpenters, because they remain straight when you're measuring long distances. A tape that's too thin will fold and bend, making measuring difficult, especially if you're working alone. Whenever possible, use a *metal* tape for measuring, because a cloth tape stretches and produces inaccurate results.

- **60-inch cloth measuring tape:** Used by seamstresses and tailors for measuring areas that can't be measured as well by a steel measuring tape, you can use this on any curved surface, like the top of a chair.

  When you're measuring, be sure you don't pull the tape, because you'll come up with inaccurate measurements. *Remember:* You're measuring your room, not your mid-section!

- **Clear plastic straightedge or ruler:** Use this for drawing straight lines.

- **French curve:** This plastic or metal template made up of several large and small curves comes in handy for drawing curvy shapes that look "free hand."

- **Three-sided scale ruler calibrated with different scales:** This ruler allows you to draw to a larger or smaller scale, if you decide you want a drawing other than the standard "$1/4$ inch equals 1 foot" scale. If the $1/4$ inch scale suits all your needs, you won't need this ruler.

- **Clear plastic furniture template:** Use this for drawing outlines of furnishings on graph paper. You can also buy furniture templates that consist of punch-out shapes in a kit with graph paper. Use whichever you prefer. You can usually find packages of furniture templates at stationery and office supply stores and sometimes in craft shops.

✔ **Camera:** Snapshots of the room from various angles help you when you're on shopping expeditions.

✔ You can also take a camera on shopping trips to get snapshots of pieces you may buy. (Be sure to get permission from the shop owner, of course.)

Measuring your space

Measuring is a science, which means that anyone can follow the rules and come up with good results. Use a steel measuring tape to take down the room's measurements, and write down the figures as you go along. Rectangular rooms are the easiest to measure, of course. Unusually-configured rooms with odd combinations of walls and features (common in Contemporary homes) are a little more challenging, but definitely doable.

Before you start measuring, make a rough, approximate sketch of the floor plan, on which you can note your measurements as you make them. (Don't worry about getting all the lengths of the walls and placements of the windows perfect — this is just a rough working drawing.) Remember to mark or indicate any openings (such as doors, windows, fireplaces, niches, or built-in bookshelves) and any other irregularities on your sketch. After you take each measurement, note it in the appropriate place on your rough plan, and then when you finish measuring, you'll be ready to create an accurate, scaled drawing.

To accurately measure a room, follow these steps:

1. **Measure along the baseboard the length of one wall, from one corner of the room to another.**

   For accuracy, measure to the nearest $1/4$ inch. Record this number on your rough floor plan and in your notebook.

2. **Measure the remaining walls the same way you measured the first.**

   Most rooms have four walls, but if you're measuring an L-shaped room, you'll have to measure more. Include every wall in your sketch, even and *especially* if you plan to give one part of the L-shaped room different flooring or wall covering.

3. **Measure the doorways and other entries into the room.**

   Be sure to note whether the door opens into or out of the room and indicate the direction (with an arc) on your rough floor plan sketch. Also measure the distances of all openings — doors and open archways — from the ends of the walls so that you can accurately locate these openings on your final plan.

4. **Determine the size of the windows.**

When you're taking your measurements, include the window frame from outside edge to outside edge. Record the measurements for any moldings around the window separately. Gauge the distance from the floor to the bottom of the window frame, from the ceiling to the top of the window molding, and from the window (on each side) to the corner of the wall (or next window or opening).

If you're also taking measurements for window treatments, see Chapter 15 for more information.

5. **Measure any and all architectural features, including fireplaces, brackets, shelves, and any other built-in feature.**

6. **Measure the walls from the floor to the ceiling.**

7. **Measure where the electrical outlets, switches, and other controls are located.**

You may also want to note where heat and air conditioning ducts, radiators, chases (coverings for electric wires and plumbing pipes), and perhaps exposed pipes are located.

Drawing floor plans

After you finish measuring, you're ready to draw your floor plan to scale. Graph paper works perfectly for this job. The standard graph has four squares to an inch, which translates easily to a scale where $1/4$ inch — or one square — equals 1 foot. The following steps guide you through the drawing process:

1. **Lightly pencil in the major areas of the room on your graph paper before firmly committing to hard-to-erase dark lines.**

Be sure to include the irregularities of the room, such as support columns or any other intrusions.

2. **Note on the paper the directional orientation (north, south, east, and west) of the room.**

The quantity and quality of natural light affects a number of decisions you'll make. (For more information, see Chapters 15 and 16.)

3. **Draw the specifics of the room, using a thicker straight line for walls, windows, and fireplaces.**

Note also the inside width of the doors and other room openings so that you'll know for certain if your sofa (or any other large piece of furniture) can fit through the opening, up the stairs, or around a turn in the hallway.

4. **Indicate where all permanent switches, outlets, controls, TV cable, and phone lines are located.**

   These factors all influence furniture placement (see Figure 2-1). Don't make the mistake of putting bookcases in front of the only phone jack in the room, loading up all the shelves, and then discovering that you can't plug in your phone!

5. **Draw the elevations of each wall (see Figure 2-2).**

   The wall elevations are two-dimensional representations that help you figure out art and accessory arrangement or window treatment. Again, remember to mark all the permanent features, such as light switches and so on.

   After you've drawn the elevations of each wall, make several working copies and keep the original in your file, in case you need to make more copies.

Figure 2-1: A floor plan that indicates windows, doors, telephone jacks, and electrical plugs will help you determine the best places for various pieces of furniture.

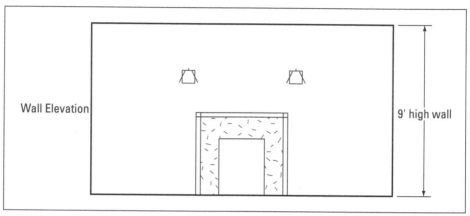

Figure 2-2:
Drawing a simple elevation (or standing wall) will help you place tall pieces of furniture and wall groupings of art and accessories to their best advantage.

Wall Elevation

9' high wall

After you've generated a basic two-dimensional floor and wall plan (see Chapter 12 for more information on walls), note the square footage of the room on your plan. To do this, multiply the room's length by its width. For example: a 10-x-15-foot room is 150 square feet ($10 \times 15 = 150$) in area. If you're measuring an L-shaped room, break the room into as many four-sided sections as necessary, get the square footage of each area, and add these together for the total.

One size does *not* fit all

Careful measuring is a must. Do not make the same mistake one designer made when she asked a friend, who occasionally worked as a carpenter, to measure windows for custom metal mini-blinds. The blinds were supposed to reach the floor so that colored lights could be projected on them. Her friend only measured one window and one wall. After all, didn't all 12 windows look alike, and weren't all 4 walls the same? Who was to know — but careful measuring would have revealed — that from one side of the room to the other, the floor sloped downward more than two feet! The result of negligent non-measuring? The blinds didn't all fit precisely. And, horror of horrors, the light show was a complete bust. Moral of the story: It pays to measure meticulously!

Photocopy or print several copies of your plan. Always keep your original plan in your file and work with the copies. Keep the additional copies in your file to take along on shopping trips. This basic information is handy for estimating how much paint, wall covering, and flooring you'll need. However, before processing your order for carpeting, window treatments, or other non-returnable items that must fit *exactly,* insist that the retailer send a professional to measure.

Analyzing the space

Evaluating your floor plan helps you decide which elements or features can stay as they are, which can be emphasized or downplayed, and which need correction. As you study your floor plan, ask yourself the following questions, then note ideas and options that occur to you (and whether you want to turn to specific chapters of this book for more information):

- ✔ **Is the room a good size?** Deciding the room seems small will guide you in selecting a color scheme to make it look larger (use a light palette) or one that plays up its small, gem-like character (vivid jewel tones).

- ✔ **Do I like the shape of the room?** Or does it need correcting with color tricks to create an illusion of better proportions? (See Chapter 4 for more on color.)

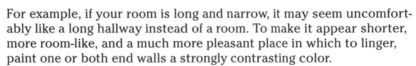

  For example, if your room is long and narrow, it may seem uncomfortably like a long hallway instead of a room. To make it appear shorter, more room-like, and a much more pleasant place in which to linger, paint one or both end walls a strongly contrasting color.

- ✔ **What are the strong features of the room?** Does it have a fireplace or any other interesting feature you can play up as a focal point, or will you need to create one? Realizing that you need to create a focal point, will lead you to consider a number of options — installing a fake fireplace, devising a wall mural with paint or paper, or choosing an important piece of furniture to serve as a focal point.

- ✔ **Is there enough wall space to allow room for your furniture?** If so, count your blessings. If not, consider ways in which to deal with this problem, or note whether you may need professional design help in solving it.

- ✔ **Are the windows located in good places?** Is the view out the window attractive (or does it need camouflaging with draperies or shades)? Is there a good balance of sunlight (or will you need blinds)?

- ✔ **Does this room relate well to others nearby?** Is there easy traffic flow from one room to the next (or will the furniture arrangement need to compensate)?

This general analysis is an important step, because the better you know your room, the better you'll do at decorating!

Putting function first

After you've completed a general analysis of your floor plan, you're ready to determine the best use of that space. Ask yourself the following questions to figure out what you plan to use each room for:

- ✔ **What is the primary function of this room?** Sitting and talking, watching TV, dining, sleeping — all of these activities are clues to the kinds of furniture you'll need and where you should put that furniture after you have it.

- ✔ **What other functions will the room serve?** For more information on the functions of specific rooms, check out the chapters dedicated to those rooms in this book.

- ✔ **How many people normally use the space?** The number of people who use the room is a clear indicator of what kinds of furniture and how much seating you'll need.

- ✔ **What's the maximum number of people who may be using the space?** For example, will you need additional seating, such as folding chairs? If so, where will you store them? What kind of furniture, appliances, and/or equipment do you need?

Putting Furniture in Its Place

Trying to figure out where to put your furniture can be a difficult job. But having a floor plan is a big help. You can arrange your furniture easily — and look at all the different options — by using the plastic or metal templates (to-scale tracing guides for most popular pieces of furniture) or to-scale cardboard cut-out pieces of furniture that you can push and shove around your floor plan. Both templates and cardboard cut-out pieces are available in kit form at most office supply, stationery, and craft shops. Whether you choose a template or cut-outs, you should be able to find all the most common pieces of furniture (sofas, chairs, dining table, beds, and so on) in your kit. If not, you may have to draw a particular item to the same scale as your floor plan, using your scale ruler.

Moving furniture on paper

Pushing furniture around on paper is much easier than moving the real thing. So experiment! Make two or three possible plans and tape them on a wall, where you can see them and weigh the pros and cons of each. If you're still not sure where to begin, take a look at the following suggestions for arranging furniture on paper:

✔ **Find the architectural feature that will serve as your room's focal point.** A fireplace naturally fits this starring role. But other possibilities include a picture window or window wall with a view, or even a super chandelier hanging from an unexpected dome. Arranging important seating groups around such focal points is natural. Then let the rest of your room's arrangement fall logically into place.

✔ **If the room has no focal architectural element, make an important piece of furniture stand out.** Usually, the wall opposite the main entry into the room becomes the *focal wall,* or the wall on which the focal point is located. An antique armoire, a beautiful sofa and its supporting cast of upholstered chairs and art (as shown in Figure 2-3), or perhaps a grand piano are good substitutes. If you don't have any of these pieces of furniture, use a cluster of tall bookshelves. Give them added importance by pulling one or two central units out away from the wall to form a faux breakfront.

✔ **Locate traffic paths on your graph.** Use an arrow to indicate an entrance or pathway. If you've lived in your house for a while, you'll know where these traffic patterns are. Traffic not only must flow through the room (to get from one room to another) but within the room as well, so note those pathways if you can.

Don't place furniture in traffic paths. Traffic should flow logically behind and around a sofa and chairs, for example, not through this conversation area. If this means moving a sofa away from a wall, be brave! Some rooms have problem traffic flow situations that make creating conversation areas almost impossible. But you just need to do some creative thinking to solve these problems. (For some ideas, see Chapter 7.)

Figure 2-3:
A large, important piece of furniture can serve very nicely as the focal point in any room.

✔ **Allow adequate space around individual pieces of furniture and furniture groupings.** How much space should you allocate for furniture? Make sure you allow ample space for opening doors, drawers, cabinets, and pull-out shelves. (The minimum in a kitchen is about 36 inches, to allow pull-out and walk-around space. Less space may be required in a living room or bedroom.) For seating areas, you need a comfortable conversation distance of two to three feet (at a minimum) to ten feet (at a maximum) between people. The farther people are from one another, the more formal; the closer they are to each other, the more intimate. Some furniture pieces simply require breathing space to be properly appreciated. The larger the piece, (for example, a large china cabinet or armoire), the more space it needs.

Keep in mind that furniture templates on graph paper look smaller than furniture does in real life. You may be tempted to start cramming in more and more furniture. You may even think about getting super-large furniture. But don't be deceived! In real life, not only does every piece of furniture need a certain amount of empty space surrounding it, but three-dimensional objects take up a lot of visual space. For example, a fully upholstered sofa with a skirt to the floor stops the eye completely and, therefore, looms larger than a table of the same size, because the base or legs of the table allow you to see through to the space beyond it.

Don't block doorways or passages with sofas and big pieces that psychologically push people away. Your room's first message should be welcoming. And a big sofa blocking the path is hardly a welcome mat!

Evaluating your plan

After your furniture is in place on a floor plan, ask yourself the following questions in order to make sure the plan meets your needs:

✔ Does this plan meet all my requirements for function?

✔ Is the plan flexible? Does the space offer different situations for different times of day and different circumstances?

✔ Does the plan take advantage of the room's good architectural features and correct or disguise the bad ones?

✔ Does this plan have the look and feel that I want?

✔ Will my guests feel welcome in this room?

✔ Will I enjoy living in this room?

If you answer "no" to any of these questions, it's time to go back to the drawing board. If you create only one plan, you may want to experiment with at least one alternative.

This is a discovery exercise. You may be amazed at what you learn about your room, your furniture, and yourself as more and more possibilities reveal themselves. So go ahead — create another plan.

Virtual Planning

With access to a PC and computer programs that make simulating endless options as easy as clicking a mouse, you can remodel and redecorate to your heart's content. You can use your floor plan measurements (see "Measuring your space" earlier in this chapter) to create a three-dimensional cyber version of your room. Virtual planning allows you to see two-dimensional plan views and 3-D realizations that let you "walk around" the room through the computer and see it from almost any angle. Some programs let you easily toggle between the two views for comparison.

Virtual planning also lets you see how changing furniture styles may affect the room's look or how altering flooring and wall covering may change its character. You can change just about everything in the room, from wall coverings and fabrics to art and accessories. You're able to see how the spaces between your chair, sofa, and table look — and figure out if you need more or less. You also get to experiment with hanging art and accessories on your virtual walls, so you won't have to knock real nail holes in your real walls until you're sure they belong there.

You can view the results of your virtual planning exercise on-screen and print them out. Save all these variations for comparison later.

The following list includes some of our favorite CD-ROMs for creating your customized virtual floor plan:

- ✔ 3D Home Interiors by Brøderbund
- ✔ Visual Home 1.0 by Books That Work
- ✔ Planix Home Design Suite by SoftDesk
- ✔ Custom Home by Sierra Home
- ✔ Picture This Home by AutoDesk
- ✔ Complete Home Designer 1.0 by Alpha Software
- ✔ IMSI Floor Plan PLUS 3D

These programs contain thousands of examples of materials, furniture and accessories, windows, doors, and other architectural features. A few of the programs feature Internet download capabilities that let you hook up to a Web site to download new furniture styles, prices, and other information needed for ordering products. Some feature direct links to manufacturers, too. Still others feature additional house plans, landscaping, and complete sets of CAD (computer-aided design) tools.

Not all of these programs are created equally, so read the package information for complete information.

- ✔ Expect to spend from $40 to $60 on the software.
- ✔ Make sure that your computer system meets all the minimum basic requirements.
- ✔ Unless you've worked on CAD or other similar programs, anticipate a learning curve.
- ✔ Many of these programs feature a tutorial to make learning and working with the program easier.

These programs are meant to be easy to use by almost everyone. After you get the hang of it, you'll be "virtually decorating" like a pro!

Chapter 3

Conceptual Designing

● ●

In This Chapter

▶ Defining the elements of design

▶ Defining the specific components of room design

▶ Focusing on focal points

▶ Looking at lines

▶ Sizing up scale and proportion

▶ Harmonizing and unifying

▶ Contrasting and diversifying

● ●

*Y*ou may be in a hurry to start decorating. After all, you just slap some white paint on the walls and drag in some furniture that you like. Right? Right — unless you care about how the whole thing looks, feels, and functions. To get all these elements right, you need to understand both *theory* and *practice*. First you need to understand the *how* and the *why* — known as the *theory* — of any good artistic design. Theory involves five basic elements — line, color, texture, mass, and form. After you understand these, you're ready to tackle the *what* — known as the *practice* — of room design. The fundamental components of *room* or interior design are the concepts of focal point, scale and proportion, harmony and unity, contrast, and variety. In this chapter, we cover these principles, which are the building blocks of good design. And don't worry — reviewing these elements and components is like playing with building blocks!

Defining Design

A design, or a composition, is an orderly arrangement of five basic elements, which we break down into line, color, texture, mass, and form. All artists — whether painters or sculptors, architects or interior decorators — work with these same basic elements. All of these elements must work together to form a unified whole.

A successful room or interior design needs other components, including, for example, contrast. Without sufficient and distinct contrast (which can be subtle), a room can look very static and flat. On the other hand, if a room (your composition) has too much contrast or too much variety, it will look busy and confusing. Your job is to find a happy medium, one that suits you. You do this by developing an eye for good design based on an understanding of basic design elements and the vital room design components discussed in this chapter.

Design elements and components are important for everyone to understand — including the beginner. If you're having trouble figuring out why this information matters to you, take a look at the following reasons:

- ✔ These definitions form a foundation on which you can better build your own personal style.

- ✔ These defined ideas are *variables,* which just means that you use some of each of them in different amounts, under different circumstances, and according to your own personal taste.

- ✔ In a sense, working with these notions is like working with basic cooking ingredients. By varying the amounts of the basic ingredients, you can create different recipes and very different products.

- ✔ Understanding basic design ideas helps to clarify what we intuitively know to be true. And clear thinking along the design process is usually a lot more fun and much less costly than muddling through blindly.

- ✔ If you understand design ideas, you can use them to get back on track when you've wandered off, which happens to all of us at one time or another. Thinking your way out of decorating trouble is less costly in time and money than the trial-and-error purchase method.

The following sections provide all the information you need to know to understand design.

Living with lines

Whether vertical, horizontal, diagonal, or curvy, lines create movement and establish mood. Line can be implied by points that the eye naturally follows or by planes and surfaces that come together. Line can also be denoted by stripes of any thinness or thickness, direction, length, and orientation. Lines used together create various effects, including focal points and a sense of rhythm (discussed later in this chapter), as well as pattern (which is discussed in Chapter 5).

Lines occur in architecture (doors, windows, columns, arches, plank panel-ing, and flooring). They are often real and sometimes perceived. Furniture, patterned wall coverings, and textiles all add lines to a room. Too many lines can make a room look very busy. Too few lines (in a room without pattern) leave a room looking a little empty. After you're aware of line and have some idea of what it should and should not be doing, you'll be better equipped to keep line under control. The following sections explain the different kinds of lines.

Straight lines

Straight lines are strong, masculine, and static. The eye sees very quickly where it is going, and after it is there, it stops. Straight lines come in three forms: vertical, horizontal, and diagonal.

- **Vertical lines** draw the eyes up and down, producing alertness. Vertical lines also suggest stability, dignity, and formality.

  A too-vertical room isn't restful. So if you're faced with this problem, introduce some horizontal lines in window treatments, furniture, and accessories.

- **Horizontal lines** move the eyes from side to side, creating a sense of restfulness. Horizontal lines are less formal and more relaxed and are associated with physical rest (see Figure 3-1).

  A room with too many horizontal lines may put you to sleep! Wake up a too-relaxed room with vertical lines — maybe in the form of striped wallpaper.

- **Diagonal lines** promote rapid movement of the eyes and suggest fast movement in general. Used in excess, diagonal lines can be not just dynamic, but downright disturbing!

  For a restful dining room, avoid dynamic diagonal lines (often found in wallpaper). Use diagonals in entry halls, or wherever you don't want people to linger.

Curvy lines

Curvy lines suggest the organic, the natural, and the feminine. They are also dynamic, creating movement, because the eye must follow them up and down, to the side, and back again. Some curves are very dynamic and others are less dynamic, depending on how simple or complex the curves are. Simple, flowing curves (like those found in the front legs of Queen Anne chairs) are gentle. Tighter, more exaggerated curves are more exciting.

Figure 3-1:
A wide red band, bold border, and swath of checked wall coverings creates strong horizontal lines that give a young boy's bedroom a relaxed, casual look.

Photograph courtesy Blonder Wallcoverings

Considering color

Color's great contribution to interior decorating is its ability to create a mood by sending messages to the human brain that exert an emotional and intellectual effect on the viewer. Color is used to create a wide variety of illusions, and when used to its best advantage, it reinforces your design idea. Color does so much that it deserves — and gets — its own chapter in this book! (For more detailed information, see Chapter 4.)

Feeling the texture

Texture is the way a surface looks and feels to the touch — smooth like nylon or nubby like chenille; fine like silk or coarse like hemp; cool like marble or warm like wood. Texture is another powerful mood maker. Although it's important in all rooms, texture is even more vital when you're using a neutral (almost colorless) color scheme and little or no pattern. (Chapter 6 provides more information on working with texture.)

Visually weighing mass

All objects have mass, or "bulk," which refers to how much space an object occupies — or seems to occupy — and how much weight an object seems to have. Individual objects such as an 80-inch-long sofa and a grand piano have mass. Groupings of objects, such as a love seat and two upholstered chairs, also have mass. (See Figure 3-2.)

Figure 3-2:
The overstuffed sofa and chair create a sense of mass that stands up to the heavy fireplace and generous bookshelves in this handsome living room.

Photograph courtesy La-Z-Boy, Incorporated

Be sure to balance mass in your room. For example, balance one heavy object on one side of the room with an equally heavy object on the opposite side of the room.

Often, our perception of mass is determined not by how much something weighs or how much space it actually takes up, but by how it *appears*. A sofa with exposed legs, for example, seems light and even delicate. The very same sofa with a skirt seems heavier and more masculine. Objects in dark colors take up more visual space and seem heavier than objects of the same size in light colors.

Placing a lot of big, heavy-looking objects together in one end of a room makes that end of the room look as though it's sinking, while the "light" end seems to fly up and away.

Working with form

Form refers to actual shapes in both architecture and furniture that carry a message. For example, we sometimes hear people say that a room's "bones are good," which means that the architectural form is pleasing. Although, to really appreciate the room, you may want to know whether the "bones" refer to tall walls and a high ceiling, which represent elegance; or short walls and a low ceiling that roar rusticity. Furniture form is important and should echo the architecture. For example, tall, straight, slender chairs seem more formal and fit well in elegant surroundings. Short, squat, curvy chairs seem casual and fit in rooms with low ceilings and relaxed, casual moods.

Working with Design Components

Good room design comes from two things. First, understanding the five design elements of any artistic composition. Then, understanding and working with certain basic room design components, like the ones we cover in this section.

Remember to look at a room as though it were an artist's canvas. Doing this will help you analyze what you see and experience. And if adjustment, revision, correction, or amplification of any of these elements seems necessary, critical analysis will guide you through the process. Designing and decorating are areas in which you can and should be critical or even judgmental.

How we perceive

When it comes to decorating, the eyes have it. We experience an interior primarily through sight. Understanding a little about how we not only see, but also *perceive* a room should help sharpen our perceptions and decorating skills. Although seeing sounds simple, due to the slightly different vision that comes to us through each eye and the movement of the head and the body, seeing is a complex process. We don't really see things all at one time either. The eyes move rapidly from point to point, and as our eyes move, we piece together an overall view of a room in our mind's eye.

In addition to relying on sight to experience a room, we add to that all of our other collective experiences of things in the past. Our sense of temperature, touch, smell, and mood are associated with visual clues. After we feel with our hands the smoothness of velvet, for example, we tend to experience a sensation or emotion, too. We see a warm color and we feel warmth, whether the velvet is actually warm or not. All of this perception, on many different levels, becomes complex, because we, as human beings, are complex. An awareness of the involvement of all of your senses is important to a truly satisfying personal design.

Creating a focal point

All rooms, like paintings, contain points and lines. A *point* is simply a location. Two points, however, create a beginning and an end, or a *line*. A cluster of points or lines help to create a strong point of interest that we call a *focal point*.

All compositions, including interior spaces, need a focal point. This occurs architecturally when there is a fireplace, a bay window, or a built-in bookcase. You're fortunate when you have one architectural focal point in a room. If there are two or more, then one element or object in the room should be given special status and all other objects and furnishings should play supporting roles. That is, don't make secondary areas more interesting by adding stronger color and pattern that compete with the focal point.

Fireplaces, as shown in Figure 3-3, are natural focal points in many living rooms. Big enough to be architecturally impressive, fireplaces are a source of warmth and comfort. Fires are visually interesting, and even captivating, so they're natural stars. And with mantels to decorate, they easily steal the show. Drawing seating around the fireplace plays up the fireplace and designates it as the star of the room.

But what if you don't have a fireplace in your living room and you're not keen on artificial ones? Picture windows or any large windows are natural focal points. Beautiful moldings and trims make them even more interesting. And if you have a gorgeous view, the window will really shine. The sofa fits in naturally on the wall opposite the window.

Figure 3-3: In this living room, a fireplace, surrounded by beautiful cabinetry, is a focal point.

Photograph courtesy Rutt Custom Cabinets

Finally, if you're left without either a fireplace or a beautiful window, you still have hope. A large piece of furniture, such as an armoire, wall unit, secretary, or highboy, can fill the bill. A lovely sofa, accented with a high stack of pillows and with a large important painting hanging above it, works very nicely as a focal point in any living room.

There is no "right" or "wrong" object or item to use as a focal point. A focal point just needs to be prominent. But it may be anything that you wish to focus attention on. The choice is up to you.

Just be sure that all other furniture and furnishings help make the focal point stand out.

Balancing size, scale, and proportion

Size is always relative. We tend to relate everything to the size of our own bodies, and we need a certain amount of space around our bodies for psychological and physical comfort. We also compare the size of one object to the size of another. These relative size relationships are important. In interior decoration, absolute size is not important; relative size is what matters.

That word *relative* is important. Remember that interior design and decoration is not a study of individual items, but of relationships. Included with the idea of relative size is *scale,* which is the relationship among objects, human beings, and the space they all occupy. Proper scale just looks right — things look their actual size and look right when people are in the room. When furniture scale is too small, an adult may feel like he or she is in a doll's house. And when furniture is too large for a room, both we and the room seem too small.

In homes with double-height ceilings, choose furniture that's scaled larger and taller than ordinary furniture (shown in Figure 3-4).

Harmonizing without sacrificing variety

Harmony describes how various elements and principles come together to make a total unified look. Every element of the room plays a role. As all these elements come together, they form a composition, which we experience as a whole. This sense of unity is created by elements that relate well together.

Figure 3-4:
A tall-backed sofa relates well to the high ceiling in this garden room.

DECORATING MAGIC

Scaling up to larger rooms

It's not unusual for newer houses to feature entry halls and rooms with two-story-high ceilings that cry out for dramatic, grand furniture and accessories. If you find yourself in such a wonderful predicament, here are five ways to "scale up" existing furniture and furnishings.

✔ Make a low-backed sofa look taller by standing a continuous row of extra-large toss pillows along the inside back.

✔ Hang a big vertical picture above the sofa, and group two rows of several smaller pictures on either side for greater impact.

✔ On a really big wall — such as a two-story-high entry wall — hang a collection of three or four quilts in compatible colors and patterns.

✔ Group or "gang" three to five bookcases as one single, massive unit, and top your arrangement with a super big container of faux or fresh vines. (We have a friend who used a wicker laundry basket, spray-painted shiny black, and filled with dried hydrangeas on top of a similar arrangement.)

✔ Steal a trick from retail store display people who make any piece of furniture — whether a secretary, an armoire, or a china cabinet — look more important by placing it atop a simple platform built of 2-x-4s on edge, topped with $5/8$-inch-thick plywood and covered with carpeting.

Relationships count. If any one general decorating maxim applies, it's "Birds of a feather flock together." But don't have so much concern for unity that you end up overdoing the matching patterns and colors.

If you strive for too much unity, you'll end up with a monotonous room. Variety — in color, texture, pattern, mass, and line — is the spice of any room. The trick is to use them like good medicine — in small doses, or in decorating terms, as *accents.* Contrast of various elements, particularly color and values of color, heightens our perception, but shouldn't bowl us over. Unity and harmony are a complementary pair of terms.

Feeling the rhythm

Repeated visual elements establish a pattern that is described as *rhythm.* Rhythm is necessary to insure that the eye and the mind move about and through the room (although the eye should always return "home" to a strong focal point). Architecturally, rhythm happens in rooms that have a series of columns, arches, doors, openings, niches, or panels. (In the room shown in Figure 3-4, note the repeated bands that create a sense of rhythm in the barrel vault ceiling.) The repetition of the visual element used to create rhythm or movement (in a column, a window, or paneling) may be simple or complicated.

Furniture arrangement can also create a sense of rhythm. Symmetrical arrangements do this very easily, while asymmetrical arrangements have to work a little harder to achieve it. Use accessories throughout a room like punctuation marks. Accessories set up a sense of rhythm as the eye jumps from one group (for example, yellow toss pillows on the sofa and chairs) to another (a group of pictures matted in the same yellow color). The rhythmic pattern can be based on large units or small, and can be far apart or close together, but they should always be in proportion to the room and certainly not be too busy or too static. Practically speaking, if you plan to use an accent color as your strong rhythm device, be sure to spread a little of that color around the entire room. Use a deft — neither heavy nor stingy — hand.

Performing a balancing act

Balance can be achieved three different ways: symmetrically, radially, or asymmetrically (see Chapter 25 for more information). Balance is a sense that everything in a room is placed properly, bringing about a feeling of normalcy and rest. Balanced rooms are comfortable to be in; unbalanced ones, however, are disturbingly off-kilter and out of whack. One side of an unbalanced room will seem heavy, and the other side will seem lightweight.

When should you try to use which type of balance (described in the following sections)? Some rooms have bilateral symmetry due to their architecture. A fireplace flanked by identical windows, for example, would naturally lend itself to a more traditional bilateral symmetrical grouping. Other types of rooms, especially in Contemporary homes, may have irregular shapes and will dictate asymmetrical balancing.

Symmetrical balance is considered formal and traditional, and asymmetrical balance is casual and modern.

Rhythm and balance work together. So if you've got rhythm going — by giving the eye objects to view as it hops about the room — don't leave the viewer hanging in midair. Be sure that people have something to view at an expected "landing spot." In case that advice sounds vague, just glance around your room, noting any voids that need filling with an interesting accessory. Add that accessory, and then look again. Have you given the eye its rhythmic "landing spot"? If so, you've added balance to your room's design. This exercise is easier in a symmetrically arranged room, because in a symmetrically arranged room you can easily see if a necessary object is missing from one spot (and not another). You can still do this in an asymmetrically arranged room — it's just a little more difficult to see. Read on for more information, and check out Chapter 24.

Symmetry

Symmetry is a classical way of achieving a sense of proper relationships. To arrange a room symmetrically, divide the room down the middle by an imaginary line (which we call the *axis*). Repeat everything you use on one side on the other side. When you finish this repetition, you'll have a mirror image. (And you only have to plan one half of the room, and then double your order for furniture and accessories!)

For the model for this type of symmetric balance, look to nature. Humans, most animals, and many other living things in nature are bilaterally symmetrical. When it comes to interior design, if you choose the symmetrical approach to balance, emphasize the center of the room. This technique makes the center of the room the focal point. Then each side of the room is identically visually weighted.

Traditional and Historic settings rely on symmetry because it creates a dignified, stable, and restful feeling.

Radial symmetry

Symmetrical balance, when established around several axes and not just one, is called *radial symmetry*. Radial symmetry centers its balance around a central point, and like a starfish or spokes from the hub of a wheel, objects radiate outward. You can see this arrangement in a traditional entry hall with a large round table in the center of the room. Large, formal, mainly Traditional dining rooms are arranged this way because the arrangement allows for a lot of walk-around space. In this arrangement, the dining table and chairs are in the center of the room and may be "grounded" and established as the room's focal point by a glorious chandelier. Large pieces of serving or storage furniture are balanced symmetrically on each of the room's four walls, leaving open space for traffic around the table. Big garden rooms can also be arranged in this way.

Radial symmetry doesn't happen often in residences, because it demands a lot of open floor space; but it's a big hit in hotel lobbies!

Asymmetry

Unlike either radial or bilateral symmetry, asymmetrical balance calls for a *perceived,* not a *real* relationship of balance. For example, if an imaginary line is drawn down the center of a room, one side does not repeat the other. This is usually due to architectural limitations or demands such as those in modern houses with L-shaped rooms.

You can bring mismatching elements into equilibrium through clever placement and massing, using a variety of design principles. One principle is best illustrated by considering how a seesaw works. A heavier object can be balanced if a lighter object is moved farther away from the balance point.

Balance can also be achieved if more objects are placed to counterweight the heavier ones. This balance idea applies to color, shapes, sizes, and texture. Asymmetrical balance is tricky but probably more common than symmetrical balance. After all, how many identical items do most of us have in our homes? Chances are, not many.

Part II
Creating Surface Interest

In this part . . .

When you decorate your home, what you're really doing is creating surface interest. And you do that by using color, pattern, and texture to give your house the look you want. The chapters in this part cover these three basics of design and show you how you can use each of them in your own home. We also include a chapter on troubleshooting, so you can figure out how to solve some of the decorating problems you may have.

Chapter 4
Color Basics

Color works magic. In the hands of artful users, color creates optical illusions, making small spaces appear larger and large spaces appear smaller. Color affects mood, making cluttered rooms seem serene and dull interiors more dramatic. It influences opinions — sometimes eliciting warm approval, at other times evoking alienating discontent.

Color sells, or prevents sales. Publishers and editors of magazines anguish over the color of their covers in every issue. Retailers know that window-display colors either can attract or repel customers.

Make no mistake: Color has the potential to make or break the atmosphere in your house. In this chapter, we not only define color, but we also explain how color affects people's mood. You will figure out the principles behind a color wheel and discover its practical applications in your own decorating adventures. Finally, you will uncover your personal color style and look at a variety of color schemes to figure out which one works best for you.

Color 101

Color is both an art and a science — it affects emotions and can be measured and defined. As a decorator, everything you need to know about color you probably did *not* learn in kindergarten. The experimentation that children do with prisms and paints is fun, but it doesn't tell you what you need to know about the art and science of color in order to create the environment you want. Although you probably realize that there's more to color than the mega-pack of crayons you had when you were a kid, you may still not know exactly what color is.

Color is every perceived hue between white and black — the two non-colors — from red (the longest wavelength in the light spectrum) to violet (the shortest). When light waves hit an object that is white, all of the waves are reflected back. On the other hand, when light waves hit an object that is black, the object absorbs all the light waves and sends no waves back. In other words, what appears to your eye as white is really the combination of all of the wavelengths of light blended together. And what appears to your eye as black is really the absence of all of these wavelengths. The combination of white and black makes gray — the third neutral.

When you begin to decorate your home, what really matters isn't the true definition of color. Instead, just remember that color can work for you — all you need to do is learn to manipulate it.

Meaning and mood

Color selection can be one of the most enjoyable projects of the decorating experience. Who doesn't love to experience color — the excitement of red, the richness of purple, the exuberance of orange? But color can be confusing, because we experience it in its cultural, aesthetic, and personal contexts, which, when taken together, can feel like a tangled web.

Thanks to Mother Nature, some color laws do exist. But realizing that ideas and opinions about color are a mix of inborn, natural responses and learned, cultural responses is also helpful when choosing which colors to use. These responses vary from place to place, from time to time. In your own home, what color means to you and your family is extremely important. But the opinions of your friends and neighbors undoubtedly carry some weight. Expect your own ideas about color to change as you move, age, and grow aesthetically.

Two universal truths about color can serve as the foundation for all of your color decisions:

- *Warm colors* (those on the red side of the color wheel) communicate warmth and relaxation that's associated with warmth, informality, closeness, and intimacy. They seem to advance toward the viewer. Intense, highly saturated warm or hot colors such as red and orange stimulate and excite.

- *Cool colors* (those on the blue side of the color wheel) connote alertness, formality, coolness, reserve, and emotional distance. They seem to recede away from the viewer. Mildly cool colors soothe; intensely cool or cold colors depress.

Here is a rundown of some common colors. (Check out the color wheel in this book's full-color pages for a visual.)

Black

Traditionally, black represents darkness, despair, sorrow, mourning, formality, and solemnity. The modern idea about black is that it is the epitome of mystery and style. Black is best used in restricted amounts — as accents or accessories — and in rooms that aren't used frequently or for long periods of time. Because black absorbs light, when it is used in large amounts (for example, in a wall covering, as upholstery for a big piece of furniture, or as a finish for large pieces of wood furniture), additional lighting must be used in order to see details.

Because subsconsciously it is still strongly associated with death, black can look unrelentingly serious when used in large amounts.

White

Traditionally, white stands for peace, purity, faith, joy, and cleanliness. White, unlike black, can be used in large amounts without seeming overwhelming. Predominately white color schemes look modern and fresh. White fabrics and objects reflect almost 80 percent of light. Therefore, a white room seems brighter (and larger) than it would if it were decorated in a color. You may need less artificial lighting (and more stain remover!) in a white room than you would need in a colorful room.

Gray

Gray, a non-color, is a somber shade that suggests humility and penance. Gray is a cerebral shade and emphasizes spiritual and intellectual values over sensual ones. Too much gray can look monotonously boring and dull instead of chic. Avoid the possibility by adding extra textural interest. On the positive side, gray is an easy-to-live-with neutral that makes a good backdrop for other appropriate accent hues.

Red

Red stimulates and energizes. The hottest warm hue, red is associated with danger, tension, and excitability. Various reds symbolize passion, anger, warmth, gaiety, martyrdom, and revolution. Red increases desire, excitability, domination, and sexuality by increasing circulation and raising the heart rate. A welcome counterbalance to neutrals, red adds life and sparkle. Some designers are calling very dark shades of red, the newest neutral.

Red should never be used in large quantities in environments where a sense of peace is necessary.

Orange

Orange has some of the effects of red, but to a lesser degree. Orange stands for force of will and is considered an active and competitive color. Widely used in fast food restaurants, orange tends to make people eat fast and leave quickly. Softer oranges are welcoming and pleasing, adding warmth and energy to a neutral or cool decor.

Yellow

Yellow, the subtlest of the warm colors, stimulates and energizes in a positive, non-aggressive way. Yellow conjures feelings of warmth, cheerfulness, and fruitfulness. Traditionally, yellow represents spontaneity and is active, projective, expansive, and aspiring. Yellow increases originality and joviality. Tints based on yellow (such as cream and beige) are safe neutrals. With yellow, use colors nearby on the color wheel, such as oranges and reds or complementary (opposites on the color wheel) violets and blues for balance.

Overuse of yellows, or failure to balance it with more substantial hues, can create a sense of shallowness or a lack of seriousness.

Green

Green suggests hope, restfulness, and calm and is the color of defense and flight. Green connotes elasticity of will and reinforces self-esteem. Green has even been known to slow down heart rate and circulation. Green is a favorite for creating calm and restful balanced color schemes. Used as a counterbalance to hot colors like orange or red, green can add relief. Yellow-greens (bright and light) and blue-greens (cool and jewel-toned) are a great balance for strong red.

Blue

Blue, the coolest of the cool colors, depresses the nervous system and makes the body ready for nodding off to sleep. This hue has come to stand for depth of feeling and is associated with sensitivity, perception, and unification. Navy blue, for example, is the dress color of choice for major blue-chip company executives. Used as an accent, blue can counterbalance warm and warm-neutral color schemes. Teal, a favorite color of the eighties, is popular in darker shades and in its lighter, brighter incarnation.

Blues that are too dark can generate depression or zap all the pep out of a person.

Purple

Violets and purples, the cool colors closest to warm, are associated with justice and royalty, and, interestingly enough, depression and suffering. Considered unsafe or risky colors, violets tend to convey uncertainty and ambiguity. (Greens, also on the borderline between warm and cool, convey just the opposite.) These delicate and difficult shades of purple can add a surprising twist to drab or overheated color schemes.

Relating colors

Color expresses character, establishes mood, and creates a variety of visual effects. Color selection, however, is not as simple as just picking out things you like in colors you like. The successful color scheme is a whole-house scheme — one that provides a sense of harmony throughout.

If you enjoyed only one mood, it would be easy to pick the color to match that mood and use it for all of your decorating needs. But people, life, and decorating are a little more complex. Seldom is one color used alone; instead, colors are used in combinations. A pleasing combination of colors is called a *color scheme.*

Two very easy color schemes work well for small- to medium-sized homes:

- The first, a *monotone scheme,* calls for using the same background color throughout and switching accent colors from room to room for variety. This technique creates the greatest sense of continuity and unity and generally makes a house seem larger.

- The second approach, the *positive/negative color scheme,* gets its name from positive and negative film. In this scheme, one room uses a light background and a dark accent color, and the adjoining room flip-flops, using the dark accent color as the background and the light color as an accent. In this way, the same colors are used (for continuity), but in different amounts (for variety). Easy, huh?

Why are some color combinations not pleasing? Colors affect one another. Any color placed beside another will either enhance or detract from its appearance. When one color detracts from or reduces the importance of another, the scheme is unsatisfactory (and maybe even ugly).

Understanding color relationship theory is a must for home decorating, in order to avoid unsatisfactory color schemes. You need to know — before you pay for and apply it — how the paint you choose for the living room wall will look with the carpet, upholstery, and draperies. What effect will the living room wall color have on the dining room, visible through an open archway? How one shade looks next to another, how hues affect our perception of an object, and how colors look under various lighting conditions can all be predicted by applying color wheel theory (see the upcoming section "Theory in the Round—The Color Wheel" for more information).

Knowing color theory can not only help prevent costly wrong choices, but when a wrong choice is made (and your scheme goes awry), you don't have to waste time blaming the color! Applying color wheel theory will help you analyze how the color was used (or misused), diagnose the error, and correct it without costly hit-or-miss methods.

Do not use a wide variety of color schemes throughout the house, especially if your house has an "open" layout. The colors won't relate and will create an aesthetic jumble and a disturbing mess.

Theory in the Round — The Color Wheel

What is a color wheel? It's a rainbow bent into a circle (look at this book's full-color pages for an example of the color wheel). Although you can perceive hundreds of thousands of colors, a typical color wheel has the primaries (red, yellow, and blue) evenly spaced between the secondary colors (orange, green, and violet). Continued mixing of *analogous colors* (colors beside one another on the color wheel) creates *tertiary* (third) and *quaternary* (fourth) colors that usually go by exotic names but can be described more matter-of-factly with other designations.

Working your way around the wheel

The color wheel, a very straightforward arrangement of the spectrum, makes it easy for us to see relationships and describe them. Refer to the color wheel in this book for a visual idea of how colors are naturally arranged. Notice that colors have implied relationships to one another: They are next to each, across from each, at angles to each other, and so on. Color schemes are talked about in terms of where colors are in relationship to other colors on the wheel. (In real life, we'd need to factor in their value and saturation, as well as the finish and the light source.)

- **Analogous colors.** Colors situated next to each other are *analogous* or *alike.* A good example of a pair of analogous colors are red (a primary) and yellow (also a primary). Mixing these two analogous colors in varying proportions creates more analogous colors, which, because they are so closely related, always work well together smoothly in a room.

- **Complementary colors.** Colors placed opposite each other are *complementary.* Red and green are a complementary pair. Every secondary, teritary, and quaternary has a complement. If your color wheel is detailed enough, you'll see instantly how mulberry and citron (both tertiaries) are pairs. So are violet plum and yellow flame (both quarternies). Combining two complements neutralizes the hue and decreases the saturation of the hue, making them seem rich and elegant — great for Traditional rooms.

TECHNICAL STUFF

Color talk

The finish and texture of an object also affect how we see the color as light interacts with it.

✔ *Hue* is another word for the color family name. It's how we recognize and describe a whole category or family of a color. For example, all blues, from baby to navy, are blue (the hue or family name), but may be further modified or described by a word that narrows to an individual name, such as Cornflower Blue, Indigo Blue, and so on.

✔ *Intensity,* sometimes referred to as *chroma,* describes how pure or how saturated the hue is. A high intensity (or high chroma) is a pure or almost pure shade, such as primary red ("or lipstick red"). A low intensity (or low chroma) is a neutralized shade that seems browned.

✔ *Tints* are any hue plus white. For example, red plus white equals pink, a tint of red.

✔ *Tones* or *shades* are any hue plus black. For example, red plus black equals dark red, a tone or shade of true red.

✔ *Temperature* (warm or cool) refers to the way in which colors either seem to come toward you, or advance (these are the warm colors), or to move away from you, or recede (these are the cool colors).

✔ *Value* is what makes shades individual, and is the relative degree of lightness or darkness.

✔ **Warm and cool colors.** Colors also have a temperature — warm or cool. These colors exert physical and psychological effects, according to the experts, that can be relied on for predictable results. For example, a cool, light gray wall will always seem to fade into the distance (nice to know, when you want a wall to fade away instead of loom large), for example. People actually feel warm, cozy, and sometimes peppy in warm temperature rooms (a great way to save on the fuel bills if you live in a cold climate!) and cool, calm, and collected in cool temperature settings.

On one side of the wheel are the warm colors from red to yellow to yellow-green. Warm colors advance and elevate and stimulate our mood. On the other side are the cool colors from green-blue to blue to violet. Cool colors recede (visually), and calm and even depress our mood.

Each warm color has a cool color complement. Combining complements is what creates a low chroma color or neutral, as discussed earlier in this chapter. Neutrals can be either warm or cool depending on which complement dominates. The darker the value, the lower the chroma, and the more difficult it is to see what the original hue was. The lighter the value, the lower the chroma, the easier it is to see what the original hue was. Just keep in mind that all browns (from beige to cappuccino to cocoa) and all grays (from cloud to stone to anthracite) will be either cool or warm.

Green is sometimes said to be a *balanced color,* because it is the closest cool color to warm. Adding yellow would make green warmer, adding blue would make it cooler. To put it another way, green neither seems to come toward you or run away from you; it neither excites us nor depresses us, but it does seem to calm us. Violet, much like green, is also a balanced color and takes on characteristics of coolness depending on the degree of blue. Some of these purpled tints and tones, if they are cool enough, can create an open and floating sense.

✔ **Hues.** Fascinating as it is, hues are complicated, even for professionals. (see the nearby sidebar, "Color talk") In practice, however, the hues (primary and secondary colors) are identified by their initial letter (R = Red, O = Orange, Y = Yellow, G = Green, B = Blue, V = Violet).

Tertiaries and quaternaries are formed by combining primary and secondary colors. BG = Blue-Green, a tertiary. If we added more green, we'd have BGG (Blue Green Green), a quaternary. Continue adding more green, and create BGGG, and so on.

✔ **Tones and shades.** Adding black to the mix of hues will create a tone or shade of that hue. The hue remains the same, but the value (its lightness and darkness) is altered. In the Munsell System, values are ranked from white (0) to black (10), with nine steps of gray in between. Each step has a designated number. Light gray is 1, dark gray is 9. Every hue, no matter how light or how dark, can be compared to this gray scale and a number value assigned. Thus the tint of BGG might be BGG/1, a barely-there wisp of a breezy tropical color; while BGG/9 would be a decidedly bold stroke of seriousness. It's important to observe that changing BGG's value (or any other hue) changes how its character is perceived.

✔ **Chroma.** But wait, we're not finished describing our color completely. Just how saturated is this BGG at the value (let's say 5)? The purer and more saturated, the more maximum the chroma, the higher the number from 1 to 14. Adding orange, the complement of blue, in equal amounts produces a neutral at chroma 1. Not adding any, keeps its chroma or saturation at 14. (Not all colors reach saturation at the same rate, however.)

Using this system prevents any miscommunications from occurring. Despite the fact that colors with names are truly specific (someone had to create them and package them), many people just aren't experienced enough with names or simply don't understand why turquoise is not aqua is not teal. Or why the teal of the '90s is not the same old teal of the '80s. (The '90s teal is lighter in value and higher in saturation.)

Using Basic Color Schemes

There are several basic decorating color schemes that work reliably to produce very satisfactory rooms. Here are the most popular and enduring:

- **One-color neutral.** The Monotone Neutral Color Scheme uses only one single color on everything, including furnishings, accessories, walls, floors, and ceilings. White or beige (low chroma in a very limited range of values) can be very chic and quite contemporary. Make sure that all your whites and beiges are the same (either cool or warm) and that texture adds interest.

  White and beige tend to announce flaws loudly. Architectural imperfections (not to mention dirt and stains) may seem exaggerated when white is used. If a number of imperfections are present (the walls aren't perfectly smooth, for example) pick a deeper value of beige or gray. Choose the best quality materials and properly prepare every surface. These one-color, all-over looks can sometimes be drab, dull, and monotonous.

- **One-color neutral, variation.** The Monochromatic Color Scheme uses one hue, but plays with the *values* and *chroma*. More variety and depth is introduced by the inclusion of softer tints and deeper tones. The drama comes from using three or four values of a single hue. Depending upon the color chosen, the effect can be very subtle or very strong. The simplest way to discover how a color may look in different values is to pick up sample paint strips that show gradations of chroma. On an intensity scale, the particular shades you pick should be distinctly different, probably two to three values apart, so that some sense of a story is created. Key examples are blush, rose, and Bordeaux (all values of red) and cream, camel, and brown (all values of orange). If you're using strong colors — all reds or blues, for example — use this scheme in a small space such as a hallway that is not used for long periods of time, because the colors can create too much of the same emotion and may grow tiring.

- **Three-of-a-kind.** The Analogous Color Scheme uses three colors that lie close to each other on the color wheel. A typical analogous color scheme features one prime color plus two supporting colors (one from either side of the prime color). Red, for example, could be used with a red-violet and a red-orange.

- **Two-colors: opposites attract.** The Complementary Color Scheme combines and contrasts two colors found opposite each other on the color wheel. One is warm, the other is cool. Complementary color schemes build tension, so they use more of one color than the other. Use low chroma versions for best results. Examples of simple complementary schemes are in neutralized shades, such as tan and slate, maroon and hunter green, teal and rose.

✔ **Three-colors: almost opposites.** The Split-Complementary Color Scheme harmonizes one main color with two colors that are adjacent to the complementary hue (but not the direct complement itself). On the color wheel, draw an imaginary line from the one main color to its complement. Then, select for one supporting color the color that is one space to the right of the complement. Select as the second supporting color the color that is one space to the left of the complement.

✔ **Three-colors: three part harmony.** The Triad Color Scheme uses three colors equidistant on the wheel. Start with your main color and draw imaginary lines to colors that are equally spaced from the complement to form a triangle. Examples of triad color schemes are: red, yellow, and blue; and orange, green, and violet.

✔ **Four-part harmony.** The Tetrad Color Scheme ups the ante by featuring four equally spaced hues. Many traditional color schemes are tetrads of low chromas and low values. These four-part harmonies require more skill and experience, so they aren't easy for amateurs to create, but there's no reason why anyone shouldn't experiment. Using coordinated upholstery and patterned fabrics makes the effort easier. Very subdued shades can generate a familiar and traditional feel.

✔ **Neutrals: the modern scheme.** Using neutral (beige, gray, and white) colors alone or together is an easy, very successful color strategy. These color harmonies create a soft backdrop for modern living, adding just enough dynamism and no anxiety-causing tension. They always look polished and well put together.

Spreading color around

How should you go about spreading color around your room? Traditionally, the greater the area to be covered, the more neutral the color should be; the smaller the area, the more saturated the color should be. As the areas reduce in size, the chromatic intensity may be proportionately increased. Figure 4-1 illustrates the differences between the primary, secondary, and tertiary areas of a room.

The main areas or (*primary* areas) of floors, walls, and ceilings should receive neutralized hues ranging in value. The traditional scheme, based on nature, is to make the floor the darkest surface, the walls medium, and the ceiling the lightest (or white). Although this is the most satisfactory arrangement, in some situations (big rooms with high ceilings, for example), you may want to make the ceiling dark to lower it. Or, you may want to keep it all-white to make the most of volume. Make selections of color for the large areas (floor, walls, and ceiling) first.

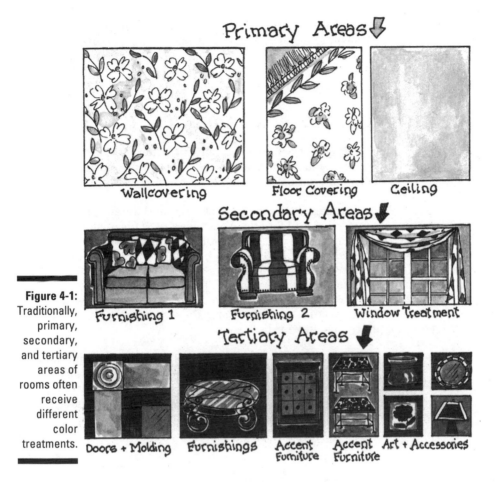

Figure 4-1:
Traditionally, primary, secondary, and tertiary areas of rooms often receive different color treatments.

The second largest or most important areas, (called *secondary* areas)such as area rugs, window treatments, and furnishings, should receive more chromatic intensity. Greater saturation of color, more pattern and more texture can be used on upholstery, window treatments, area rugs, and furnishings. Secondary color should be decidedly stronger in proportion to the primary areas.

The third area (called *tertiary* areas) may have the strongest colors and are often used as accents. Included are art and accessories such as pillows, throws, lamps, vases, and other decorative and small functional objects. Balance the colors around the room so that there are equal distributions of the accent color or colors.

As a color is introduced into these areas of your room, repeat it enough to make a statement. One small whisper of accent color is inaudible, but repeating it turns up the volume. If, for example, the accent color is an apple-green, use it in a series of throw pillows, in lamps, and in other accessories.

Make sure the accent color is in patterns on smaller upholstered pieces, in artwork, or in some other accessory. If you like using lots of patterns that feature your accent color or colors, you may use up to five coordinated fabrics or coverings.

What you see is what you get

Natural and artificial light affect color and affect it differently. When choosing colors and lighting, you need to know that objects do absorb certain wavelengths of light and not others.

Sunlight at different times of the day and year, and at different places on the globe, contains varying combinations of wavelengths. This means that a color appears different under different conditions. If too few of the wavelengths needed to make that color sing are present, you may end up with a drab hue and an unlovely decorating tune. For example, white looks crisp in New England, but dingy in the subtropics. The same pink that says elegant in Bermuda, screams bordello in New Jersey. Sunlight is comprised of different wavelengths, and it may be missing the wavelengths you need to bring out the pretty pink in your bedroom.

To select just the right color for a room, you need to know when and how much sunlight streams into that room. At different times of day, from different directions, sunlight has a different color temperature. Early morning light is warmer; rainy days and late afternoon are bluer. Add halogen light, if your colors need intensification to offset gloomy weather or northern exposures.

Creating a style board

To help craft your color scheme, collect samples and photographs and arrange them on a *style board,* a large sheet of white paper or poster board (see Figure 4-2). This is how professional designers show their schemes to clients because it shows them at a glance how different items are relating.

Collect your color and material swatches from actual samples. Some samples (laminate countertops, paint, and so on) are free. You may have to purchase others. But many sources, such as wallpaper stores, will credit your account when you actually make a purchase. In many other instances, you may have to use brochures, magazine pictures, or even colored slips of paper (available through art or design stores). Having actual carpet, paint, and fabric swatches to place together to form relationships is the best option, but pictures will do in a pinch.

Color corrections

Remember that we said color is a powerful tool? And that when it's used artfully, it can work magic? Here are some of the ways to make the magic work for you:

- To make a room look bigger, use monochromatic, light, cool color schemes to create a receding atmospheric look. Paint all surfaces the same color and match the upholstery to the floor.

- To make a room look cozier, use darker, warm neutrals. Use decorative wall features like *wainscoting* (less than full wall height wood paneling) or paneling as accents. Use contrasting paint for paneling, and either match or contrast the molding.

- To make a ceiling look higher, use white paint or the same color as the walls, and keep floors relatively light.

- To square off a long, rectangular, shotgun room, paint or paper the long narrow wall in light, cool colors to make these walls recede. To make the ends of the room advance, use a dark, warm color on the short walls.

- To narrow a wide room, use deeper, warm neutrals on long walls, and lighter cool tints on shorter walls.

- Black out a high ugly ceiling with black, dark gray, or midnight blue.

Figure 4-2:
Making a
style board
will help
you plan
and shop.

Color no-nos

Everyone experiments with color at one time or another. And those experiments aren't always a success. Here are some no-nos and, more importantly, ways to fix them after you've done them.

✔ **Too much color!** Using more than four, very carefully chosen, colors will result in visual overload. If you're guilty — for example, you've acquired a lot of furniture in different woods or different upholstery — consider painting or refinishing the woods to match and recovering or slipcovering the upholstered pieces.

✔ **Too-strong chromas!** Using far too intense colors can be overwhelming, especially in rooms that must be used for long periods of time. To fix this problem quickly, hang lots of art on walls, cover floors in quieter toned area rugs, put neutral throws on big pieces of furniture.

✔ **Too much contrast!** Using equal or near equal proportions of complementary colors creates displeasing tension. Tip the balance: Make one color dominate the other by increasing its presence in decorative accessories or decorative flourishes. A wallpaper border and wainscoting may help to alter the proportions.

✔ **Too much drabness!** Carried safe color too far, and now you're sorry? Change drab to dramatic by adding a big, important vase or some other accessory in a complementary color or value guaranteed to get attention. The surefire remedy for monotony elsewhere in the room is using accessories in the same complementary color, repeated as often as necessary.

✔ **Too little zing!** Just one monolithic monotone after another? Make this one-note scheme sing a different tune — paint the trim a crisp white or contrasting color. Add emphasis by bringing in a dramatically deeper value. Check to see whether light bulbs available in both warm and cool versions suit you and your color scheme. (If your light seems too cool, switch to warm bulbs and vice versa.)

The larger the sample, the better. Tiny snippets won't let you see enough of a pattern and won't let you get a true idea of how a color may look when it's covering an expanse of wall or floor. *Memo samples* (a yard or more) of upholstery, drapery, and other textiles are available. Also, many stores will let you take home a sample book (just don't cut or rip anything out!). If you're lucky enough to be given generous samples to play with, cut them. For large, primary areas, use large samples. For secondary and accent areas, cut proportionately smaller samples.

In addition to samples, swatches, and photographs, designers use other things to tell their sample board story, including simple floor plans. Others also use three-dimensional representations, called *macquette.* Your decorating software can generate lots of plans and often adds in the color for you. Your plan should ultimately be evaluated under the same lighting conditions that you'll be using. What you see will be what you get — your room should look as good (and probably even better) than your style boards.

Chapter 5

Pattern Basics

● ●

● ●

So, you thought you could live without pattern. Think again. Pattern gives life to dull interiors and revitalizes those that are just a little weary. Pattern is enriching but not necessarily expensive, and best of all, it's plentiful.

In this chapter, we guide you through the basics of pattern. You'll discover how to use patterns in your own home, and how to mix and match different patterns within the same room — a decorating feat many people are afraid of, but which *you* can master with ease. We also give you some ideas for ways to practice with patterns before you go all out and decorate a room. Practicing is sort of like trying on clothes in a store — you'll get a chance to know what you're buying before you plunk down the cash. This chapter gives you everything you need to use patterns with confidence — and shows you the fun behind it!

Understanding Pattern

When you hear the word *pattern,* you probably think of fabrics or wallpaper. Fabrics and wallpaper *are* powerful representatives of pattern, but they aren't the only places where you can find patterns. A pattern emerges whenever an object — even one as small as a pinprick — occurs more than once. The more the object is repeated or appears, the more pronounced the pattern. Patterns occur whether the object is real or implied, like the vertical lines in wood paneling, for example (see Figure 5-1). Those inferred or implied lines create a vertical pattern that offers relief from a plain surface.

Figure 5-1:
A manu-
factured
ceiling with
the look
of wood
planks
creates a
pattern that
adds
interest to
the ceiling.

Photograph courtesy Armstrong World Industries

The lines in wood paneling are so crisp that they often need to be tempered and softened. Floral draperies or upholstery work well and serve as a nice complement to wood paneling. Also consider painting the ceiling the same color as the walls, to keep the pattern under control.

Italian, French, and English architects created pattern by dividing walls into lovely square and rectangular boxes with moldings. These crisp patterns were softened by blurring the molding with gilding or antiquing and filling the insides of the boxes with painted floral bouquets.

While fabrics and wall coverings are the most frequently looked to sources of pattern, you can find and use pattern in a variety of things, including area rugs and carpeting, china and porcelain lamp bases, vases, and plates.

Historic patterns

Although textile designers continually create new patterns, some patterns appear again and again in fabrics, wall coverings, and carpeting. The following are some of the more common patterns, and ones you may want to use in your own home:

- **Flame stitch:** A type of tapestry that looks like flickering flames, flame stitch is often multicolored and very textural. Flame stitch is often seen with 18th century furniture and is somewhat masculine in character.

- **Gingham:** This pattern consists of monochromatic checks (blue and white, red and white, yellow and white, and so on), usually in a woven cotton fabric. Gingham is almost synonymous with Country styles.

- **Herringbone:** This pattern has a diagonal ridge that reverses direction periodically, creating a vertical stripe effect. Some people think it looks like a fish skeleton, which is how it got its name. Herringbone is often seen in wool coats and suits and is often replicated in vinyl wall coverings, especially those intended for commercial interiors. Herringbone also appears in carpeting and is thought of as tailored or masculine in character.

- **Stripes:** Stripes are, obviously, repeated vertical lines, but keep in mind that stripes come in many different varieties, including the following:

  - **Ticking stripes:** Narrow, monochromatic stripes, most often in cotton fabrics used for pillow ticking (hence the name), but a favorite slipcover fabric for Country style rooms.

  - **Rep (or irregular) stripes:** Alternating narrow and wide stripes, often in woven silk fabrics used for upholstering Traditional style chairs.

  - **Roman stripes:** Stripes in alternating bright colors and sometimes of varying widths, found in silk and synthetic fabrics for curtains and upholstery in Traditional style rooms.

  - **Awning stripes:** Big, broad, monochromatic stripes used for awnings, found in upholstery and wall coverings.

  - **Satin stripes:** Alternating plain and satin (shiny) stripes in silk and silk-like synthetic fabrics (and wall coverings), appropriate for Traditional rooms.

- **Tree-of-Life:** An ancient Oriental rendering of a sprawling tree, this pattern is often seen with other plants and animals. Usually large in size, the tree-of-life is often seen in 18th century printed fabrics and wall coverings and seems very much at home in formal and dressy living rooms, dining rooms, and bedrooms.

> ✔ **Trellis:** Garden trellises (narrow strips of wood lath joined either in a square or diamond pattern) are often repeated on fabrics, wall coverings, and area rugs — with and without accompanying flowers and vines. They add a sense of spatial depth, which provides a three-dimensional space-making effect that's very liberating. This pattern is appropriate in any style room.

Contemporary patterns

The first Contemporary home decorating patterns were called *geometrics,* a word used to describe patterns created from basic geometric figures, such as circles, squares, rectangles, triangles, and ovals. This label was an accurate description of the patterns — and a word that sounded modern at the time. Floral patterns were thought of as traditional patterns. But then artists began *stylizing* (rendering in a less than realistic or figurative manner) floral patterns, so some florals were then considered contemporary.

Historic patterns are often made more contemporary by updating the colors used in the pattern. This resulted with area rugs when designers like Manjit Kamdin Anandani of New York City and New Delhi, India, began to introduce current pastels and other popular colors to traditional dhurrie, needlepoint, and chain stitch area rugs.

Historic or traditional fabric and rug patterns also become more contemporary when designs are *edited,* or changed, to become less complex, more economically manufactured, and more widely available. The bottom line is that both modern and updated historic patterns may be described as contemporary.

Pattern Strategies

You probably *only* care whether you're decorating with a particular pattern — historic or contemporary — if you're recreating an authentic historic interior. Otherwise, you may look to certain traditions, but you don't have to follow any rules. The origin or name of the pattern you use doesn't matter, as long as it fits into your overall decorating scheme. The following sections provide ideas and suggestions on ways you can use patterns in your home.

Picking an appropriate pattern

Any pattern can serve as the basis for a foolproof color scheme. A wonderful wallpaper, beautiful bedding, upholstery, area rug, plate, or painting can all be sources of inspiration. But be alert to the possibilities suggested by a sweater, dress, or scarf — sometimes your favorite piece of clothing may have just the color scheme you're looking for. Keep in mind that different rooms require different decorating strategies. The following tips steer you in the right direction:

✔ **Small rooms:** If your room is small to medium in size, choose a pattern with a light background. Use that light background color for the largest areas in the room (the walls and the floor). Repeat the strong dominant hue on upholstery. And reserve the exciting accent color or colors for accessories.

✔ **Large rooms:** In a large room, use the dominant color for large areas such as walls and floor, the contrasting light background color for upholstery, and exciting accent colors for accessories.

Using pattern as background

Pattern can create a highly distinctive background, compensating immeasurably for a lack of architectural features. The following are some general guidelines for using pattern as a background:

✔ **Scale the pattern size to the room size.** Use small patterns in small rooms, medium-sized patterns in medium rooms, and large scale patterns in large rooms.

✔ **Choose the pattern based on the size of the room.**

- **Small rooms:** Choose softly-colored patterns with light backgrounds. Patterns with three-dimensional effects, such as a trellis pattern, ribbon-and-floral stripes, or toile de Jouy (a scenic pattern), make the room seem larger than it is.

- **Medium rooms:** Use stronger colored patterns in mid-sized rooms, but stick to light backgrounds to make the room seem larger rather than smaller. Figure 5-2 illustrates how several coordinated wall coverings with strong patterns on white backgrounds add dramatic impact without making the room look smaller. A patterned area rug and the leopard patterned pillow add to the medley of updated classical motifs and patterns in the wall coverings.

- **Large rooms:** In larger rooms, you can be bold. Choose strong, dramatic patterns with rich, exciting background colors.

✔ **Choose the pattern based on the overall style of the room and the house.**

- **Contemporary or modern rooms:** Choose geometric patterns, including stripes. Avoid floral patterns, unless they're highly stylized and obviously avant-garde.

Photograph courtesy Blonder Wallcoverings

Figure 5-2:
Pattern is
used in a
medium-
sized room
to add
impact
without
making the
room seem
smaller.

- **Traditional rooms:** Look to traditional patterns — those based on historic examples called *documents.* They're easy to find and usually created in current colors. And if you really need authentic (exact) reproductions of wallpapers and fabrics from a certain period, you'll probably be able to find them. Wall covering retailers, manufacturers, and interior designers are good sources of information.

Letting upholstery star

If you have a marvelous piece of furniture — such as a showcase sofa (perhaps a great old antique from Great Aunt Harriet) or wonderfully plump club chairs — put the spotlight on them. Cover these treasures in a fabulous fabric like a glazed chintz, a tremendous tree-of-life crewel pattern, or a woven wool plaid. Then, because every jewel looks best in just the right setting, create a plain background (walls and floors) free of pattern, which will show off that piece of furniture best.

Putting one pattern everywhere

Putting the *same* pattern on the walls and furniture is great fun. And this technique certainly removes the problems of color-matching and pattern-scaling. Wall covering and fabric patterns designed to match or coordinate make this a very easy, efficient way to create a perfectly coordinated room. You can also have fabric treated so that it can be applied to the wall. Ask your wall covering dealer or a local interior designer to recommend a source in your neighborhood.

Even a small room can be covered in the same pattern from head to toe. One of the most delightful rooms we have ever seen had the same strawberry pattern on the walls and furniture. The clever homeowner even had the pattern enlarged and made into a needlepoint rug, which covered almost the entire room!

Spreading pattern around

You can use a traditional strategy and combine a plain background on the walls and floor with patterned furniture. Then spread pattern around the room in the draperies, decorative pillows, Oriental lamps, or an area rug. This technique commonly combines several patterns in one room, which usually calls for clever mixing and matching of fabrics so that they relate (for unity) and contrast (for interest).

Mixing patterns

Mixing patterns is fun, but can definitely be a challenge. The following are some general guidelines that remove some of the guesswork from success-fully mixing patterns. Use this list as a jumping-off point, and experiment with as much creativity as you can muster.

Some of the classic fabric mixes — like the French use of big cotton checks on the backsides of solid velvet-covered chairs — probably happened because the upholsterer ran out of velvet or the client was too stingy to put velvet on the back. Or maybe, as in the case of America's patchwork quilts and their incredible pattern mixes, necessity became the mother of great inventions.

✔ **Limit the number of patterns in a room.** If you're a novice, limit the number of patterns in a given room to three. If you're more familiar with using and mixing patterns, try using as many as five patterns in the same room. (Figure 5-3 illustrates an example of a three-pattern scheme and a five-pattern scheme.)

- ✔ **Practice your scales.** Whether you're using three or five patterns, choose one large dominant pattern for the largest area. Accompany the dominant pattern with medium- and small-scale secondary patterns.

- ✔ **Up the ante.** If you're using as many as five patterns, start with a large-scale dominant pattern. Then choose two medium-scale patterns (one floral, one geometric) in the same colors as the dominant fabric. Finally, choose two small-scale accent patterns (each in either a different pattern or a different accent color found in the dominant pattern).

- ✔ **Think positively — or negatively!** A *positive* printed fabric places dark motifs (such as flowers or geometrics) on a white or light background. A *negative* printed fabric (like a film negative) places light floral or geometric motifs on a dark background. You can follow one of the easiest pattern mixes by using the same pattern in both its positive and negative prints. Mixing and matching diverse positive and negative patterns is only a little more difficult. Just remember to pick one dominant pattern and vary the scales of the others.

  Create a little easy magic by sticking to a monochromatic (one) color scheme, such as cobalt blue and white; rose pink and white; or apple green and white. Or go for real drama — choose black and white!

- ✔ **Play the trim game.** Gain additional unity by using the same trim for your pattern mix. For example, if you're making toss pillows in four different patterns, use the same moss fringe on each.

  Or for both variety and unity, make your own *welting* (a covered cord trim) for pillows or upholstery by covering a rope-like cord (available in fabric and upholstery shops) in one fabric and using it as trim for the companion fabric, and vice versa.

Figure 5-3:
If you want to combine several patterns in one room, consider either a three-pattern scheme or a five-pattern scheme.

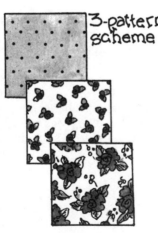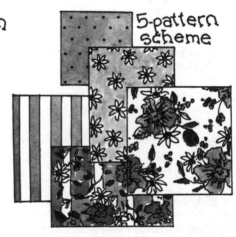

Classic fabric pattern mixes for living rooms

Why reinvent the pattern-mix wheel, you may ask, when others have done such an excellent job? Exactly! The following are some classic fabric mixes:

✔ **Traditional 18th Century.** Large scale floral chintz (sofa); crewel-work tree-of-life (wing chair); woven trellis pattern (lounge chairs); small all-over floral tapestry (accent chairs); and medium satin stripe (draperies).

✔ **American Country Style.** Large country quilt pattern (sofa); medium-scale folk-art floral print (lounge chairs); woven checkerboard checks (accent chairs); and medium stripes (window blinds).

✔ **American Southwest.** Navajo-blanket print (sofa); woven check (lounge chairs); and woven narrow stripe (draperies).

✔ **English Country.** Large-scale glazed chintz (sofa and draperies); narrow stripes (slipcovered lounge chairs); small calico or mini-printed pattern (accent chairs, pillows).

Pattern Practice

When you're mixing and matching patterns, let your eye be the final judge. The more you allow yourself to judge what you do and don't like, the better (and quicker) you'll get at making great decisions. So, don't be afraid to experiment.

The following sections provide some tried-and-true methods for experimenting without penalty. Take these trial runs before you start a real decorating project.

Making sample boards

A great way to practice mixing patterns is by creating sample or swatch boards. An 8$\frac{1}{2}$-x-11-inch sheet of bond paper or white cardboard works well. On a room-by-room basis, clip a bunch of 3-x-5-inch samples of wall coverings and fabrics that you like. Add photographs of area rugs, patterned synthetic flooring, or decorative ceramic tiles — all patterned materials you're considering using in the same room. Move samples, swatches, and photographs around until you find the mix or combination of three to five patterns that please you most. Then paste or tape those samples onto your sample board.

Experiment not only with different patterns, but with patterns in different color schemes. And make sample boards in fabrics and patterns suitable for different styles (American Country, 18th Century Traditional, English Country, Art Deco, and so on), either for real projects or just for your own education and practice. Who knows? Even though you may not be seriously planning to do Art Deco, your next home may cry out for it. And you'll be ready!

Studying magazine pictures

Magazines are chock-full of instructional and educational photographs that are invaluable when you're decorating your home. Interiors in magazines illustrate patterns on walls, floors, and furniture. Often, patterns occur on all three areas in the same room, providing great opportunities to study "the mix" (the number of patterns, the size and scale of the patterns, the use of similar or contrasting backgrounds, and so on). When you're looking at a magazine photograph that you especially like, take note of exactly which pattern or patterns capture your fancy and where they're used (on the wall, the floor, or the furniture, for example). Notice how they're used — as a quiet or dramatic background, a bold attention-getter, or a gentle accent. What you see in magazines may be exactly the answer you're looking for in your next decorating project.

Watching wall covering sample books

Wall covering pattern books have room settings that illustrate the art of mixing and matching many patterns, sometimes in adjoining rooms. Study these, and look especially at those rooms that concern you most, such as the living room, dining room, bedroom, kitchen, and entry hall. Notice especially

- The variety of ways in which several patterns are used in living rooms of many different styles and periods.
- The ways in which different designers distribute pattern differently, even in Traditional rooms!
- How designers combine patterned art, area rugs, and numerous accessories in rooms with as many as five different wall covering patterns.

Room settings in wall covering sample books are great lessons in ways to decorate with pattern. And the patterns you see there are immediately available, too — which saves you lots of time. After you look through a few wall covering books, you can't help but have some good ideas on how to furnish your rooms with pattern.

Chapter 6

Texture Basics

· ·

In This Chapter

▶ Defining texture

▶ Adding texture to walls and floors

▶ Using your furniture to make a textural statement

▶ Making a certain texture the focal point of your room

· ·

*E*verything has texture, so a room cannot avoid having texture. A room can, however, be texturally boring, due to insufficient textural content or contrast.

In this chapter we give you lots of ideas for adding textural excitement to your rooms. We discuss using textures on the walls and floors as a background in a room. We also show you how you can play up texture in the furniture you choose or create a focal point in a room through the use of texture. Finally, we provide some general decorating tips for using texture to get what you want out of your home. After you take a look at our suggestions, adding texture to your house — and recognizing it where it already exists — will be easy.

Examining Texture

Texture, the characteristic physical structure of a material, appeals to several senses. Figure 6-1 illustrates two very different textural effects — one in a living room and the other in a bedroom. The heaviness of the stone fireplace in the living room contrasts sharply with the light and airy feeling created by the satin sheets and tieback curtains in the bedroom.

When you choose different textures as you decorate, be sure to think of how each material affects your senses and the way you feel in the room.

Figure 6-1: The contrasting visual effects created by different textures.

We usually think of texture in *tactile* terms — how a material feels to the touch. As an example, when we're handling fabrics, we modify the term *hand* with the adjective that best describes how a particular fabric feels when we touch it. Velvet has a soft hand; silk a smooth hand; and linen a rough hand.

A different hand, or tactile sensation, also creates a visual perception of physical weight, which affects our choice of where and when to use particular fabrics. For example, fleece seems heavy and bulky, partly because it reflects less light than a silk fabric, which seems light, fine, and rich. Recognizing and acknowledging those differences, you would naturally choose fleece for the family room couch and a woven silk for a formal living room sofa.

Texture involves other visual perceptions. For example, paints have textures which we describe as *finishes*. These finishes have names, such as satin, matte, and eggshell, which describe not just how the paint feels to the touch, but how the eye perceives the ability of a finish to reflect light. We call that ability *sheen*.

Paint sheens also imply visual weight. A satin paint finish seems lighter in weight and more ethereal than a matte finish, which seems not only duller but physically heavier. We identify the heavier, dull matte finish with a more casual, rustic interior. A satin paint finish, which appears finer, also seems more suitable for a formal room.

Under foot, texture is important, even though you're probably not going to bend down and touch the floor. A shag rug, for example, seems duller and heavier than a velvet carpet, needlepoint rug, or marble tile floor. When we see and walk on a shag rug, our senses respond to the various aspects of texture, transmitting information to the brain. When our brain gets the texture message, it influences our choices — shag for a more rustic family room and marble tile for an elegant entryway.

Making Magic with Texture

You can think about and use texture in many ways. Of course, you won't use all of them all at once or all the time. The following sections explain the different options you can choose among.

Using texture as background

When you're planning the background (walls, floors, and ceiling) of a room, you naturally think first of color. But try to think of color and texture as inseparable. Texture has almost as much influence on the mood of your room as color does.

Generally, convention for distributing texture dictates that we use a fine texture on the ceiling (so that it never seems heavy or as though it's falling), a medium texture on walls (so that they seem supportive), and a heavier looking (hard, smooth, and even) texture on the floor (so that it appears sturdy and can be walked on). Using texture in this way creates a great background or foil for sensuously soft upholstery to sink into as well as for hand-waxed, almost matte-finished, wood furniture.

Texture on the walls

When you hear terms like grasscloth wall covering, barn board siding, decorative ceramic tile, stucco, antique brick, and knotty pine, different images come to mind. What are they? If you were asked to use these materials in different interiors, would you pair grasscloth with a tropical room? Barn board siding with a Country family room? Decorative ceramic tile with a French kitchen? Stucco with any room in a Southwestern or Tuscan style? Antique brick in a Traditional family room or a city loft? Knotty pine in an Early American or Country style den or dining room? Mirror and other glass in a penthouse? Shirred fabric for a tent-like sensation in a room with ethnic origins? These are traditional pairings of textures and styles. No wonder each term makes you think of images of whole rooms and even whole houses, full of the conventional distribution of texture.

Notice that in Traditional interiors, textural contrasts are controlled and relatively minimal. Elements may surprise and delight, but never seem in violent opposition.

Contemporary style calls for using textured backgrounds daringly, in a surprising mix of strong, sometimes even warring opposites. This technique requires a very good eye for dramatic couplings that seem contradictory but work because of at least one common element. For example, consider covering walls with barn board siding in a formal, eclectic dining room. With the grayed-to-silver barn board, you may hang an elaborate crystal and silver (not gold) chandelier that's entirely at odds with the informality of the barn board. Then restate the case for elegance begun by the chandelier, by choosing chairs upholstered in gray silk and trimmed with silver nail heads. Pit those against a glass-and-chrome dining table. Tie it all together with a soft, luxuriously thick, gray, velvet-like wool rug, which will relate in color to the barn board and other furnishings, but offer textural contrast to all other elements.

Dare to use texture in a Contemporary way by pitting a few items strongly against all others. Tip the balance one way (informal) or another (formal). Do not use equal amounts of opposites, or you'll end up with a room that seems confused and static.

Texture on the floors and ceilings

Floors are for walking on, so no matter how rustic they may look, they must have flat, smooth surfaces. This requirement still leaves room for lots of textural interest. Consider the differences between red, rough quarry tile; glazed ceramic tile; brick; wood; wool carpeting; resilient flooring; and wood flooring. Each material has a distinctive texture that traditionally works well with one or more wall textures. For example,

- Quarry tile works well with a variety of wall textures, including barn board, linen-textured wallpaper, and fine or lightly textured paint in a Casual room.

- Ceramic tile contrasts nicely with many wall coverings, such as paneled and faux-painted walls, and can look dressy or relaxed, historic or modern.

- Brick contrasts richly with wood paneling and wallpaper and adds a slightly rustic, vintage note.

- Wool carpeting with a cut pile provides a contrast to wall coverings, wood paneling, and plaster walls, and wool carpeting generally looks urbane, whether the room style is Traditional or Contemporary.

- Resilient flooring pairs nicely with wall coverings, paneling, plaster, and painted wall finishes and, depending on its pattern, is at home in a variety of room styles and periods.

- Wood flooring offers mild contrast, so it relates well to all wall materials and is appropriate for all decorating styles and periods — whether the pattern is dressy or casual.

Country style rooms, like the one shown in Figure 6-2, often have interesting textured ceilings that need no other decoration. Ceiling textures in Traditional and most Contemporary style interiors are traditionally smooth, which makes them ideally suited to any number of decorative treatments, ranging from an interesting paint color to *anaglypta* (molded plaster carvings), murals, or wall covering. Unfortunately, because it saves them time

A slanted, tray ceiling with indirect lighting behind the ceiling molding adds glamour to this bedroom (top left). Vertically striped wallcovering and a dramatic border draw the eye up, making this living room ceiling look higher than it actually is (top right). Darkly stained planks act like ceiling camouflage, allowing light colored wood cabinets to capture the limelight In this country-style kitchen (bottom).

Wallcovering borders unify coordinating patterns and serve as decorative highlights in each of these three rooms.

Appealing patterns on the hall chest (top left) and walls (top right and bottom), create movement that keeps rooms interesting and inviting.

Wallcovering borders look great with a single pattern like the gingham check (top), the simple pattern in the living room (bottom left), or with several coordinating patterns (bottom right).

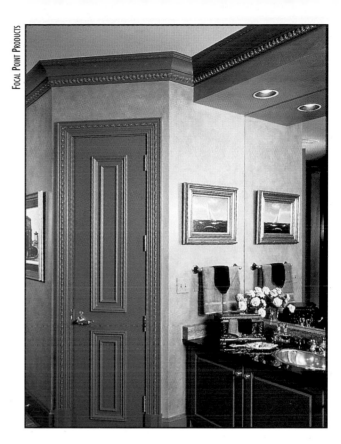

Wood moldings that contrast with the wall but match the ceiling (top left) keep walls looking tall. Ceiling moldings that contrast with both walls and ceilings (top right) make walls seem slightly lower and cozier. Two wide, contrasting borders make tall walls seem shorter and a high ceiling lower in the bedroom (bottom right).

Coordinated wallcoverings and fabrics, (top left, right, and bottom), make mixing diverse floral and geometric patterns foolproof.

Accessories on shelves, walls, and tabletops customize and personalize each of these three rooms.

The color wheel

The color wheel displays primary colors (red, yellow, blue), secondary colors (orange, green, violet) and tertiary colors (red-orange, yellow-orange, yellow-green, blue-green, blue-violet, and red-violet) in various degrees of saturation. Remember that colors directly across from one another on the color wheel are complementary.

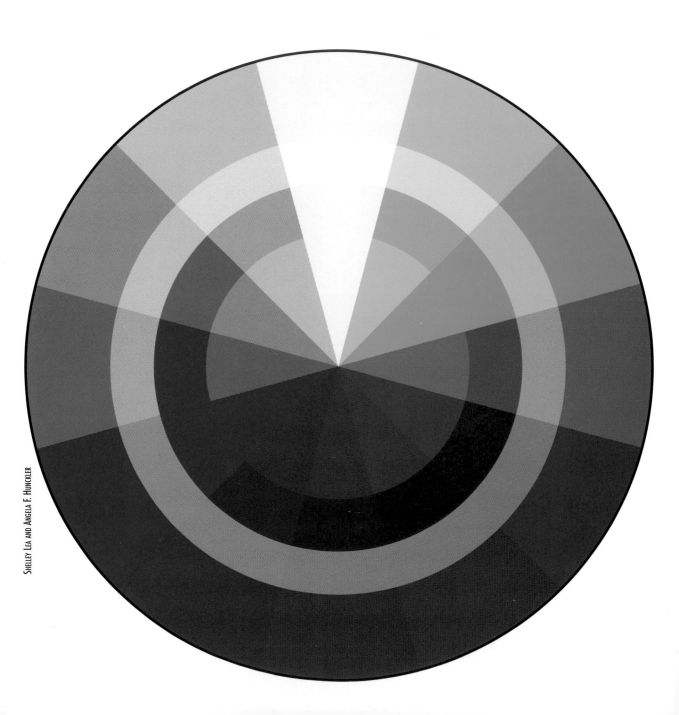

and labor, some builders cover ceilings in a textured paint sometimes called *popcorn*. If you're building a house or gutting a room, consider eliminating this ceiling treatment from the picture, because it severely limits the number of decorating techniques that can be used on the ceiling.

Figure 6-2:
A ceiling gains textural interest from plaster and the addition of rustic beams and planks.

Photograph courtesy La-Z-Boy Incorporated

Using texture in furniture

Mixing upholstery textures in both Traditional and Contemporary rooms is always a good idea. Traditional schemes call for textures that are different, but not *extremely* different. Choose some sturdy fabric — woven wool, velvet, quilted cotton or linen, or leather — for the sofa, which is usually the largest and most dominant upholstered piece. The textures of these fabrics are the boldest, nubbiest, wooliest, and shiniest in the room. Lounge chair fabrics should be just a little finer and lighter in weight. Accent chairs, used less often in a room, may be covered in finer, more delicate fabrics. The object here is unity first, and diversity second.

Contemporary texture mixes tend to be more dramatic and more extreme, pitting opposites against each other for the greatest diversity. Contemporary texture mixes are also unified by a common color or mood. For example, a sofa in matte velvet could be contrasted with sleek lounge chairs in lacquered leather. Both the sofa and the chairs may be in the same scarlet red. Or the sofa may be in red and the chairs in white, united only by a common, city-slick chic.

Frames count, too! Many pieces of upholstered furniture have exposed frames made of wood or metal. Count them, along with upholstery fabric, into your texture mix.

Other materials, such as woven wire, aluminum, wrought iron, and wicker (shown in Figure 6-3), are very textured. Woven wicker furniture gets even more textural interest when bamboo is mixed with sea grasses and other unique textures, or when one of these materials is woven in a distinctive chevron, cable knit (like the sweater), big basket check, or trellis pattern.

Figure 6-3:
Wicker
furniture
adds
complex
textural
interest that
makes it a
natural star.
Here, a
duck
slipcover
transforms
the sofa
and its
texture.

Photograph courtesy Lexington/Henry Link

Using texture as an accent

One of the quickest ways to spice up a ho-hum room, where just about every item has the same safe texture (not too rough, not too shiny, not too smooth — not too *anything*) is to bring in accessories that shout texture.

Hand-thrown pottery, straw baskets, dried plants, palette knife paintings, wooden carvings, quilts, macrame hangings — any of these accessories do a great job of adding texture to your home.

Texture is a powerful decorating tool — just use it with respect. A little may go a long way, so proceed with caution. When in doubt, add one major highly textured accessory at a time until your eye tells you that you have enough.

Using texture as focal point

A neat trick is to use one strongly textured decorative item as a focal point. The focal point should be a strong counterpoint to all of the other surfaces. Think in terms of opposites: smooth versus rough, bumpy, or prickly; hard versus soft; an undulating line versus a straight line; multi-depthed versus a plane. This technique is easier to do in a Contemporary room where people expect to see surprising juxtapositions and daring extremes.

Country style rooms also welcome exaggerated textural focal points such as quilts, woven wall hangings with stones, features, and interesting bits and pieces of wood incorporated.

Traditional rooms can handle strongly textured but not terribly extreme focal points. Tapestries, embroidered wall hangings, and sculpture are some examples of things that work well in Traditional rooms.

Working with texture

You want texture to work with, not against, your decorating plans. So take into consideration some of the following tips for using texture in your house:

- ✔ Texture is all about contrasts. But remember that with more contrast, a room has less unity. And with less unity, the space seems smaller. So, keep the contrasts minimal and subtle in small spaces. You may increase textural contrasts in larger spaces.

- ✔ Window shades and blinds in natural wood and metal are relatively high-contrast textures. Reduce contrast by blending shades and blinds with walls of the same color in small rooms.

- ✔ Shag rugs with furry textures seem bulky, even in light colors. Use this texture to make a big room seem smaller. Avoid shags in small rooms.

- ✔ Sleek textures seem streamlined, fast, smart, Contemporary, and lightweight and appear to take up very little space. You can see why sleek textures are ideal for small spaces. Rooms with backgrounds in these textures may need help from more heavily textured furniture and accessories that add depth, warmth, and comfort.

✔ A great method for selecting textures is to create a *swatch board.* On a large piece of white cardboard, paste samples of fabrics, wood finishes, mica surfacing, wall coverings, and any other materials you like. Pasting them on the board helps you see how these textures relate. If you don't like what you see, keep experimenting until you find the combination that makes you happy.

✔ Some textures reflect all light, creating luminous, ethereal moods. Other, rougher textures capture and hold some of the light, creating shadows that add a sense of mystery. Contemporary interiors celebrate light; Traditional interiors embody great light-shadow play, which is an effect that occurs between textures that absorb light and those that reflect light.

No matter what your style, texture adds a lot of interest and sometimes a whole lot of attitude! Texture is one more terrific thing to have in your decorating bag of tricks, and it's a great tool for creating decorating magic.

Chapter 7

Troubleshooting Basics

- -

In This Chapter

▶ Spotting the problems you need to fix

▶ Coming up with solutions

▶ Looking at examples of decorating problems — and the solutions that worked

- -

When it comes to figuring out what's wrong with a room, many people don't know where to begin. You may have a general feeling that something just isn't quite right. But a general feeling doesn't help much unless you can come up with some specifics and work from there.

In this chapter, you'll find all the tools you need to rescue yourself from the decorating doldrums. We take you step-by-step through the process of figuring out what's wrong with that room that you just don't like. You also discover how to solve the problems with a few simple rules. Finally, we provide three case studies — real-world examples of decorating problems and solutions.

Spotting Trouble — Before It Spots You

When you walk into a room and look around, you can usually tell right away whether you like it. And if you like what you see, you have no problems. In fact, you probably don't even think twice about *why* you like it — you just do. Seeing rooms you don't like in *other* people's houses is one thing. But what if you walk into a room in *your* house, you don't like it, and you can't leave it? This situation calls for some serious troubleshooting.

Before you can do anything to fix a room, you have to keep in mind some very basic decorating rules. Check out Chapters 3–6 for all the information you need on conceptual planning, which just reduces decorating down to the three main elements of line, color, and texture.

Applying these rules or standards one-by-one — like an automobile mechanic using his checklist to eliminate potential sources of the problem — gives you immediate feedback. If you check the list and find that one item is okay, just keep going until you find the root of the problem.

When you walk into a room and you don't like what you see, just follow these steps, based on the three main elements of design, to discover the root of your problem:

1. **Assess the situation.** State the problem you have with the room. If you're having trouble figuring out what the problem is, try thinking about how you feel when you're in the room. Be as specific as you can, and try to jot down just a few words or sentences, just to get yourself thinking.

2. **Spot the Problem.** Ask yourself three main questions:

   • Do I like the color of the room?

   • Do I like the lines (or patterns) in the room? Are there too many lines (making the room seem too busy)? Too few? Do the lines seem contradictory?

   • Do I like the combination of textures in the room? Are there too many? Too few? Are they incompatible, or just tasteless?

   After you answer these questions, you should be able to narrow the problem down to one or more of the three categories (color, line, or texture).

3. **Examine the issue.** Take a closer look at the area (color, line, or texture) where the problem seems to be. Try to come up with a list of things you could do to improve this facet of your room's design.

After looking at the preceding steps, you know where the problem is and you can begin coming up with solutions.

Zeroing In on a Solution

After you've spotted the problem with your room and considered some things you *might* do to correct it, you're ready for the creative part — determining a solution. Address the problem head-on by following these easy steps:

1. **Choose a solution.** To find a solution to an unsatisfactory color scheme, try to narrow your problem down even further. Then you can apply some simple color rules to solve your problem (see Chapter 4 for more on color). Is the room too warm, making you feel uncomfortable, overstimulated, and unable to relax? If so, you can apply the "cool

colors are calming" rule and make your room less warm by adding cool-color accents. Is the room so cool that you feel depressed? Apply the "warm colors are stimulating and therefore more cheerful" rule. Warm up and cheer up the cold room with accents from the warm side of the color wheel. Is the color bland and boring? Spice it up with complementary colors (colors from the opposite side of the color wheel).

2. **Apply the rule.** A good technique for applying the rule that will solve your decorating problem is to work in steps, gauging your response as you work. For example, what if your color problem were too-red walls that made you feel hot and jumpy? Assuming that you love the color but just want to simmer it down a bit it, consider cooling the room by degrees.

Here's how you can do this: First, switch to a cool-colored, neutral upholstery. Not enough cooling? Lower the temperature further by adding a neutral rug. Better? Determining just the right color climate (like deciding how high or low to set the thermostat) is a personal thing. If the room's still too hot, hang cool-colored paintings or pictures with white mats on the wall for more relief. Your eye, and your body will tell you when you've cooled your room down to your comfort level.

Looking at Troubleshooting Case Studies

Sometimes the best way to solve your own decorating problems is by looking at real-life examples of problems other people have faced and the ways in which they solved them. The following sections let you do just that.

The case of the plain, paneled room

Elizabeth had been looking forward to converting her large garage into a generous spare bedroom. She chose handsome wood paneling for the walls, and teal blue carpeting for the floors. The two samples looked great together before the redecorating began. But after the wood-colored paneling was on the walls, the solid, teal blue rug was on the floor, and the wood desk was in place, Elizabeth still wasn't happy. The room wasn't as interesting as she had envisioned. So we suggested that she take a look at the three main elements:

✔ **Texture:** The smooth paneling didn't contrast too strongly with the tightly woven carpeting. In fact, the textures looked great together. Texture wasn't the problem.

✔ **Color:** The teal carpeting looked okay with the brown paneling in the swatch stage. But now that they were in place — in large quantities — Elizabeth could see that both colors were equally intense.

When colors match each other in intensity, they vie for attention, and in the end, they cancel each other out.

In this example, there was not enough contrast between intensities. One item should have been appreciably lighter for contrast and the relief that contrast provides. In this case, the colors were not so far off; there just needed to be contrast and relief. Would it be necessary to change either the wall or the floor, or was there another way to save this color scheme gone slightly sour? If so, how? And, was color alone the culprit? Before deciding, it's always a good idea to run through all three elements on your composition checklist.

✔ **Line:** Architecturally, the room's lines were okay — not too many verticals, not too many horizontals. And the furniture did nothing to tip the balance either way. But the room was full of plain and solid surfaces and completely lacked pattern — and pattern *is* line!

The problem in this case seems twofold: a lack of pattern and an absence of color relief.

The solution to this problem room was simple: Add pattern in a great color mix (shown in Figure 7-1). The problem was solved with draperies made of a pattern with lots of line content, a light colored background for relief, and colors that included some of the brown and teal along with an accent color. The draperies also provided two bonuses: privacy and some much-needed soft texture. Case closed.

The case of the unmade bed

Furniture with chipped and peeling paint has been such a rage lately that furniture manufacturers are starting to make new furniture that looks like it's been stashed in a barn for a hundred years. Whether antique-looking furniture is authentic or brand new, it may look marvelous in magazines, but, in real life, it doesn't always work out. Jennifer's iron bed is a case in point.

Figure 7-1: Pattern adds line and color interest to a room with plain surfaces and little textural contrast.

Jennifer loved the way the old iron bedstead looked when she bought it. But after she saw it in her bedroom, its charm quickly wore off. What was the problem? The line or design of the bed was beautiful. A clear-eyed look revealed the truth: The bed was simply too rusted (therefore, the wrong color) and too primitive (the wrong texture) for the refined setting of Jennifer's room. The solution? Get rid of that rusted look, and paint on a prettier face.

How should you paint an old iron bed? Just follow these easy steps:

1. **Sand away any loose paint on the bedstead, or use a paint remover recommended for use on iron.**

2. **Wash the bedstead with a dishwashing detergent to remove any grease.**

   Be sure to rinse off all the detergent and let the bedstead dry completely before painting it.

3. **Take the bedstead outside to a place sheltered from the wind.**

   Choose a day with low humidity and temperatures between 70 and 95 degrees Fahrenheit for the best results.

4. **Spray-paint the bedstead with a primer that is close in color to the top coat you've chosen.**

   Let the bed dry completely, according to the directions on the can.

5. **Spray-paint the bed in the finish and color of your choice.**

Before you refinish your iron bed, check with your local paint dealer to be sure you're using the right primer and topcoat finish. If you mistakenly select the wrong type of primer and paint, all your hard work may peel away in just a short time.

The case of the crowded room

Many rooms that looked great without any furniture when you were house hunting can look dreadful after all your furniture is piled in. After moving into his new apartment, Joe suddenly realized that all the doors and windows in the combination living room/dining room were in the wrong places, not enough wall space existed, and a traffic pattern between the sofa and the television seemed unavoidable. He got a headache trying to unscramble the mess. But we had an easy solution.

The main problems Joe faced were overcrowding and an architectural design that wasn't very accommodating of furniture placement. We helped Joe consider the three main elements of design to solve his decorating problems:

▶ **Line:** Joe's living room had too many lines (because of all the furniture he wanted to fit in this limited space). The room looked chaotic—somewhat like a used furniture store. So the answer to this problem was simple: Simplify.

Joe arranged the bookshelves, TV, armoire, and drop-leaf dining table along the long, uninterrupted wall, creating a sense of unity and a focal wall (see Chapter 3 for more information). He kept the traffic pattern between the kitchen, the bedroom, and the patio clear by leaving room behind the sofa for a walkway. (The sofa then faced the bookshelves, TV, armoire, and drop-leaf table.) Finally, he flanked the sofa with side chairs (you can use dining room armchairs with cushions to fill this role).

The result of this furniture rearrangement was better visual and practical organization, eliminating confusion and inconvenience.

▶ **Color:** We already determined that with all the furniture, Joe's living room felt busy and cluttered. So he brought a sense of calm and order to the room with a monochromatic color scheme. Because the walls were light, Joe painted the bookshelves, drop-leaf table, and armoire a light color, which helped them blend in and seem to take up less space. He kept the floors light, like the walls, and also covered the sofa in a light color that blended with the room. Finally, we recommended that Joe use only one accent color, to continue the calming effect of the monochromatic color scheme.

▶ **Texture:** Continuing in his efforts to keep the room calm, we recommended that Joe use textures that were smooth and simple, with low textural contrast. This plan meant that Joe had to get rid of the shag carpeting he had from his fraternity house days, avoid furry upholstery, and move the fuzzy macramé wall hangings his grandmother had made to another room. Instead of complicating the room with more texture, we recommended that Joe keep the carpeting low pile and simple (not deeply carved). He chose leather and tightly woven upholstery for the furniture. And finally, Joe completed the simple look of his living room with low-textured, linen horizontal blinds (enameled blinds would work equally well).

After Joe recognized the main problems of his living room — a cluttered, chaotic feeling — he was able to make some fairly simple changes and end up with a great result.

Part III
Style and Substance

The 5th Wave   By Rich Tennant

"It was Jack's idea to have a home office, but I picked out the artwork."

In this part . . .

An important facet of home decorating is discovering your style. So the chapters in this part help you do just that. We provide chapters on the differences between Historic and Contemporary furniture styles, as well as one that helps you choose the right furniture for your home. We even devote an entire chapter to finding your own personal style so that you can easily decide which pieces will work for you.

Chapter 8

Historic Decorating Styles

· ·

In This Chapter

▶ Introducing key historic periods and styles

▶ Decorating today with yesterday's favorite styles

▶ Choosing your favorite historic style

· ·

*S*tyles endure because they're appealing. Many styles seem to live forever, and most work equally well in authentically re-created environments or paired with other more up-to-date furnishings in what we call an Eclectic style. In this chapter, we review the most popular historic styles. We also show you how you can use these styles in your own home, and we guide you through the process of selecting a style or two to use.

Considering Style

A whole world of historic style is out there for you to discover and enjoy — and maybe even use in your own home. Mixing compatible historic styles — from Classic to Modern — creates an eclectic atmosphere that adheres to good design principles.

You may love the look of super sleek Contemporary accented by a few clean-lined Neoclassical Louis XVI pieces. Go right ahead — both styles emphasize pure line. Or you may adore the "inherited over generations" look typified by English Country. Feel free to mix a range of fine wood pieces from different periods — just don't forget the important accessories like "instant ancestor portraits" that pull the whole look together.

Historic styles continue to influence everyone from interior decorators to architects and beyond. Most homes feature one or several historic influences. By playing up the mood of the architecture with the right historic style, you'll create a dramatic, consistent mood.

For firsthand experience of the high styles of bygone eras, do some research that will entertain as well as educate you. Decorations and designs of past centuries and other cultures can be found in grand museums and stately mansions. Don't pass up a chance to visit museums and houses open to the public.

Understanding historic style will help you develop your own taste. You'll also avoid decorating mistakes. Not everything can be mixed and matched successfully. But by knowing which style is which, you'll be able to develop your own judgment, and ultimately, your own personal style. Discernment — the ability to tell good from better from best — is fundamental to developing personal style.

Choosing the Right Historic Style for Your Home

You can choose furniture using at least two approaches. One approach involves choosing one style and sticking with it throughout the house. The second approach — practiced by most people — involves using one style in the public rooms and at least one other style in the private rooms.

You can transition from public to private areas by using distinct period styles best suited for each purpose and to suit your individual style. You may choose, for example, 18th Century Traditional (a mix of English, French, and American furniture from this era is the norm) in the living and dining rooms. You may even carry this style into the master bedroom. Or you may switch over to Louis XV (French Provincial) in the master bedroom. A natural for a young girl's bedroom is a painted French Provincial or American Country style. For a young boy, Shaker, Arts and Crafts, California Modern, or Southwestern (a ranch house style) all work well. Variety offers a "something for everyone" approach by meeting everyone's need to express personal style.

Of course, nothing is wrong (and a lot is right) with using one style throughout your house. If you like the idea of choosing one style as your very own, but you're not sure which is right for you, we suggest that you take a good look at the furniture styles that interest you. Checking your impression against our descriptions of the design philosophy (for example, is the style too fine or too rustic, too formal or too friendly?), keep narrowing down your selection until you find the one style that fills your decorating bill.

Understanding Styles of the Past

When you hear the phrases "Neo-Renaissance" or "Post Modern" do you have any idea what they mean? Does the mention of "Louis Quinze" (Louis XV is pronounced *louey canz*) lead you to think that people are talking about the latest recycling plan? If you're in quandary about which style is which, read on. Grasping the defining characteristics of styles will help you create the interior of your dreams, whether you're sticking to just one style or varying your style throughout your home. Personal style, after all, builds on all the other styles that have come before.

When you hear the words *Old World,* for example, you probably think of a permanence and elegance that adds meaning to the everyday. Touches of Old World influence (rounded archways, richly textured rustic wall surfaces, Spanish tile roofs, for example) add a sense of exotic splendor to many Contemporary homes. In home furnishings, the phrase *Old World* refers to an amalgam of a range of continental European styles beginning with the earliest Gothic or Medieval style in northern Europe and the Renaissance in Italy and France. Old World — a trendy look that's hot right now — is just one current example of hybrid historic styles.

Gothic design (12th to 16th century) is considered the high point of the Middle Ages. The characteristic feature of Gothic design is the pointed arch and vault, a technical development that made building taller ceilings and putting in large windows possible. The great hall also emerged during this time. Gothic design continues to be adapted by us today, as you can see from the bed shown in Figure 8-1. Gothic design from England, France, Italy, and Germany vary considerably. Spanish design is heavily influence by Islamic art, with elaborate decoration inspired by myth, allegory, and religious themes. An abundance of Gothic and Gothic-inspired furniture and accessories (including stained glass windows) is available for every room in your house.

The 16th and 17th Century Early Renaissance (Quattrocento) was a transitional period between the Gothic arts of northern Europe and a rather restrained use of Classical decorative elements, originating in southern Europe (especially Greece and Rome). During this time, Medieval austerity continued and residential interiors were minimally furnished. Today we see some mixed use of Gothic and Renaissance elements in both architecture and furniture.

Italy

The Renaissance produced some of the world's greatest architecture and decoration. Designers through the ages keep going back to rediscover its greatness. Unlike the strict revivals of yesteryear, we tend to prefer updated and streamlined versions of elaborate Renaissance design.

Figure 8-1:
A bed
inspired by
the Gothic
style is at
home in a
Country
style room.

Current-day versions of these classic designs may alter proportions,
heighten or tone down color schemes, or simplify the heavy carving or
detailed painting. Architectural elements based on Renaissance architecture
(your home may feature the classic windows or embellished columns so
distinct to the style) may inspire you to add decorative touches reminiscent
of the Renaissance. Renaissance touches add spice to almost any other
style.

The High Renaissance (Cinquecento) was the high point of Renaissance art
and architecture. Artists, architects, and designers in this period loved
system and classical order. The great architect, Palladio (1508–1580),
reinterpreted Classicism for this new era. (We remember him for his famous
Palladian window, which features a big central window flanked by two
shorter ones and topped by a sunburst window.) From 1500–1600, furnishings grew more significant, and new varieties of furniture types were con-
ceived. Classical forms and beauty of line were key elements. Mass was
emphasized over surface ornamentation, but as the skills of cabinetmakers
increased, so did their desire to express themselves. Furniture became more
specialized and more highly detailed. Storage cabinets, for example, were
designed to hold various personal and valuable objects. Walls featured
painted scenery and life-like *trompe l'oeil* (fool-the-eye) paintings, which are
very popular now.

The Renaissance look actually never went away, and today it's still popular. To get that Renaissance look, select the furniture, wrap your walls in deep reds, hang lots of tapestry, pile on gold and other metal accessories, and add lots of stained glass and sparkling jewel-covered ornaments. A touch of the Renaissance is especially suited to Contemporary homes that feature the key elements of the period.

France (17th and 18th centuries)

All French styles convey love of romance and order. The French adopted and adapted Italian styles, making them uniquely their own. Walls and textiles were darkly colored during the Renaissance, but lightened and brightened as furniture designs became more delicate, formal, and feminine. The key French periods include the following:

- **Louis XIV:** Under the Sun King, large-scale furniture, excessive ornamentation, and strong color contrast reigned. This style is revived from time to time.

- **Regency:** A transitional style that lasted from 1700–1730, it was characterized by an economy in architecture and decoration. France's version of Baroque was elaborately decorative but still based on classically ordered character. Graceful scrolls and curves display the restraints and classical discipline of characteristic Rococo design.

- **Louis XV:** This style was feminine, sentimental, and delicate. Smaller rooms and smaller furniture ruled right along with delicate color schemes, curved forms, and Oriental influence. Louis XV chairs have never left fashion and are very popular even today.

- **Louis XVI (Neoclassic):** This style was a major rediscovery of Greek and Roman design. From 1760–1789, Louis XVI's clean lines and balanced decoration dominated. Naturalism; simplicity in decorative forms; straight lines; compass curves; classical orders; and Pompeii, Greek, and Adam influence was keenly felt. (For more about the Adam influence, see "England" later in this chapter.) For those who love French period furniture, many of the original cabinet-making companies continue to produce original designs precisely as they were made during their heyday. The Louis XVI chair is everywhere. And the Neoclassic style is found even in wall coverings, such as the one shown in Figure 8-2.

- **Empire:** Seen from 1804–1820, Napoleon commissioned this style to reflect the masculine military style symbols of his victories, including Egyptian motifs and Roman allegorical influences. Color schemes of this style tended toward pale tints of neutralized colors for large areas such as walls, floors, and ceilings. The pretty pastels were used lavishly in textiles during the 18th Century. By the 19th century, Napoleon's wife, Josephine, influenced color sensibility with her pale, muted blues, grayed purples, medium browns, and almost flesh tones. Chairs influenced by Empire designers who loved the curved, saber leg are as popular today as they've ever been.

French style is always elegant, refined, and a bit more formal than most other styles. Add French flair by bringing in a bit of the glorious touches of French period style. Look for hand-painted tables, commodes, or other accent pieces to lend instant grace and delicate charm.

England

Renaissance trends didn't become popular for 100 years after they had faded into the past in Italy. Though introduced to England during Tudor and Elizabethan times, Renaissance styles weren't easy to understand. It would be after a great deal of political, social, and religious disorder that the Renaissance design concepts could take hold. Inigo Jones, who brought Palladian architecture and High Renaissance style back with him to England during the1600s, and Sir Christopher Wren, who became the leading influence of all the arts (leaving some to speak of England's "Wrennaissance"), had great influence on architecture and design.

Figure 8-2:
Neoclassic style, based on Greek and Roman motifs, shows up even in wall coverings!

Photograph courtesy Blonder Wallcoverings

TIP

The design of chair and table legs is a clue to the style of a particular piece of furniture (see Figure 8-3).

The important styles of England (usually lumped together by furniture retailers as Traditional) are the following:

- **Queen Anne:** Seen from 1702–1714, this style featured curvilinear design and Oriental influence. The Queen Anne chair, with its generous curved leg, is an enduring favorite.

- **Georgian:** Classical details from Greece and Rome influenced the great furniture designers of that era. The tendency was toward heavy proportion and detail. This style is still imitated and used today.

- **Chippendale and Rococo:** These styles featured generous scale and chairs with a straight leg. Some chair backs reflected Oriental influence in the shape of the top of the chair and in fret-like patterns in lieu of back splats. By contrast, Chippendale chairs seem more masculine than the curvy Queen Anne chairs and the lighter-scaled Sheraton and Hepplewhite chairs. Colors popular with Chippendale's furniture were neutralized color schemes that were deeper than the French colors of the same time.

- **Hepplewhite:** This style is characterized by well-scaled chairs with a distinctive shield-shaped back.

- **Sheraton:** This style includes more delicately scaled furniture with neoclassical elements and design motifs.

- **Adam:** The Adams brothers were influenced by French Rococo and Pompeii styles. They reveled in finely designed, delicately scaled, elaborately detailed interiors and furnishings. These furnishings were covered in rich distinctive colors of dulled blue, pale yellow-green, light gray, and lavender.

Figure 8-3:
The design of chair or table legs are great indicators of the style of a particular piece of furniture.

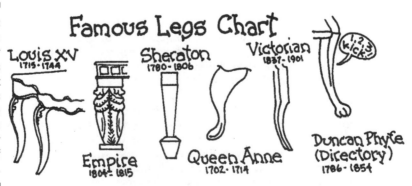

Famous Legs Chart

Louis XV 1715-1774

Empire 1804-1815

Sheraton 1780-1806

Queen Anne 1702-1714

Victorian 1837-1901

kick 1,2,3

Duncan Phyfe (Directory) 1786-1854

✔ **Victorian:** This period was known as the mauve decade, thanks to the love of dark, dramatic aubergine (eggplant). Other colors favored during this period included bottle green, tobacco brown, red, and purple. Furniture was factory-made and available to the new middle class, which was fond of decorative excess. A smorgasbord of design influences were a part of the Victorian era, including nostalgic renderings of Gothic, Renaissance, Moorish, and Oriental designs.

Victorian decorating has never lost its charm and appeal. (An entire magazine, *Victoria,* is even devoted to extolling the look.) Lacy curtains, layers of patterns, and armloads of accessories create the Victorian feel. Feminine and frilly, Victorian style is just right for those who love the magic of pretty things. Your home needn't be Victorian to be decorated in the style but it does work best in older homes or newer homes that lack a different, distinct style.

Germany

Biedermeier is the best known and perennially popular German style from the early 19th century. Unlike other furniture styles named for monarchs and furniture designers, the Biedermeier style is named after a popular cartoon character. This solidly masculine furniture style is based on English 19th Century and French Empire styles, and it incorporates some neoclassical elements.

Biedermeier's most distinctive feature is its dramatic use of light and dark wood. For stylistic impact, mahogany, ebony, or ebonized fruit-woods were offset by blond or light fruit-woods. Inlays of dark wood would accent light wood, and sometimes vice versa. Heavy gold hardware was sometimes used as drawer pulls or decoration. Generally, the proportions of desks, chairs, tables, and so on would be heavy and stout compared to French or English furniture.

Biedermeier furniture was also produced in other Eastern European countries as well. Regional differences influence the proportion and ornamentation. Some Biedermeier pieces may be more graceful and more embellished than others. The main drama, however, comes from the mix of the woods and the boldness of the silhouette.

There's nothing dainty or fussy about Biedermeier. Biedermeier tends to be less ornamented, carved, or decorated than other styles, which is probably why it continues to be popular today. The simple but bold elegance of Biedermeier makes it very well suited for those who favor masculine style. Add eclectic touches to a contemporary home with Biedermeier. The style can be used in either public places or private spaces, depending on your preference.

America

American style, although sometimes based on European, is unique thanks to its cleaner, simpler design approach. In the early days of American design, furniture makers had little choice over materials and finishes. They were limited by the kinds of woods and other materials they could obtain. Craftsman and designers were also somewhat isolated from the trends of Europe and were forced to create according to the demands of their new environment. They adapted trends from the various books from cabinetmakers like Chippendale and created regional or vernacular styles.

American furniture and interior decoration, though not as fancy as European styles of the same periods, does feature quality craftsmanship and good design suitable for the New World. American political idealism (democracy and equality) affected more than the government, influencing designers to create furniture that could be used by everyone. The rocking chair, one of the earliest American furniture designs, has been used by everyone and in almost every room from President Kennedy's Oval Office to grandma's front porch. Basic American style (before 20th century, when everything became international) is characterized by its lack of pretentiousness.

American style can be broken down into the following categories:

- **Early Gothic:** Early settlers brought with them the traditions of their homelands. The earliest colonists, still under the Medieval influence, built homes and furnishings based on Gothic period style. Gradually, as the colonialists grew more affluent and an increasing number of newcomers came from aristocracy, the homespun Colonial Gothic style was replaced by the more refined English style. Georgian influence inspired early American craftsmen, who replicated the noted styles of established cabinetmakers. Today we may use Gothic-inspired Windsor chairs in a modern kitchen (see Figure 8-4).

- **Greek Revival:** Federal style is the name given furniture designed for the Greek Revival houses during the early years of the new United States. These 18th century furnishings were inspired by Greek ideals and images seen on Greek vases. One of the best known furniture designers of this period and style was Duncan Phyfe (1768–1854), whose name was given to a saber-legged chair and a distinctive pedestal table with three saber legs.

- **Gothic Revival:** Gothic style has never died. A resurgence of Gothic forms kept the style going. Carpenter Gothic architecture, with pointed arches, tracery ceilings, and stained glass windows, also became popular. Today Gothic is bigger than ever. You can see Gothic elements in architecture, furniture, and accessories.

Figure 8-4:
The clean surface and simple lines of Gothic-inspired American hoop-back Windsor chairs make them compatible with a thoroughly modern kitchen.

Photograph courtesy National Kitchen & Bath Association

Touches of pure Americana can add decorative — and patriotic — appeal. Scour antique and junk stores for eagles, flags, and other icons of independence. Think red, white, and blue for a dynamic color scheme. Don't think your interior need be traditional either. Some very contemporary Americana continues to be created by artists like Jasper Johns (who is famous for his versions of the American flag).

Styles may come and go suddenly. Any style that makes a comeback is generally tagged with the terms "Revival" or "Neo" to distinguish it from its predecessor.

American Country

Around the time of America's bicentennial, in 1976, a new decorating style was developing in America. It was not quite Early American, Southwestern, English Country, or any known style. Instead, it borrowed from a large variety of European provincial styles. It was decidedly casual and incorporated up-to-date fabrics and furnishings with old but attractive, mix-and-match furniture. Painted and even distressed finishes added a colorful, light-hearted note. Accessories were practical, such as on-hand, country-made things like baskets and quilts, displayed in an ad hoc way. The new style was labeled American Country, and it continues to evolve. But, even as it changes, the key elements remain: comfort, casual informality, a generous helping of country-made or countrified accessories, and a certain lack of pretense.

Don't confuse the American Country style — essentially a no-nonsense farmhouse style — with the English Country style, which is based on a loftier, richer, manor house style. Simple, carefree, and relaxed, American Country style is down home living at its best. Formal and fussy English Country style, on the other hand, is based on the lifestyle of the aristocracy. If you accidentally mix the two terms, you may miscommunicate your vision to others, including your decorator.

Country is a state of mind. Enrich any room with views of country landscapes for an instant breath of fresh air. Idyllic scenes may be used in virtually any interior — simply match the mood and level of formality.

Decorating with Historic Styles

Only museums bother to re-create an authentic historic period or style. However, most manufacturers offer furniture based on the styles mentioned in this chapter. And, chances are, you'll decide that one is just right for your decorating project.

The information we provide in this chapter should give you the helpful big picture. Keep in mind that most of the new versions of historic styles generally are designed to meet the needs of our technology-driven homes. As a society, we're far more interested in comfort, convenience, and function than people of the past. We're also just a bit larger in height and weight, too. So our homes tend to have higher ceilings and more space in general. Keep all these factors — and your preference for personal style — in mind when choosing period style furniture.

For example, the heavier the furniture, the darker the colors, the rougher the textures, and the more masculine the mood. Delicately scaled furniture is generally formal and feminine and is well paired with formal, feminine colors, textures, and accessories. If you know these two things about the extremes, you'll probably automatically and correctly conclude that a medium-scaled style offers the greatest versatility. You can use a wide range of medium weight fabrics and textures. This mid-range also allows for wider choices in color schemes ranging from dark (but not too dark) to light (but not too light).

Practical people have always mixed furniture styles. But for the happiest mix, remember the old maxim, "Birds of a feather flock together." The general guideline is: Combine large scale furniture with other large scaled styles; fine with fine; formal with formal; dark with other dark woods; and fancy with fancy styles. Avoid confusion by not mixing casual (pine or oak) and formal (mahogany or cherry) furniture in the same room.

We're not suggesting that you treat historic furniture reverently and with awe. Create decorating magic by adding a big scaled buffalo plaid fabric (maybe even a blanket) to a big Louis XIV chair in a family room or den. Or, for spray-painted Edwardian or Victorian wicker chairs around a glass-topped dining table, make cushions of raw silk in a variety of wild, jewel colors.

Chapter 9

Contemporary Decorating Styles

● ●

In This Chapter

▶ Introducing 20th century styles

▶ Noting the differences between Modern and Contemporary

▶ Decorating Contemporary style

● ●

*T*he radical shift from the heavily decorated styles of the past to the sleek, minimal styles was anticipated by several design schools, movements, and trends near the start of the 20th century. Each had its own distinct philosophy and unique style.

During the 1800s many free-thinkers — from Shakers and Utopians to artists and intellectuals — anticipated the need for a new way of furnishing the home. Driven by lofty ideals and a hunger for something different, groups of craftsmen, designers, and artisans began making everyday items that reflected (or reacted to) new technology, social conditions, and values. More honest, simple, and utilitarian styles emerged. This trend toward essentials would continue and finally heighten in the earliest part of the 20th century. Many designers, even ones of the 20th century, sought to free people from what they perceived as materialism. Spiritual values became a primary creative force that drove the emerging designs.

In this chapter, we go into detail on Modern and Contemporary styles. With this information, you can determine if your personal style meshes with this category, and if so, which decorating techniques you can use to incorporate this style in your home.

Twentieth Century Styles

The 20th century is usually associated with Modern and Contemporary styles, but it actually brought on many other new styles. We associate some of these styles with Country or Cottage style decorating; others we associate with Romantic styles. The following list outlines the major styles of the 20th century. Many of these pre-Modern designs work well in Contemporary settings. For lovers of the eclectic, look for styles that reflect a similar design approach for best results. Mixing in a few pieces of Shaker or Mission into Country style interiors may work for those interiors based on natural materials.

- **Shaker (1830–1850):** Traditional furniture designs stripped to bare essentials (few turnings, no decorations), producing furniture plain in appearance. Natural materials; no ornamentation; strong emphasis on function. Familiar rush-seat Shaker style chairs are available as antiques or as knock-offs.

- **Arts and Crafts/Gothic Revival (1851–1914):** Emphasized natural materials. Designs based on nature. Hand-crafting versus machine-made.

- **Adirondack (1890–Present):** Rustic; natural; often made of bark-covered logs or simple planks. Look for junk shop finds when in the country (for authenticity) or purchase hand-made new versions of these comfy furnishings.

- **Art Nouveau (Circa 1900):** First new style not using any historical reference. Based on flowing lines of leaves and vines. Influenced by Japanese art.

- **Arts and Crafts/Mission in America (Circa 1900):** Simple designs executed in natural wood. Emphasized hand craftsmanship, quality materials, and strong, clean lines. Also called Golden Oak.

- **De Stijl (1917–1929):** Design based on geometric principles and primary colors. Highly abstract. No historical references used.

- **Art Deco (1918–1939):** Fashion-oriented. Influenced by primitive art and cubism (see Figure 9-1). More color, pattern, and grand ornamentation, including motifs such as zigzag, electricity bolts, and skyscrapers.

- **Bauhaus (1919–1933):** Design based on unifying art and technology. Little ornamentation. Function, form, and materials (metal tubing, glass, and other technological, machine-made materials) most important. Emphasis placed on machine-made, efficient production. Neutrals, black, white, and primary colors.

- **Modern/International (1925–1947):** Collective grouping of Modern styles, also called Classic Modern. No regional influences or historic references. Based on geometry. No ornamentation or unnecessary elements. Details come from interesting use of modern materials.

- **Classic American Modern (1945–1965):** Clean-lined, comfort-oriented, featuring little ornamentation or excess. Popular materials of this style include molded plywood, glass, chrome, steel, and leather.

- **Late Modernism (1966–Present):** Modernist principles of abstraction and efficiency underlie designs. More ornamentation, stronger color, and broader range of materials used.

- **Post-Modernism (1966–Present):** A particular form of Modernism that includes witty and ironic historical references and ornamentation.

Greek, Romanesque, and Georgian design motifs may be used to produce disconcerting effects that look deliberately odd and off-putting yet witty and urbane.

- **Minimalism (1970–Present):** Less is more; simple is best. Emphasis on quality materials and subtlety. Few accessories or ornamentation.

- **Memphis (1980–1990):** Witty, irreverent, fun designs. Challenged austerity and seriousness of furniture designs. Strong color play, strong forms, strong design statements.

- **High Tech (1980–1990s):** Emphasis on exploitation and exposure of elements of science and technology. Shows construction of interior. Use of industrial materials for the home. Electronic and space-age details important. Celebrates the machine.

- **Contemporary (Present):** Broad umbrella term for furniture being produced *now,* not based strictly on traditional style. May feature any use of materials and ornamentation to produce a pleasing design. Stylish and functional.

Figure 9-1:
An Art Deco end table, inspired by Jacques-Emile Ruhlmann, features spiky legs and a simple silhouette.

Photograph courtesy Milling Road

Moving into the 20th Century

The first wave of 20th century design has recently been rediscovered by everyone from art historians to museums to furniture buyers worldwide. Mixing all the styles together into one piece is the newest trend in the furniture industry. So is combining various Modern and Contemporary Styles. Modern is very much in style as this century comes to a halt. Call it end-of-the-century nostalgia, if you want, but even people far too young to have seen the original pieces are falling in love with the new-again Modern style.

In Europe, the precursor to Modern and Contemporary style occurred during the mid- to late-19th century and was known as the Arts and Crafts movement. William Morris, a creative force behind the movement, spurred the development of furnishings and textiles that were handmade and nature-based. This return to Gothic-inspiration was a revolt against overwrought Victorian furniture that was essentially thought to be cheap and tasteless. Machine-made carvings, turnings, and other embellishments on poor quality materials rankled the sensibilities of designers. Charles Eastlake, the big taste-maker of the Arts and Crafts Movement, called for less ornamentation and more discernment in furniture decoration. William Morris's textile and furniture designs are still in production today.

In the United States, Shaker, Adirondack, and Mission styles were growing popular. Shaker furniture was based on clean lines derived from "spiritually correct" mathematical proportions and was highly functional. Shakers believed that some proportions and furniture silhouettes were more other-worldly and would help them in their quest for strict celibacy and cleanliness. For example, chairs could be hung on wall pegs for easy cleaning and instant storage. Lounging was certainly not encouraged by these ramrod-straight, rush-seated chairs. Honesty of materials was stressed over luxury. Adirondack style with its homespun use of unrefined timber was a counter-point to all the machine-made and ornate Victoriana furniture. Mission Style, inspired by the Arts and Crafts movement, called for an emphasis on natural woods, honest craftsmanship, and simplified ornamentation. Mission Style, a masculine and natural look, continues to be discovered by new generations of style-lovers.

Art Nouveau, the first truly new style, drew nothing from design's historical past. The flowing asymmetrical lines of abstracted and conventionalized plant forms inspired by Japanese design was an "art for art's sake" approach. Art Nouveau's greatest champions were Charles Rennie Mackintosh (his work is enjoying a major revival right now) and Antoni Gaudi. Paris was the primary center of this movement.

Modern and Contemporary Styles

Modern is a distinct style pioneered by architects and designers such as Frank Lloyd Wright, Walter Gropius, Ludwig Mies van der Rohe, Le Corbusier, and Marcel Bruer. Modern styles from the '20s through the post-World War II era were based on mathematical abstraction and lofty notions. Structural or sculptural qualities were emphasized. All details were abstract, not from nature, and certainly not symbolic. Technology and economy (maximum value, minimum expenditure) were important, as were comfort and convenience. No ornamentation, such as carving, hand-painting, or forms of decoration, were introduced into these pure designs.

Classic Modern refers to the Golden Age of Modern design. World War II brought most of the European designers to the United States. Meanwhile, great designers like Charles Eames and his wife Ray, also a designer, were creating furniture that emphasized comfort. Their executive chair, shown in Figure 9-2, was the first design in history that fully supported each area of the human body from head to toe. The style continues to be manufactured and is readily available.

Figure 9-2:
Modern Eames chair and ottoman. Charles Eames and Ray Eames created the first truly comfortable lounge chair.

Photograph courtesy Herman Miller

The terms *Modern* and *Contemporary* may sound as though they mean the same thing, but they don't. The main differences between the two include the following:

✔ **Modern:** A distinct style of very clean-lined furnishings, Modernism lasted from the '20s through the '60s and produced scores of classic furnishings that are now trendier than ever due to our nostalgia for the past. Modern, as a style, is *history* and is not of the moment.

✔ **Contemporary:** Contemporary furnishings, strictly of the moment, may combine influences, trends, and new technologies without strict adherence to a philosophy. Contemporary trends include furniture designs that are amalgams of various periods and trends, combined in fresh and exciting ways.

Modern styles of the 20th century now have other names, including Post-Modern, Memphis, and Late Modernism. Many versions of more current Modern furniture include witty references to '50s Modern, Memphis, and Post-Modern, without being strict statements of these particular styles. Consider these pieces to be the equivalent of "traditional" furniture that is based on a wide variety of English, French, and Italian styles of the 17th and 18th centuries (see Chapter 8 for more information on Historic styles).

While most current Contemporary styling (including the new Modern) is fairly sleek, clean, and tailored, a hallmark of Contemporary design is functionalism, without being strictly utilitarian. Over-scaled, overstuffed big sofas, for example, are the cornerstone of the living room or family room and are actually "a room within a room." Along with the satellite-linked TV, these big "room sofas" are the true center of the home. Regardless of what it looks like, Contemporary style is mainly about comfort, function, personal style, and a new sense of luxury based on high quality materials and excellent craftsmanship.

If Traditional furniture, lots of accessories, and ruffles and flourishes are not your style, maybe Contemporary is. Let your choice of sleek, pared-down furniture be your guide to decorating the rest of your house. Keep decorations throughout your house just as simple as the furniture. Also, keep backgrounds simple by looking to texture instead of pattern to add visual interest. Choose a few necessary pieces of furniture and arrange them for greatest comfort. Make a few well-chosen, big, important accessories work for you. Avoid any sense of fuss, but be as witty as you want to be.

Chapter 10

Personal Decorating Styles

• •

• •

*H*ome decorating is all about choosing the look *you* want and making it come alive in your home. But when you face the task of decorating — whether you're starting from scratch with your first home or redecorating the home you've lived in for 20 years — you may not be sure where to start. The most important aspect of home decorating is figuring out what you want. After you do that, you have a starting point, a place to begin.

In this chapter, we guide you through the process of figuring out what style you can call your own. You'll take a quiz that will get you thinking about what you like and don't like. We also show you how to use what you find in the quiz to develop your own personal style. Decorating a house is about making a place reflect your personality, and in this chapter you'll also see how some little touches can make a huge difference in making you feel at home.

Determining Your Own Personal Style

Personal style is all about making a unique design statement that's an expression of your character, viewpoint, and personality. Style isn't about right and wrong, or even good, better, and best ways to decorate. All of your life experiences and expectations contribute to creating and defining your personal style. Your education, experiences, travels, and exposures inform your preferences. The trouble is that you can easily feel overloaded with input from so many sources. You've heard so many "shoulds" and "oughts," "outs" and "ins," that you've never taken the time to decide something as basic as whether warm colors or cool colors make you feel better. Do the hot citrus colors of Provence turn you on, or is beige more beautiful? Are you torn between Country and Modern rooms (see Figure 10-1)? Not having the answers to all these questions is completely normal, but in this section, we help you figure out how to find the answers you need.

Figure 10-1: Choosing a personal style — Country or Modern — is about selecting a look that makes you feel happy.

Country   vs.   Modern

The numerous options you have can make choosing just one style — or even two or three — difficult. When you're having trouble making up your mind about which decorating styles you want to include in your home, knowing more about yourself may help you make up your mind. So take a few minutes to answer the questions in the following quiz, and let your natural preferences shine through.

Section I: Personal Style Pursuit

To get an idea of your decorating mood, answer the following questions (circle your responses, then total your scores):

1. **My favorite mood is:**

   A. Buttoned up

   B. In control

   C. With it

   D. At peace

   E. In love

2. **My favorite historic site is:**

   A. Monticello

   B. Falling Water by Frank Lloyd Wright

   C. The Louvre

   D. King Ranch

   E. The Taj Mahal

3. **If I had to live with only one color, I would choose:**

   A. Royal blue

   B. Pure white

   C. Beige

   D. Hunter green

   E. Dusty rose

4. **If I could pick only one pattern, it would be:**

   A. Paisley

   B. Solid color woven design

   C. Leopard print

   D. Laura-Ashley-type mini-print

   E. English chintz

5. **If I could choose only one piece of furniture, it would be:**

   A. A wing chair

   B. A white sectional sofa

   C. A hutch

   D. An entertainment center

   E. A canopy bed

Now total up the number of responses you had for each letter and enter the totals here:

A _____ B _____ C _____ D _____ E _____

If you answered mostly A, your mood is Traditional. Warm wood colors and interesting printed fabrics enrich your life.

If you answered mostly B, your mood is Contemporary or Modern. Stream-lined furniture and fabrics with woven patterns add up to the "clean" look of Contemporary that satisfies you.

If you answered mostly C, your mood is more Eclectic. The mix is what matters to you. To make mixing easier, try to limit your furniture to two or three compatible styles.

If you answered mostly D, your mood is Country. A great gathering of friendly objects and the heart-warming look of time-worn furnishings appeal to your instincts.

If you answered mostly E, your mood leans toward Romantic. Gorgeous colors, soft fabrics, and pretty objects provide the environment that you need in order to flourish.

Section II: Frills or No Frills?

To see whether you prefer more or less frilliness, circle any of the following items that you especially like:

Category A	*Category B*
Florals	Stripes
Pretty colors	Neutrals
Lots of pillows and throws	Important accessories only
Several different collectibles	Investment collections
Several patterns	Textures
Fresh flowers	Bowls of green apples
Displaying keepsakes and mementos	Leather
Paintings of mother and child	Still-life paintings
Rooms with a view	Rooms with a television
Painted furniture	Natural fine woods
Sleek surfaces	Glass and chrome

Count the number of circled items in Category A and Category B, and enter the totals here:

A _____ B _____

If you answered mostly A, add lots of frills and flourishes to your home.

If you answered mostly B, downplay frills in your house, for rooms that are tailored to perfection.

Section III: Am I Formal or Informal?

To determine whether your home should lean toward the formal or the informal, answer the following questions (True or False):

1. I feel it's best for the host or hostess to serve his or her guests. True or False?

2. I prefer lots of texture and easy-to-care-for, durable materials. True or False?

3. I prefer meals served in the dining room. True or False?

4. I prefer fine fabrics and luxury materials. True or False?

5. I like touches of wit, humor, and whimsy in my rooms. True or False?

6. I most often entertain guests in the kitchen and family room. True or False?

7. I most often entertain my guests in the living room. True or False?

8. I prefer symmetrical room arrangements. True or False?

9. I like lots of furniture groupings placed around a room. True or False?

10. I like very serious interiors. True or False?

11. When others are in my home I tell them to put their feet up and help themselves to whatever they want. True or False?

12. Everyday is Casual Friday. True or False?

Give yourself the following points for each question:

1. True = 5, False = 0	7. True = 5, False = 0
2. True = 0, False = 5	8. True = 5, False = 0
3. True = 5, False = 0	9. True = 0, False = 5
4. True = 5, False = 0	10. True = 5, False = 0
5. True = 0, False = 5	11. True = 0, False = 5
6. True = 0, False = 5	12. True = 0, False = 5

If your score is higher (with 60 being the maximum), you tend toward the formal. If your score is lower, you tend toward the informal.

Writing a Personal Style Statement

After you take the time to answer the questions in the preceding quiz, you should have a better idea of your personal style. But writing out your ideas in the form of a statement usually helps to make it more concrete in your mind.

Take a look at the following example of a personal style statement, and then try to write your own:

"I like a *casual, eclectic* style, with *frilly* touches."

Take your personal style statement with you when you go shopping. Then if you can't decide between two fabrics, you can look at your personal style statement and let it help you decide.

Developing Your Personal Style

So, you've taken the quiz, but you're still not absolutely sure how to express your likes and dislikes.

Try out some of the following techniques for developing your personal style:

- ✔ **Experiment with color.** Tape a large piece of colored fabric or paper to the wall. Reenter the room, gauging your immediate response to the color. Then repeat the process with other colors. How does each color make you feel? Happy? Sad? Calm? Depressed? Better? Worse? Rate each color, beginning with the one that makes you feel best.

- ✔ **Treat a small room (hallway, laundry, or playroom) as your "color lab."** If you'd like to experiment with a color, but you don't want to use your living room as a guinea pig, paint one or all four walls of a smaller, more private room in the new color. Because paint is easily and inexpensively changed, if you decide you can't abide by that color, you can paint the walls a safe color again. All you've lost is a couple of bucks and a little energy (and look what you've gained!).

- ✔ **Visit designer showcase houses for avant-garde ideas and daring pairings of furniture and accessories.** Take a notebook and jot down your likes, dislikes, and criticisms. Review your notes occasionally as you continue decorating and redecorating your home.

- ✔ **Look at department and furniture store vignettes and room settings.** Take note of the relationships between furniture, backgrounds, and accessories that underscore a particular theme. Make a note of the ones that appeal strongly to you. What did you like best or least about the room? Getting a sense of your most extreme likes and dislikes is important.

- ✔ **Keep a notebook of all the magazine pictures of rooms you like.** Take note of the elements that worked together to create a look. Note special architectural features (such as moldings, windows, fireplaces, and doors), surface treatments, furniture styles, color schemes, and other nuances.

- ✔ **Keep all your notes and ideas together in a folder.** Review your ideas from time to time, especially after you've seen a showcase house or room that strongly appeals to you. You may be able to adapt these things to your own rooms.

- ✔ **Make short lists of colors, furniture, and accessories that you like.** Take your lists with you on shopping trips so that you don't become overwhelmed by all the options.

- ✔ **Keep an eye out for new decorating books on subjects and styles that you like.** Glance through the books in the bookstore or library and maybe even add them to your library for ready reference.

Admitting that you're crazy about a certain color today doesn't mean you're stuck with it for life. Expect your personal style to evolve as your awareness grows, your knowledge builds, and your taste develops. Above all, don't be afraid to experiment (especially when you can do it easily and inexpensively).

Adding Personal Touches

Every item you select for a room is an expression of your personal style. If you love pattern, for example, chances are you'll seize every opportunity to express that love, starting with walls and including curtains and other fabrics. Wall covering offers up pattern galore, especially if you choose coordinating patterns.

If too much pattern is not your taste, decide just how much is enough. None? Or just a little, for relief from plain and simple surfaces, as shown in Figure 10-2. If this plain-and-simple style suits you, probably only a few, important accessories are necessary.

Figure 10-2: Thin horizontal lines on the walls create a sense of rhythm and rest in this master bedroom. An earth-tone pattern in the bedding and a few strong accessories underscore the simplicity of the room.

Photograph courtesy Broyhill Furniture

So take the opportunity to add personal touches to your house to make it feel like your home. If you're not sure how much is enough, add just a few items at a time. You'll be able to tell when you've reached your limit.

When shopping, if you're not sure if something will work well, ask the salesperson before you buy it whether you can return it. Keep your receipts and observe the store's policy for returns and exchanges.

There are lots of reasons you should hesitate to add personal touches of a permanent sort. But if you plan on selling your house in the near future, or you're renting and the lease forbids you from painting the walls, you may wonder how to make the place you live in feel like home. Here are some tips and techniques for adding exciting personal touches that only *seem* permanent:

- **Paint just one, focal wall your signature color.** You can paint it white or beige later, if you need to — and painting one wall is a lot easier than painting four!

- **Repeat your favorite color — magenta, tulip yellow, cornflower blue — around a neutral room.** You can achieve this by adding the color to various accessories, such as toss pillows, picture mats, and lamp bases.

- **Choose fabrics in your wild, favorite color for draperies and upholstery.** These portable pleasures will leave when you do.

- **Make a color statement with a large, room-size rug, and then repeat the colors throughout the room in accessories.** A rug is one background surface you can roll up and truck away to work its magic at your next destination.

- **Display collections in a distinctive cabinet.** Choose a cabinet or other piece of furniture that both establishes your interests and enthusiasms and is a good traveler (a large piece of furniture made of parts that disassemble for easy transport).

- **Leave large spaces neutral and satisfy your craving for powerful colors by using those colors on the walls of a smaller room.** Such rooms are easily repainted an innocuous neutral tone.

- **Look to accessories such as area rugs, baskets, and slipcovers for strong textures.** All these things are quick and easy to add or subtract when you move or improve.

Chapter 11

Furniture Facts and Fancies

*F*urniture shopping can be overwhelming. You don't know whether to buy furniture already assembled or opt for pieces you have to put together. You may not know how to tell if furniture is well-constructed or if the wood frame is worth the money you're paying for it. In this chapter, we answer all of these questions, and more. You'll discover tips for buying furniture. You'll also see how you can make an old piece of furniture seem like new again with just a little creativity. This chapter has all the information you need to make your next furniture-buying excursion a big success.

Looking at the Different Types of Furniture

Furniture can easily be divided into two categories: pre-assembled and ready-to-assemble (see Figure 11-1). When you're in the market for furniture, you're better off knowing the differences between the two, as well as the advantages and disadvantages of each kind. In this section, we provide you all the material you need to make an informed decision about which kind of furniture to buy.

Figure 11-1:
Furniture is available either fully assembled (pre-assembled) or ready-to-assemble.

Pre-assembled furniture

Pre-assembled furniture is furniture that is delivered in one piece, ready to be used. Occasionally, the legs of a pre-assembled sofa may need to be removed before it's delivered, so that the sofa can fit through the door of your house. But if this is the case, the furniture dealer or delivery person attaches those parts at the time of delivery. You, as the homeowner, only get involved with the furniture after it has been completely assembled.

Pre-assembled furniture is available in a variety of price ranges. The prices vary based on the materials used in construction, the techniques used to build it, and the kind of finishes used on the frame. You can generally figure that furniture that costs more is of higher quality. High quality furniture has several distinguishing characteristics, including the following:

- The frame is made of strong, hard woods.
- The *veneer* (a thin layer of wood covering the surface of a lower quality wood) is made from the finest hardwoods (such as mahogany or oak) instead of other, less costly hardwoods, like maple and birch.
- Multiple coats of finish cover the wood frame.
- The hardware for the glide rails of the drawers and for the drawer pulls is sturdy and has a protective finish for long wear.

If you want your furniture to last for years, buy the best furniture you can afford.

You can buy pre-assembled furniture in traditional furniture stores. But don't forget to check out other sources, including estate, garage, and moving sales; flea markets; auctions; consignment shops; and charity outlets (such as Goodwill, the Salvation Army, and church thrift shops). One person's trash can become *your* treasure!

If you shop at places other than traditional furniture stores, you may be able to buy older, higher-quality furniture for less money than you'd spend on new pieces at a traditional furniture store. If you live near an alternative source of furniture that benefits from the castoffs of the wealthy, you can find some especially good deals. So get to know the people who run the store and ask them to alert you to new arrivals. Many experienced shoppers — even antique dealers — know to shop in these places, so competition can be fierce.

You may buy furniture from these second-hand sources with the intention of refinishing and perhaps restoring your new find. Refinishing furniture and making it look like new isn't as difficult as you may think — and a lot of materials are available in paint and craft shops to make the job easier and faster.

To make an odd assortment of furniture seem less odd, paint all the pieces either white or black, or refinish them in an identical stain. To make a unique piece stand out, you may want to decoratively paint it or cover it in a mosaic or in some other special finish.

Ready-to-assemble furniture

Ready-to-assemble (RTA) furniture is furniture that you need to put together, and it's more available and more acceptable now than it's ever been. Ready-to-assemble furniture is so popular mainly because it's much less expensive than pre-assembled furniture. Plus, it's instantly available — you don't have to wait for delivery.

The most popular kinds of ready-to-assemble furniture are bookshelves and desks. Ready-to-assemble furniture can be made from a variety of materials, but laminates are the easiest to assemble.

Even if you're a do-it-yourselfer, before you buy, be sure to find out how the piece should be assembled. Some ready-to-assemble furniture requires a lot more work than other furniture. Check to see whether you have all the tools you need to finish the job (some manufacturers include the tools you need in the box, but others don't). So be sure you know what you're getting into before you get your new furniture home.

Buying Quality Case Goods

The term *case goods* refers to furniture such as dressers, table, chests, armoires (mainly storage pieces) *that is not upholstered,* and is usually made of wood or metal. When you're buying furniture, the quality of the case goods plays a huge part in determining the price. Several factors affect the overall quality of case goods, including the following:

- Wood pieces should be joined in either a *mortise and tendon* (in which one piece fits into a pocket on the other) or a *dovetail* (in which the pieces fit together like meshing gears). Then the pieces should be glued together for greatest strength.

- Drawers should glide easily on heavy-duty glide rails, and the drawers shouldn't move or wobble from side to side.

- The insides of drawers should be smoothly sanded.

Ask the salesperson to point out these and other excellent furniture construction features so you know what you're getting.

High quality case goods come in a range of prices, so if your budget is limited, you're not limited to cheap furniture. You may even be able to find high quality case goods in your favorite style, *and* at a price you can afford. Be sure to check out the section called "Pre-assembled furniture" for more information on non-traditional places to buy furniture.

Think twice before buying inexpensive, ready-to-assemble pine case goods — especially those that require a lot of effort to finish. Think about where, when, and how often you'll use these pieces, as well as how long you want them to last. Inexpensive pine case goods don't stand up to hard use. So you may not want to spend much time or money on them.

Case goods come in a variety of materials, including wicker, chrome, stainless steel, wrought iron, wire, plastic, glass, and laminates. Take a look at the following tips on some different case good materials before you choose which one you want to buy:

- **Wicker:** Make sure the wicker you buy is finely and smoothly woven. If a second-hand piece of wicker is unraveling, it can be reglued. Ask your paint or hardware store dealer to recommend the best adhesive for this job.

- **Metal:** You can choose from a variety of metals, including chrome, stainless steel, wrought iron, and wire. Whichever metal you select should be smooth and have no sharp edges. If you live in a tropical or high humidity area, make sure new metals have a protective coating.

- **Plastic:** Make sure the plastic is smooth and without obvious seams.

- **Glass:** Usually used as tops for tables and for shelving, the glass should be at least $3/4$-inch thick for durability. For the sake of safety, make sure you only buy tempered glass.

- **Laminates:** A plastic surface bonded to particle board substrate, laminates are durable and affordable, and they usually look very modern.

Double-check to be sure whether you're buying *real* mahogany or *mahogany-stained* furniture. Many manufacturers stain maple or another less expensive wood to look like a more expensive mahogany, cherry, or fruit wood. The manufacturers don't intend to deceive consumers with this style-making, cost-cutting technique — it just allows them to offer more affordable, good looking furniture. Usually the price of the furniture is an obvious clue — if you find a piece that looks like mahogany for a relatively low price, check to be sure you know what you're buying. Mahogany-stained furniture is often a great buy, but not if you think you're getting the real thing.

Finding Quality Upholstered Furniture

You can find upholstered furniture at the same second-hand sources where you can find case goods. But for sanitary reasons, you may want to re-cover second-hand upholstered pieces. If you plan to reupholster, choose furniture without exposed wood frames — you'll save a lot of money in labor charges, because exposed wood frames are more difficult to cover.

If you buy new (or newer) upholstered furniture, keep the following points in mind:

- High-quality upholstery frames are made of kiln-dried hardwood, as opposed to lower-quality frames, which are made of cheaper, less durable pine.

- Steel coil springs should be hand-tied (not machine clamped) in as many as eight different places where the adjoining coils and the frame meet, for greatest stability.

- Layers of cotton batting, a quilted pillow of high-quality foam, and a layer of muslin should cover the steel coil springs. (Ask a salesperson to show you samples and explain the differences in foam quality.)

- You can specify the degree of softness or hardness of your sofa seat if you have it custom-made. Otherwise, take the time to try out every sofa until you find the one that seems most comfortable. Expect sleeper sofas to be harder or more rigid than other types of sofas.

  Custom-made sofas feature padding of horsehair and burlap, which retain their shape, topped with layers of goose down.

- Upholstery fabric should be upholstery-weight velvet, tapestry, woven wool, leather, or another heavy-duty material. (Avoid even quilted chintz, if you want the upholstery to last a long time.)

  If you're choosing a fabric, look at fabrics available in all price ranges. Compare the *thread count* (threads per square inch). Generally, the higher the count, the more tightly packed the thread and the stronger the fabric. Don't select a loosely-woven fabric for upholstery — it won't last long enough for you to get your money's worth.

✔ Don't assume that your sofa and chairs need to be the same style or covered in the same material. The styles of the different pieces should, however, be compatible and the coverings should coordinate, just for the sake of unity.

✔ For longevity, choose neutral-colored upholstery coverings in durable materials. Neutral colors never go out of style. Add a dash of color with patterned pillows.

✔ If you choose a distinctive pattern (such as a large, bold stripe) for your sofa and chairs, the pattern should match at the seams and align on the pillows to create an unbroken pattern.

✔ Sofa pillow edges should align smoothly, without gaps between pillows or the sofa back and arms.

✔ Make sure the frame of the furniture is sturdy. The sofa should not flex in the middle when you lift it at either end.

✔ All exposed wood parts should be smooth, without any discernible air bubbles or blemishes.

Decorating Furniture

You can decorate furniture to achieve the look you want — or just for fun. But either way, decorating furniture is easy to do. So take a look at the following decorating tips, and try some of them out on *your* furniture:

✔ **Dress up a plain-Jane, upholstered side chair by using a hot-glue gun to attach interesting *gimp* (an ornamental braid or cord), fringe, or other trim along the bottom of the seat.**

✔ **Paint a wooden chair that has an interesting shape and a dull finish many different colors and patterns, like a Victorian house.**

✔ **Individualize dining room chairs for your children.** Paint mismatched chairs the same or different bold colors. (Let each of your children choose his or her own color.) Then stencil your children's names on the chair backs.

✔ **Create an instant slipcover by throwing a king-size sheet, quilt, or bedspread over an unsightly sofa.** Tie it in place with rope or grosgrain ribbon.

✔ **Take a tip from Colonial homemakers and cover simple side tables in flat-weave rugs (dhurries, needlepoints, or chainstitch) that drape nicely to the floor, covering all four sides.** These tables make wonderful desks and display areas for framed family photos.

✔ **Let your ottomans double as coffee tables by adding big tin trays that protect the upholstery and hold cups, magazines, and snacks.**

- ✔ **Convert a glass-topped dining table for use as a handsome desk.**

- ✔ **Use a deep, glass-fronted china cabinet to hold a small TV or serve as a mini-bar in the living room.** Punch a hole in the back to slip through the wires for any appliances.

- ✔ **Consider new uses for old furniture.** We bought an old combination radio/phonograph in a beautifully veneered cabinet for $5 from the Salvation Army. Now it's an elegant foyer console.

- ✔ **Adapt unique items for use as furniture.** Drums can be used as tables. Bunch together a trio of tribal drums and use them as individual coffee tables.

- ✔ **Use loose-back and seat pillows to convert even a slab of lumber into a sofa of sorts — outside or inside, as shown in Figure 11-2.**

- ✔ **Add casters to bookcases for convenient mobility.**

Figure 11-2: Convert hard surfaces to soft seating by adding simple pillows and solid comfort.

Photograph courtesy IKEA ICSAB

CHEAP CHIC

Making a footstool

My late grandmother, Minnie Kelly Ephlin, taught me as a child to make my own footstool, using recycled large dehydrated mashed potato or coffee tins as a base. You might say my grandmother was very canny. Making a footstool out of cans or coffee tins is a fun project — and the end result can add a personal touch to any room.

If you want to try this project, you need the following materials:

(continued)

(continued)

- 3 empty, 28-ounce cans with plastic lids
- 1 yard fabric, 45 inches wide
- 1 package synthetic batting
- 3-inch-thick upholsterer's foam (you'll need about 1 yard)
- Strapping tape
- Double-faced tape
- Dressmaker's chalk
- 1 large piece of paper
- String (26-inch shoestring works well)
- 4½ yards grosgrain ribbon

After you've assembled your materials, just follow these easy steps to make your footstool:

1. **Wrap synthetic batting around the sides of each of the three cans to keep them from rattling when they touch.**

   Fasten the batting with strapping tape. Be sure to wrap it completely around the cans, near the top and the bottom.

2. **Place the three cans snugly together in a clover leaf shape.**

3. **Tape the cans together tightly across the top and bottom.**

   Consider the plastic lid the bottom. Plastic won't rust and damage the fabric or floor.

4. **Cut the 3-inch upholsterer's foam to fit the top of the cans and secure it to the cans with double-faced tape.**

5. **Create a slipcover pattern by tracing around the circumference of the clover leaf of cans (add ³/₈ of an inch for seam allowance width as you trace) on a large sheet of paper (a newspaper will work).**

6. **Cut out your pattern and put it on the fabric.**

   Trace around the pattern with dressmaker's chalk and then cut it out.

7. **Cut a piece of fabric long enough to sew around the clover-leaf top.**

   Make this length of fabric the same height as the can plus ³/₈ of an inch top and bottom for seam allowance, and add 8 inches to form a bottom that ends with a drawstring pocket.

8. **Fold 1 inch of fabric under at the bottom and stitch this in place.**

   This folded section is wide enough for a cord drawstring to slip through.

9. **Stitch the end of the side panel together, but don't stitch across the drawstring pocket.**

10. **Place the right (face or outer) sides of fabric together (turned inside out, or right-side-in) and machine stitch the clover leaf shaped top to the side panel.**

11. **Turn right-side-out.**

12. **Slip the finished slipcover over the foam-covered cans.**

13. **Run the drawstring through the pocket and draw it snugly tight.**

    Tie the string in place.

14. **Tie 1-inch wide grosgrain ribbon around each of the leaves so that each of the three leaf junctures is decorated with a big bow.**

Now you have a footstool that is sure to add personality to any room!

Part IV
Creating Backgrounds

The 5th Wave   By Rich Tennant

"Hellfire or brimstone - which one's it gonna be?
I can't hold these all day."

In this part . . .

The background of a room is essential in decorating. So in this part we cover the backgrounds you focus on when you decorate: walls, floors, ceilings, and windows. We also include a chapter on lighting, because the kind of lighting you choose can greatly affect the appearance of the backgrounds. These chapters cover the main things you think about when you decorate your home and provide all the information you need to create the look you want.

Chapter 12

Ways with Walls

In This Chapter

▶ Creating unity in your house

▶ Decorating according to the style of your house

▶ Choosing appropriate wall coverings

*W*alls form the background of rooms and lives. Covering them with the right materials is important, but it's not a matter of life and death. You'll discover in this chapter that many wall materials (including paint, wallpaper, and fabrics) are easy to change. If you decide you've made a mistake — or just want something different — a change is no big deal. If all the choices confuse you, do what the rest of us do: Take a look at how other people use materials.

This chapter helps you create unity in your house by using your walls to tie together each room. You'll also discover the style of your house and the kinds of wall covering that works with that style. Finally, you'll find out everything you ever wanted to know about the many possibilities in the world of wall covering — everything from tile to fabric and from stucco to paint. Read on to uncover more information on covering your walls.

Creating Unity First

Walls, the largest surface area of any room, create the backdrop. They can be bold or they can fade quietly into the background. Either way, they play a major role in creating a particular mood or style. They also serve as a major unifying element between the ceiling, floor, and furnishings.

Not all walls are the same. Generally, older interiors offer organized, symmetrically arranged spaces with a great sense of architectural unity. Play up that unity by treating all four walls alike.

Typically, more Modern or Contemporary interiors offer four totally different wall designs that can add up to a sense of disunity. One solution to a modern room is to unify the walls, floor, and ceiling with the same all-white or all-beige color. (This is an especially good solution when attention focuses on a piece of furniture, art, or the view, as shown in Figure 12-1.)

Some decorating daredevils jump at the chance to paint every wall a different color in a Modern home! Of course, unity is still a must, so this technique can create a problem. To create some sense of togetherness in this situation, each wall must relate to some unifying element. An easy solution can be found in a large room-sized rug or furniture of many different colors. Each wall relates to one of the prominent colors in the rug or furniture, tying everything together. Creating unity and bringing order out of chaos without sacrificing excitement is easy!

Remember that if you want to create a unified look, all background elements — walls, floors, and ceilings — should make one another look better. None of these elements should compete unfairly for attention. Each should contribute to the particular mood of the room as a whole. For example, if one surface is formal, then the other two will look more unified if they're also formal.

Figure 12-1: To create a unified backdrop for a spectacular ocean view, choose neutral colors for the walls, ceiling, and furnishings.

Photograph courtesy Sura Malaga, American & International Designer's Network

Decorating by Design

Perhaps the most important thing to keep in mind when deciding how to decorate your walls is the design of your house as a whole. Is it basically a Traditional style with regularly-shaped, box-like rooms? Or is it a Contemporary style, with Ls and other irregularly shaped spaces that flow into one another? The design of your home can answer many of the questions you may have about how to cover and decorate your walls.

Traditional wall design

Typically, Traditional rooms are box-like, with a few doors and small windows. These rooms have a lot of wall space against which to place furniture. Often, the architect creates a focal wall by building in a fireplace — a decorating plus. The walls can be broken into three areas: the lower wall, a mid-height chair rail, and the top of the wall. Traditionalists panel the lower part of the wall, paint the chair rail a contrasting color, and then add paint or paper to the top. Traditional color distribution calls for a dark color on the bottom, a medium color in the middle, and a light color on the top.

If your Traditional room is spacious and the walls are high, you can create a sensational room with beautifully colored paneling, a boldly contrasting or complementary-colored chair rail, a heroically scaled and patterned wall covering, and a magic mix of patterned fabrics (see Figure 12-2).

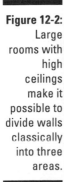

Figure 12-2:
Large rooms with high ceilings make it possible to divide walls classically into three areas.

Photograph courtesy Shelbourne's Nature's Gallery Collection, Blonder/Cleveland

If you want to make a Traditional room seem more Contemporary, any of the following techniques work well:

✔ Flip-flop the color scheme, placing darker elements on top and lighter elements nearer the floor.

✔ Paint the entire wall the same color.

✔ Eliminate the Traditional three wall areas, and paper the wall floor-to-ceiling in a non-Traditional, textured or patterned wallpaper. Either forgo using a traditional chair rail or paint it to blend with the background.

Traditional rooms do not work well with restless diagonal lines, so don't introduce them in graphics, wall coverings, or chevron-patterned planks.

Contemporary wall design

Contemporary rooms are irregularly shaped, with more doors, huge windows, and not much wall space against which to place furniture. Baseboards and cove or ceiling moldings, devices used to maintain some sense of dividing the walls into three areas, are often dispensed with in very contemporary rooms. Such walls (when they're long enough) are great backgrounds for hanging large art works, which help visually divide the wall into areas.

Sometimes, what little wall space there is in a Contemporary room competes with the view through enormous *window walls* (exterior walls devoted almost entirely to windows) or a large expanse of sliding glass doors. In this case, in addition to creating some sense of unity, you should either relate or contrast interior walls with the exterior.

If you're unsure what you should do, take your cue from the local color. For example, we chose atmospheric blue-gray paint for the walls of a New York City high rise apartment so that they would blend, and not compete, with the daytime sky. We kept the flooring and furniture in the same gray family so that the window view and the sky beyond seemed like a soothing extension of the room. Bright artwork on the wall opposite the windows provided ample color and accents. On the other hand, for a Florida living room with a similar wall of windows, we chose hibiscus pink paint that made the view of the bright blue sky and ocean pop out by contrast. (The pink also blended with a too-heavy terra cotta floor that would have cost a fortune to remove.)

Texture also can make materials seem lighter or heavier. Mirror, for example, can make walls seem light and airy, whereas creek stones and boulders make for a heavy-looking wall. Take care that a textured wall (fieldstone, for example) doesn't look heavier than the floor (such as bleached white planks). Such "top-heaviness" upsets the sense of balance.

Wall magic

In the best of all decorating worlds, a terrific wall treatment creates illusions of beauty and almost magically makes problem areas vanish. Here are some favorite "wall magic" decorating tricks:

✔ **Cut too-high walls down to size by dividing them into three horizontal bands.**

In a Traditional room, paint the wainscot (less than full-height wood paneling) a dark color to contrast boldly with a wide chair rail. Above the chair rail, use a boldly patterned wall covering in a strong, contrasting color. You may even decide to paint ceiling moldings a different color and make the ceiling appear lower by adding color to it, too. Or you can bring the ceiling color down onto the ceiling molding and even several inches below the molding along the top of the wall to achieve a stronger effect.

In a Contemporary room, create three distinct areas by applying two horizontal bands of wood or metal molding. Paint the areas between the bands contrasting colors.

✔ **Make too-low walls seem higher by keeping the wall all one light color.**

In Traditional rooms, keep wainscot paneling, a narrow chair rail, and the paint above the chair rail all the same light color. If you use wallpaper, instead of paint, above the chair rail, choose a narrow stripe with a light background color that matches the light-colored paint used on the chair rail and paneling. Use a simple narrow baseboard and ceiling molding.

You can also stretch any short wall to new heights by adding vertical lines from the floor to the ceiling. Do this by painting stripes, applying striped wall covering, applying planks vertically, or installing *bead board* (a paneling that looks like narrow planks) vertically.

✔ **Transform an awkward rectangular room into a more graceful square by painting the shorter end walls a much darker, warmer color than the two longer side walls.**

This technique makes the end walls seem to advance toward the center of the room, and, as a result, the room seems less rectangular.

✔ **Make a square room seem less static by painting one focal wall a different color from the other three.**

If your square room is small, keep your palette light and cool. If you're lucky enough to have a big square room, you may use warmer, darker colors.

✔ **Calm down busy walls by painting all the moldings and trims (including the trims for mechanical devices, like vents) the same color as the wall.**

✔ **Create interest in an otherwise dull room by outlining moldings in a color that's complementary to that of the wall.**

✔ **Eliminate the feeling that a room has too many doors by painting the doors and trim the same color as the walls.**

✔ **Accentuate beautiful doors and make the surrounding walls recede by painting the walls a plain neutral color and the doors in a strongly contrasting antique color.** We recommend an antique color kit to achieve this effect.

✔ **Make unattractive trim around the doors and windows less obvious by painting it to match the walls.**

Considering Your Options

An abundance of materials is available for walls. This section gives you a brief look at old favorites and their special virtues. Don't hesitate to consider using them in new ways to create walls with the look you're after.

Ceramic tile and natural stones

Ceramic tile has long been a natural choice for shower stalls and bathtub areas, as well as for bathroom walls. Increasingly, ceramic tile is a popular choice for walls of kitchens with Old World or Vintage charm — and not just for small areas, such as backsplashes (the space between the sink and wall-hung cabinets), but for entire wall areas (floor to ceiling) as well. Using tile makes good sense in any area that must stand up to heavy traffic and be cleaned often and easily (see Figure 12-3), including entry halls and especially mud rooms. Porcelain tile (a fairly new material), which has color throughout, is an excellent choice for areas where glaze may be worn away through especially heavy wear or repetitive cleaning and scouring. Porcelain's *vitreous,* or glass-like, nature makes it nonabsorbent, which means that it's stainproof and sanitary. Glazed and porcelain tile comes in an endless array of colors, patterns, textures, and sizes. Generally, small sizes are used in Traditional settings; large format tiles are more compatible with Contemporary styles.

Figure 12-3:
Using ceramic tile for backsplash and walls enhances the antique finish on these kitchen cabinets.

Photograph courtesy Rutt Custom Cabinetry

Marble, a fine and usually formal material in its polished state, is seen more frequently in sophisticated, formal bathrooms. Lately, marble is taking on a newer, rustic look because it is being *tumbled* (placed in a rotating bin with an abrasive, which rounds off the edges and roughs up the surface) instead of *polished* (which smoothes the surface). In elegant Old World style kitchens, tumbled marble (which must be treated to a sealant to make it less porous and easier to clean) adds the rustic charm of natural stone to walls and floors. Granite, an especially hard and durable stone is increasingly popular for countertops; but, because it's expensive and perhaps "commercial" looking, granite is less popular for walls. Soapstone, a softer stone than granite, adds a vintage touch to kitchen counters, but isn't terribly popular with fussy homeowners because it stains.

Fabrics

Fabrics are a favorite wall covering for almost any room in the house. They work well for powder rooms and fancy bathrooms. But fabrics are impractical for use in kitchens, where they're also a fire hazard. Generally, in living rooms and other public areas, fabrics are professionally mounted on a backing material that makes them easier to install. The face of the fabric may also be treated professionally with a protective coating that makes it easier to clean and maintain.

Fabrics used in bedrooms are often gathered or sheared at the top and bottom on curtain rods that are attached to the wall. Another method is to gather fabric on top and bottom wood slats, which are screwed or nailed into the wall. A third do-it-yourself method is to gather and staple fabric directly onto the wall. In some cases, fabric is used to create tent effects in bedrooms and bathrooms. The effect is both elegant and romantic, and it's also a very practical way to disguise disfigured walls and ceilings.

Favorite fabrics for walls are velvet, linen, silk, cotton chintz, and cotton corduroy.

Mirror

Mirror is a valuable ally in the battle to expand small spaces visually and to reflect both light and views. Use it in wall-to-wall, floor-to-ceiling applications in Contemporary rooms. Mirroring a wall above a *wainscot* (wood paneling) or *dado* (the area below a chair rail) in a Traditional room and especially in small- or medium-sized dining rooms is also considered a good idea. Large, wall-sized mirrors above vanities are practical and very decorative.

Mirror is available in large sheets for installation by professionals in wall-to-wall applications. Do-it-yourselfers find mirror strips in various widths and lengths and large mirror tiles easier to handle. Both are available in plain or beveled edges.

Paint

Paint offers so much for so little. You can choose virtually any color, including one to match your favorite blouse or shirt. Just take it with you to the paint store and the computer there will match it perfectly. Not sure what color or colors you'd like? Some stores have computerized aids for selecting just the right color scheme for any room. Want a texture, as well? No problem. New faux-finish and special decorative effects come in a can or kit, complete with instruction booklets and videos. Choose any sheen from matte or subtle eggshell to semi-gloss to high-tech, high gloss. Expect to find *green paints* — paints formulated with ecology in mind. These paints take a little longer to dry than the old oil-based paints.

And if yours is a high-traffic household, pick a finish that's not only beautiful but washable. Paint technology is always improving, so that one coat of quality paint is sufficient. You may have to pay a little more, but you save a lot of labor.

If you're in doubt about just which paint to buy for a particular area, ask your salesperson. Follow directions for properly preparing the surface you plan to paint. (For example, don't paint over wallpaper or peeling paint.) You'll be much happier with your finished job if you exercise care up front.

You can use paint in many different ways and achieve totally different looks depending on the technique you choose. Figure 12-4 illustrates several different painting techniques, and the sidebar "Special effects with paint" provides suggestions for using paint in creative ways. For even more information about paint and painting techniques, check out a copy of *Home Improvement For Dummies* (IDG Books Worldwide, Inc.). There you'll find more than you ever needed to know.

Figure 12-4:
You can apply paint in a number of different ways to achieve very different effects.

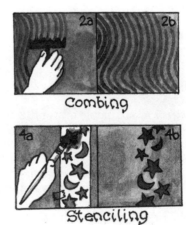

CHEAP CHIC

Special effects with paint

Paint, probably the least expensive wall covering material, is also the most versatile. Here are some special decorative paint effects to enliven walls:

✔ **Classic faux finishes:** Faux paint finishes have never been more popular. They include sponging, ragging, rolling, combing, feathering, stippling, spattering, masking, marbleizing, and tortoise and bamboo finishes. All are do-it-yourself projects, and kits and instructions are readily available at hardware stores and hobby shops.

✔ **Other faux finishes:** If traditional faux finishes aren't your cup of tea, check out the Ralph Lauren Paint "Techniques" booklet and learn step-by-step how to make a painted wall look like denim, chambray, linen, or antiqued leather. If that's not enough, consider the historic crackle or aging finishes; or unique finishes that

simulate such sophisticated textures as gray flannel, duchesse satin, suede, and river rock. Kits, how-to booklets, and videos are available in paint stores and home centers.

✔ **Gilding:** Call attention to molding and decorative trim by *gilding* (covering in gold leaf).

Because gilding with *real* gold leaf is very expensive, you may want to consider using inexpensive gold that comes in a tube. You can apply this less-expensive finish with your fingertip, and it's available at most arts and crafts stores.

✔ **Stenciling:** Stenciling is a classic art form that seems to grow more popular every year. It's a charming touch to Colonial, Early American, Country, and Romantic rooms. And it's easy to do, even for amateurs. Books and kits abound.

Stucco

Stucco (a textured plaster) is a great traditional finish for Country style walls. Ask your paint dealer about stuccos that come premixed, ready to spread from the can. Practice your spreading technique on a piece of plywood or gypsum wallboard so that you get the precise texture you're aiming for.

Wallpaper and wall coverings

Wallpaper isn't just paper anymore. Much of it is really vinyl or vinyl-coated, so it's tougher, longer wearing, and can be washed or scrubbed. For these reasons, it's called *wall covering*. No other surface really does what a well-designed wall covering does for any room — introduce unique pattern, color, and texture simultaneously. The range of patterns is so vast that you're virtually certain to find anything you want or need.

One necessity when shopping for wall covering is patience. So give yourself time to search for and find the perfect wall covering.

Remember that you may need a specific wall covering pattern to solve a difficult decorating problem, so finding the perfect wall covering can be very important. For example, you may need a tiny geometric on a light background to simultaneously create a sense of unity and dimension in a small attic room. You may need a large floral pattern to make a big bedroom look better-scaled. And you may need just the right pattern to visually furnish a hallway that's too small for furniture and too large to look empty. In sophisticated, Contemporary living rooms, textured wall coverings add a richness that paint cannot completely mimic. Certain embossed wall coverings take on the look of leather, carved wood, and ornate plaster, and they can be painted. Coordinating patterns and borders expand the possibilities. Many wall coverings come pre-pasted for easier installation.

Wood

Wood comes in many guises. One of the most ancient forms is logs. Unless you have a log home, logs are probably not something you'll add to your walls. But paneling may be.

When shopping for wood paneling, be prepared to see an infinite range of panelings in an assortment of colors, wood patterns, and finishes.

- Paneling commonly comes in 4-x-8-foot sizes for easy, efficient installation.

- Popular again is *bead board,* which resembles tongue-and-groove planks that feature a distinctive, thin, vertical stripe. Bead board is particularly good-looking in Cottage-style interiors and is used in just about every room in the house, beginning with the front entry and ending with the kitchen. (Bead board can even be applied to ceilings!)

- Real planks — especially knotty pine — are popular wall surfaces and are great for cottage and lodge-look interiors and for dens and family rooms.

- Wood moldings, of course, have been used for centuries to create designs on walls that simulate or enhance paneling. These can be painted to blend or contrast with painted walls or stained to match wood paneling or planks.

Chapter 13

Fancy Floors

Most people don't realize this, but flooring and floor covering are two different things. *Flooring* is the hard, finished surface, such as wood, tile, or stone, that is permanently attached to, and an important part of, a building. *Floor covering* is a material, such as carpeting or an area rug, that is laid on top of finished flooring. Floorings and floor coverings are available in many different materials. Many rooms use both a flooring and a floor covering — for example, a rug used to soften a hard surface like wood.

In this chapter, we show you some of the most popular of these materials — wood, stone, synthetics, carpeting, and rugs. We highlight some of the advantages and disadvantages of each material. And we explain various ways you can decorate with them.

Pondering Hard Surfaces

Hard surface flooring is available in a wide range of materials, including everything from wood to natural stone to ceramic tile. Recently, some designers have even used concrete flooring for very modern rooms. Synthetic flooring (either resilient vinyl or the newer laminate flooring) is less expensive than other materials. And linoleum, one of the first man-made floor coverings, is making a comeback.

Each flooring material has both pros and cons, and you have to weigh these to determine what's best for you. The following sections provide a quick review of several popular hard surface floor covering materials. But when you're choosing your floor covering, shopping around and looking at what's available is still your best bet.

Wood

Wood flooring is available in two forms: *traditional* (which is installed and finished by professionals) and *engineered* or *pre-finished* (which you can install yourself).

Traditional solid wood flooring comes in two configurations: planks (in wide or narrow widths, and in same-size or random widths and lengths) and parquet patterns. Usually installed and finished by professionals, traditional wood flooring costs more than its pre-finished counterpart. But traditional wood flooring can be refinished several times, so it lasts for many years. Some pre-finished wood flooring, which you can install yourself, is thinner than traditional wood flooring and usually can be refinished only one time. What you gain in lower costs and ease of installation you lose in longevity with pre-finished wood flooring. After they've been installed, distinguishing pre-finished from traditional flooring is difficult. The only thing you notice is the characteristic warmth of a wood floor (see Figure 13-1).

If you think you may need to refinish your pre-finished floor, be sure to ask how thick the wood is before you buy it. You need at least $\frac{1}{8}$ inch of sanding surface.

Figure 13-1: Wood planks add natural warmth to a kitchen full of French charm. Coats of polyurethane keep wood in wet areas looking beautiful.

Photograph courtesy Rutt of Atlanta

Both traditional and pre-finished wood flooring are available in a variety of colors, wood grain patterning, texture, and finishes. Hardwoods such as oak, maple, and walnut are common favorites, because they wear well and can be finished in a wide range of dark to light colors. Brazilian cherry, an especially fine hardwood, is very dressy looking and increasingly popular. All hardwoods stand the test of time and are very durable. Pine, a favorite in Country style interiors, is a softer wood in a medium color. Pine does show the effects of hard wear, but if you want this kind of worn, lived-in look, this is the wood for you. Pine doesn't refinish as well as hardwood. However, some people like to install pine (because it's relatively inexpensive) and then paint or stencil patterns on it.

Planks come with either strait or beveled edges. Beveled edges create a rich-looking, recessed groove, but those grooves are dirt-catchers that can slow down a vacuuming job.

Plank floors can be fancied up with elaborate borders and decorative medallions, thanks to new laser-cutting technology that makes cutting and manufacturing planks more affordable than they've ever been. Ask your wood flooring dealer about these exciting new options.

Parquet patterns — available in a wide range of woods — are available in numerous styles in traditional wood flooring and in a limited number of styles in pre-finished floorings. You can choose simple trellis patterns as well as historic styles based on floors from famous châteaux and mansions. The more elaborate the parquet, the more at home it is in a grand room — and the higher the price.

Wood reflects sound. If a quiet atmosphere is your main goal, wood is not your best bet. However, adding padded carpeting in walkways lowers the boom on wooden floor noise.

Stones

Stone, which is both durable and elegant, brings to mind images of palaces and huge houses, but you don't need a mansion to incorporate stone in your home. Many different kinds of natural stones are available, and they all must be properly sealed and maintained. (Ask your dealer for more specific information about the stone that interests you.) The following are some of the more popular varieties:

- **Marble:** Available in an enormous variety of colors and patterns, marble is usually highly polished, fine, and formal. You can create elaborate patterns in contrasting colors of marble, but it's often used in pale, sophisticated colors in Contemporary interiors. *Tumbling,* which is a new finish that gives marble a more casual, rustic look, is at home in Old World kitchens. Marble is relatively soft, so it scratches easily and is not good for heavily used areas.

✔ **Slate:** Sometimes called flagstone, slate looks great in hallways and garden rooms. It comes in several natural colors, including dark gray, red, and green. Usually cut in large rectangles, grout lines add pattern to this surface. Slate is handsome in Traditional as well as Country and Contemporary rooms.

✔ **Granite:** Making its way into today's homes, granite is the hardest of the natural stones, and is long-wearing, durable, and expensive. Granite comes in fascinating colors and patterns, ranging from casual earthy looks to fine and formal colors, and in textures from polished to *honed* (rough). (Both polished and honed surfaces must be sealed for protection and proper maintenance.)

✔ **Terrazzo:** A poured concrete with inset marble chips, terrazzo was popular years ago, especially in Florida and warm-weather climates. Originally, terrazzo was an inexpensive alternative, but today it's not all that cheap. Terrazzo is a distinctive material with great appeal and it lasts forever.

✔ **Concrete:** Once the stuff of sub-floors, garages, and basements, concrete is becoming trendy in homes, thanks to new colors, textures, and finishes. In addition to new color techniques (added to ready-mix concrete, applied to the top of a still-moist concrete slab, or acid-stained by professionals), concrete can be stamped with brick, slate, and other patterns. Like natural stone, concrete must be sealed to protect the color and finish. Less costly than natural stones, concrete is easier to maintain.

✔ **Ceramic tile:** Available in an endless number of colors and in patterns that mimic other materials, including natural stone (see Figure 13-2), ceramic tile is a great option. A wide range of tile sizes and shapes, as well as different colored grouts, make ceramic tile one of the most versatile decorating tools. It also mixes beautifully with wood and carpeting in complex floor designs. Most ceramic tile gets its color from a surface glaze that's baked on for durability. When the tile is chipped or scratched, the color is lost and the clay body is revealed. The only way to solve this problem is by replacing the damaged tile.

Newer *porcelain* tiles have color throughout the tile so that the color and pattern aren't lost if the tile is chipped or worn. Porcelain tile is particularly great for kitchens, because it doesn't stain. But porcelain tiles do cost more than glazed tiles.

Tiles are classified according to use for walls, floors, and countertops. Don't install wall tiles on the floor, and vice versa. Wall tiles aren't strong enough to withstand the pressure applied on a floor. And floor tiles may be too heavy to use on walls. Make sure that your tile dealer knows which surface you're buying the tiles for, and follow the dealer's advice for installing them.

✔ **Mosaic:** Made of tiny pieces of cut natural stone or ceramic tile, mosaics used to be an inexpensive flooring, while larger pieces of stone were expensive. Today the tables are turned, and mosaic can be pricey. Every little piece in a mosaic is hand-cut and applied to a backer — and labor is expensive. Some newer mosaics are applied to a cement backer board that's appropriate for installation in such damp areas as the shower and the kitchen backsplash. Mosaic is also pre-grouted, so it can be installed quickly and easily without disrupting or losing any of the tiny pieces. Because mosaic is so distinctive when it's used as a border, a wall mural, or a floor medallion, you can easily understand why, in some instances, nothing else will do! (And if you're using only a small amount, you may consider it affordable.)

✔ **Brick:** Not to be forgotten as a candidate for floors, brick is a very handsome material that looks just as great in a Traditional setting as it does in a Modern loft. Like many natural stones and some Mexican tiles, brick is porous and must be sealed against stains to make cleaning easier.

Synthetics

Synthetic (man-made) flooring is available in a number of materials, and it comes in two varieties: *resilient* and *laminate*. Resilient flooring has been around for some time; and laminate flooring is relatively new.

Figure 13-2: Stone-like ceramic tile in subtle grays provides textural contrast to the glass tabletop and sleek maple cabinetry in this Contemporary kitchen.

Photograph courtesy The Rutt Collection/Los Altos, CA

Resilient flooring is sometimes called vinyl flooring, but to qualify as a solid vinyl product, it must contain at least 40 percent polyvinyl chloride (PVC). Once considered an inexpensive flooring alternative, vinyl isn't necessarily the lowest-priced material anymore, thanks to value-added manufacturing techniques and materials that are used to increase wear- and stain-resistance. Resilient flooring wears well, as long as you don't wear stiletto heels on this impressionable surface. Cushioning makes resilient flooring easy on feet and legs. This kind of flooring is a favorite material for kitchens and baths because it cleans easily. Patterns are based on everything from granny quilts to porcelain china to natural stones (as shown in Figure 13-3).

Laminate flooring is a relatively new facet of synthetic flooring. It's made by layering printed paper and coatings, and then fusing them together under high heat and pressure. Laminate flooring comes in strips, planks, and squares, and it is made to look like wood or stone. But this kind of flooring must be properly installed, because water (from mopping and cleaning) can damage the edges. For this reason, you may not want to use it in a kitchen, bath, or entry hall where water will be tracked in. Like pre-finished, do-it-yourself wood floors, laminate can be installed as a *floating floor* (not attached to the wall at the edges) over most existing floorings.

Figure 13-3: Luxury vinyl tile adds the elegance of marble to the entry of a luxury condominium, but this classic pattern's good manners make it at home anywhere, even in a country cottage.

Photograph courtesy Azrock Floor Products and Resilient Floor Covering Institute

Going with Soft Surfaces

Although hard surfaces last longer, you may prefer softness underfoot. You can have it in the form of wall-to-wall carpeting — considered a flooring because it's installed as part of the building — or a rug, which covers only part of the floor.

Carpeting

Wall-to-wall carpeting, preferred by those who hate damp mops, fills the floor area with pattern, color, and texture. When properly padded, it's extremely comfortable and among the least expensive floor coverings. As if that weren't enough, carpeting muffles noise and doubles as a sound controller.

Builders consider carpeting a blessing because it can be installed directly and economically over unfinished sub-flooring. Carpeting can also be replaced with little effort and is available in endless natural and synthetic fibers, colors, patterns, and textures, thanks to many different weaves and construction techniques.

Give a second thought to buying a continuous loop rug carpet, because after a loop starts to unravel, it has no natural stopping point. (Continuous loop is a construction technique, not a style. So ask about the construction technique of the rugs you consider buying.) We know, because our puppy started pulling on a loose thread in a living room carpet. Before anyone noticed, a large part of the rug had become one long and very loose thread, lying in a heap at his paws while he tugged away at the connected end, delighting in his new game!

Carpeting can assume either a very laid-back or a very in-your-face role. If you pick a show-off pattern, keep the upholstery and window treatments in a solid or all-over pattern or texture that doesn't compete with the carpeting.

Residential-quality carpeting is available in an extraordinary range of colors, patterns, and textures, but we often prefer commercial-grade carpeting in handsome stripes and geometrics that not only look good, but work hard in heavy wear-and-tear areas like family rooms. If you haven't considered commercial-grade carpeting before, be sure to look it over.

Commercial-grade carpeting is slightly more expensive than residential-grade carpeting, but it's well worth the price if you intend to keep it for a long time.

Don't use ordinary residential carpet in baths and kitchens, where water spills and easy cleanup are important issues. Instead, look for bathroom carpeting (which can be laundered) and kitchen carpeting (which doesn't allow water to pass through to the floor beneath). If you're happier scrubbing hard-wear areas, combining kitchen carpeting in the dining area with ceramic or vinyl tile in a sink and stove work area can be a great idea.

Be sure to use the correct padding with the carpeting you choose. Ask the salesperson for guidance in choosing the right one. And, to protect your investment, ask your carpet dealer about a stain-resistant protective coating to prolong the life, appearance, and performance of your carpeting.

When you're considering wall-to-wall carpeting, don't forget sisal and other floor coverings, made from a variety of exotic grasses and plants. These materials, once available only in mats or small, area rug sizes, are now available for wall-to-wall installation. Sisal floor coverings provide unique texture and color (but they're too rough to lie down on comfortably). Cleaning may be a problem, so ask your dealer about maintenance. If you like the look, but prefer a traditional, softer, and easier-to-maintain fiber, many companies are now making sisal looks in wool and synthetic fibers.

Rugs

Rugs come in many different sizes. But generally, a *rug* covers most of the floor, while an *area rug* defines a smaller area.

An area rug, like the one shown in Figure 13-4, is an accessory that adds an exciting touch of color and pattern and defines a special spot in a room. You can use area rugs just about anyplace in the house — in the entry hall, bedrooms, dens, and even kitchens. Our friend placed a vibrant, watermelon red, Oriental rug in front of the sink in her Traditional kitchen, with a black-and-white vinyl tile floor. She painted the insides of the white cabinets the same luscious fruity red as her rug so that opening the cabinet doors became a magic trick.

The larger the room, the larger your area rug can be. For example, we placed a 10-x-12-foot rug on a diagonal angle in the middle of a long, rectangular, combination living and dining room. A sofa, coffee table, and two easy chairs sit on top of the rug. So the rug defines a conversational area that's a kind of island. It also orients the sofa and chairs toward both a TV set and a big window with an ocean view. Although seating faces more toward one end of the long room, the angled rug directs the eye to both ends of the room so that no one area seems neglected.

You can find rugs that have been manufactured in several different ways: machine-made, handmade, and homemade. Machine-made rugs are the most plentiful and least expensive. Handmade rugs are costly but may increase in value over time. And homemade rugs have tremendous charm — just right in Country and Cottage interiors.

Figure 13-4:
In this lively living room with a traditionally dark hardwood floor, an Oriental area rug with a distinctive border defines the seating area and quiets sound.

Machine-made rugs

Many more people can own handsome rugs now than in the past because of machines. Machines produce rugs quickly, eliminating the high cost of labor. Traditional weaves include the following:

- ✔ **Wilton:** Woven on a Jacquard, tapestry-like loom that permits as many as eight colors, Wilton rugs are considered the best of the machine-made rugs.

- ✔ **Velvet:** A cut-pile rug which looks like, but is less resilient than, a Wilton, Velvet rugs are usually woven in a solid color.

- ✔ **Axminster:** These are rugs that look hand-tufted and have unlimited pattern complexity and color selection.

Handmade rugs

Historic Western handmade rugs include *Savonnerie* (made in France and constructed similarly to Oriental rugs, but with French patterns) and *Aubusson* (similar to a heavy tapestry with distinctive floral patterns).

Oriental rugs come from both the Near and Far East. The six most recognized types are Chinese, Turkish, Turkoman, Caucasian, Indian, and Persian. Each has distinctive and traditional colors and patterns and comes in a variety of sizes. Knowledgeable salespeople are usually eager to point out the merits of a rug. But remember that, in general, better rugs have more knots, are heavier, have a more distinct pattern, and have finer (more distinct) lines.

Oriental rugs are a decorator's delight. Almost any color you could wish for is available, even though you may have to search a while. Patterns and colors range from the fine, feminine, and formal to rustic, heroic, and casual. And, while it's true that Orientals go with any style, not every Oriental goes with just any style. Select your Oriental rug carefully. Like a beautiful jewel, it deserves the right setting. Ask whether you can try out your rug at home and, if it doesn't look just right, return it for another.

Homemade rugs

A number of rugs are either made at home (as they were years ago) or are commercially made with a homemade look. These affordable rugs — made in both wool and cotton — are highly decorative and make great floor and wall accessories. Homemade rugs include the following:

- Needlepoint rugs (made in large quantities in such places as Portuguese convents)
- Chain stitch rugs (made in India by attaching a chain stitch pattern onto a backing)
- Hooked rugs (made by pulling and knotting yarns through a coarse, canvas burlap backing)
- Dhurries (flat weave rugs, usually with floral designs, made in India of wool or cotton — originally for use on summer-house floors)
- Navajo rugs (flat weave rugs in geometric patterns woven by Navajo Indians in the American Southwest)
- Kilims (flat weave rugs in geometric designs and strong colors made in the Near East)

Floor Shows

If you're faced with an awkwardly shaped room, you can use floorings to reshape it (as shown in Figure 13-5). The following is a list of ideas that can be worked out in all types of flooring materials, including carpeting, laminate, ceramic tile, stone, or wood. Draw on these suggestions when you're ready to redecorate — and reshape — rooms in your house:

✔ **Square rooms:** Sometimes static and stodgy, you can make a square room appear more rectangular and dynamic by drawing an X from corner to corner through the middle of the room and dividing the room into four triangles. Install one color of flooring in the top and bottom triangles and another, complementary color of flooring in the remaining two triangles. This technique is effective in any room that's intended for fun, including a play room, child's room, or garden room. It can even be done in a sophisticated Contemporary room, using tints and shades of gray or another elegant neutral.

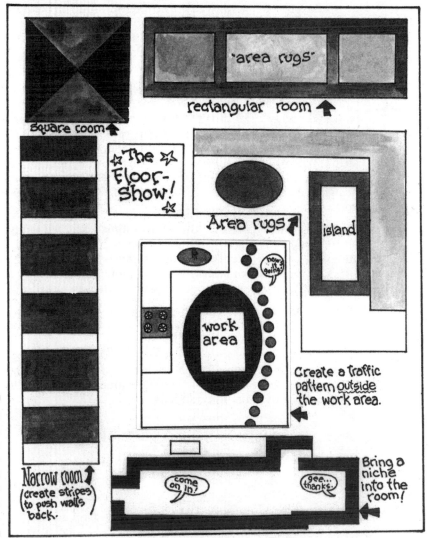

Figure 13-5: Use flooring materials in designs like these that reshape awkward spaces.

✔ **Rectangular rooms:** These rooms can seem uncomfortably long. You can divide and conquer a rectangular room with floor covering inserts in contrasting colors that are positioned so that they look like area rugs surrounded by deep borders. The largest area rug should occupy the center two-thirds or so of the room and be flanked by smaller area rugs. Work out your design on graph paper, until you get just the right area rug size.

✔ **L-shaped kitchens:** Kitchens shaped in an L can seem disorganized and disjointed. If you have an island in your kitchen, surround it with a strongly contrasting, captivating, decorative border. If you don't have a centrally located island, create a strongly-colored circular or oval medallion in the middle of the main work area. If the room is large, create a border around the perimeter in a color that matches either that of the border around an island or a central medallion. This technique creates lively, interesting interaction.

✔ **Narrow rooms:** These rooms can make you feel as though you're caught in a squeeze play. But you can visually stretch a narrow room's width with a series of broad stripes on the floor. The longer the room, the broader the stripes can be, and the more (and darker) the colors that you can introduce. If your narrow room is not very long, keep the stripes narrow and restrict your palette to two light colors that are either complementary or contrasting tints. (Rough out your stripe design on graph paper and show it to the floor covering dealer before you order material.)

✔ **Confusing traffic patterns:** Give busy rooms with confusing traffic patterns a green light by creating a "yellow brick road" pathway of stepping-stone-like inserts (circles, triangles, or rectangles) in a different color, texture, or pattern. This technique is a great way to create a pathway that keeps traffic outside a busy, kitchen work area.

✔ **Disappearing niches:** Niches can seem divorced from the rest of a room, so rein a niche in with the same decorative border that circles the rest of the room.

If you combine different types of materials (wood and stone, carpeting and wood, and so on), make sure the finished heights are the same, in order to prevent stumbling over uneven surfaces.

Chapter 14

Scintillating Ceilings

● ●

In This Chapter

▶ Balancing form and function

▶ Using paint to change the look of a room

▶ Covering your ceiling with different materials

▶ Building to get the ceiling you want

▶ Solving common problems in rooms by changing the ceiling

● ●

The ceiling in any room is as big as the floor, but it seldom gets as much attention. Most of us paint ceilings white and then forget them. But ignoring ceilings in certain rooms is difficult. In small baths, for example, stark white ceilings stand out like sore thumbs. In large family or great rooms, 8-foot-high ceilings loom threateningly low, and 18- to 20-foot-high cathedral ceilings overwhelm. In either case, vast, empty ceilings disappoint the eye. Any ceiling offers tremendous opportunities for adding visual interest.

This chapter helps you recognize and deal decoratively with potential problems. We explain the importance of keeping the style of your ceiling consistent with the style of your house. We also explain dozens of different techniques — from simple painting to serious rebuilding — that can change the feel of a room for the better. Finally, we offer solutions for some common ceiling problems, including quieting a noisy room and camouflaging mechanical devices such as smoke alarms. Whatever the effect you hope to achieve, you can find the answers to all your ceiling questions in this chapter.

Combining Form with Function

Ceilings serve several very practical purposes. Not only do ceilings disguise whatever is directly above them, such as heat and air conditioning ducts, but they also anchor in place things like lighting, smoke alarms, and sound equipment. In addition to serving these purposes, ceilings (and the insulation above them) affect the temperature and noise level of a room. When a house is built, all of these things need to be carefully planned with practical, as well as aesthetic, requirements in mind.

Without proper insulation, ceilings are a source of tremendous heat loss and sound transmittal. Even a well-insulated ceiling may not totally silence a room. In that case, decoration can help ceilings play a second role in sound reduction.

In addition to paying attention to the practicalities, integrating your ceiling design into your overall room scheme is extremely important. For guidance in deciding which look is appropriate for your ceiling, you may want to look to historic ceiling treatments that are key elements in various decorating styles. For example, beamed ceilings are identified with many different architectural styles, including Colonial and Early American interiors. Mirrored ceilings are often associated with Hollywood and movie bedrooms.

If you choose to use mirrors on a ceiling, be sure they're securely attached!

Base your ceiling treatment on the architectural clues provided by your house. Do you see any interesting elements in your dwelling that suggest Old World, Renaissance, Victorian, Modern, or Country? Or is your house strictly Contemporary, without any historical references? In either case, your ceiling treatment should reflect the style of architecture and interior design of your house. Most houses (and apartments) are not one distinct style, but instead blend and mix many "vernacular" interpretations of architectural styles. For more information on styles, see Chapters 8 and 9.

If you're building or remodeling, ask the builder *not* to finish the ceiling with "popcorn" (a rough textured spray-on), shown in Figure 14-1. Instead, ask the builder to give you a plain, smooth surface that you can treat decoratively. Smooth ceilings not only appear higher than their "popcorn" counterparts, they are also easier to paint or embellish.

Figure 14-1:
If you can, choose a smooth ceiling instead of one with a "popcorn" surface.

Painting Your Ceiling

Painting a ceiling is an easy — and often overlooked — way to change the appearance of any room. Whether you want to make your white ceiling look more interesting or you want to use the ceiling as your canvas and create a work of art, this section gives you all the answers — and ideas — you'll need.

Going with not-so-basic white

Okay, we admit it — a white ceiling reflects more light than any other color. It's also one of the most expected and accepted ceiling treatments. So if you're looking for a surefire solution, white may be just the color for you. But you can add interest to a white ceiling by extending the white paint onto fancy cove moldings. Available from home improvement stores, cove moldings extend from the wall and onto the surface of the ceiling. They range in width and come in a variety of decorative carvings or other treatments.

Carry your wall color onto the ceiling by creating a focal point of the same hue. A vibrant spot of color — in the form of an oval or circle painted on the ceiling — can be located over points of interest such as dining areas, conversation areas, or the center of a room.

Using color

Unify the ceiling and the wall by painting them the same color or by painting the ceiling a tint or shade of the wall color. Create drama by painting the walls and ceiling contrasting colors.

In a small- or medium-sized room, paint the ceiling lighter than the walls to help "open up" the room. In a room with an awkwardly high ceiling, you can lower the ceiling visually by painting it a darker color than the walls.

Designing your own pattern

Create your own modern art graphic design and paint away! If wallpaper covers the walls, use colors from the pattern for your ceiling design. This is an inexpensive technique and adds a sense of fun and play. Graphics are especially cheerful in a child's room, bathroom, play room, or laundry.

Creating a sky

Painting clouds on a ceiling is a popular technique for adding instant atmosphere. You don't need to be much of an artist to duplicate the effect of soft wisps of clouds. Plenty of faux painting books give step-by-step instructions and list all the materials and best colors. But, if you're no Monet, consider hiring an artist from a local art school (but be sure to see samples of the student's work first).

Gold stars and a moon on a midnight-blue sky may be just the cure for insomnia. A friend, who is not an artist, painted a starry night scene on the ceiling of her small daughter's bedroom. Her daughter now counts stars, not sheep. You may prefer to glue on shiny stars, which are available at any craft shop.

Stenciling

Stenciling is easy, even for an amateur. It just takes time and patience. For inspiration, look at decorating magazines and art history books. They show designs as simple as trailing ivy borders that spill over onto the ceiling. Stencil patterns, paints, and idea books are available in craft shops.

Creating a mural

Take a tip from Michelangelo — turn your ceiling into a giant mural. If you're a rolling stone, make sure the mural is painted onto a canvas and attached in such a way that it can be removed and carted off to your next home.

Using Materials to Cover Your Ceiling

Many people focus entirely on the walls or floor of a room in need of decorating help. And, if they *do* think of their ceiling, they think painting is the only option. But as this section explains, the sky's the limit when it comes to ways to make your ceiling come alive. We give you ideas for using different materials — everything from fabric to straw matting — to cover your ceilings in an innovative way.

Covering your ceiling with lattice

Lattice can be bought in 4-x-8-foot pieces at garden shops. Painted white and attached to a dark green or bright blue ceiling (and even to the walls), lattice-work creates a great garden room mood. If you know basic carpentry, you're on your way. If you're all thumbs with a hammer and nails, call a carpenter.

Using wall coverings

A wall covering adds a finishing touch to a ceiling. The treatment that's required depends on the room itself. For example, you can decorate a small bathroom by covering the walls and ceiling in the same small, non-directional print. We used this technique in a tiny, cramped, attic master bedroom, using a Laura Ashley navy blue print on a white background. We surrounded the bed with hangings in a matching fabric. The effect was spacious and charming.

In a larger room, use a small print for the ceiling that coordinates with a larger pattern for the walls. In a Florida bathroom, we hung a jungle pattern with a dark background, light dimensional flowers, and leaping leopards by Ronald Redding on the walls, and then covered the ceiling in a coordinating all-over leopard print. Dark walls and a papered ceiling make the bathroom cozy, but the 3-D wall covering pattern keeps it from seeming claustrophobic.

Creating a tent with fabric

Tenting calls for yards and yards of fabric, but it creates a great sense of fun. For the best method, yardage, and other vital information, check with your local upholsterer. In addition to looking wonderful, tenting absorbs sound, quieting a dining room, bedroom, bathroom, or garden room.

Tenting is not necessarily a do-it-yourself project unless you're very handy with fabric and you have assistance putting up the material. (Some how-to decorating books give instructions.) But it's best installed by professionals.

Creating a ribbon trellis

Grosgrain ribbon glued onto the ceiling in a trellis pattern creates a feeling similar to a wooden lattice. This technique is slightly less dimensional, but cheaper and quick and easy to install.

We created a ribbon trellis in the tiny New York City kitchen of a celebrity client, matching ribbon color to the wall paint color. He loved it. We used a one-inch wide ribbon, but you can use any width you want. Use a grosgrain ribbon (glue seeps through satin ribbon, marring it). Design, measure, and lightly mark where the ribbon goes before you start gluing. Plain ol' white school glue works well for applying the ribbon.

Applying straw matting

Straw matting adds an exotic touch to the ceiling of a garden room and adds to an Africa-inspired decorating scheme. Mats come in a variety of sizes and shapes. Attach the matting with glue so that it doesn't sag. And don't use straw matting in a high moisture area.

Using ceramic tiles

Ceramic tile is frequently used to cover shower ceilings. But it can be very colorful and is effective for ceilings in garden rooms and in decorative niches and alcoves in kitchens and other rooms as well. Tile stores carry huge selections of distinctive tiles. Ask which ones are better suited for ceilings (some are thinner and work better than others). You'll need to have tiles installed by a professional for the best results.

Reducing noise with acoustic tiles

Acoustic tile has its place — and that's wherever noise is a problem. A basement practice room for your rock-and-roll teenager's band may be one such place. More interesting designs and patterns are available every year, including painted plank looks. Ask at your favorite home center.

Applying decoupage

You can apply favorite motifs onto your ceiling using a technique called *decoupage,* which involves covering paper cutouts with several layers of lacquer or varnish. Try angels in your little cherub's bedroom, big cabbage roses above your bathtub, super veggies in the kitchen, and so on. Look for a decoupage kit at your local craft shop — they come with easy-to-follow directions.

Building the Ceiling You Want

Sometimes a simple paint job or the use of other materials just isn't enough to achieve the look you're after. If you're thinking that big changes are in order, this section is for you. Read on to find more information on everything from raising and lowering your ceiling to other techniques, including adding beams or creating *coffers* (recessed panels).

Building a false ceiling

Take the idea of a dropped or lowered ceiling to new heights by asking your carpenter to drop (lower) only the outside perimeter of a too-high ceiling. Then have a carpenter install a light in the center area and cover it with a stained glass (real or faux) or other translucent cover. (An alternative may be to install a prefabricated plastic dome that looks like stained glass. Ask your local lighting dealer for sources.)

Raising the ceiling

Liberate your room. Raising a ceiling is definitely a job for carpenters and other craftsmen, but ripping out a too-low ceiling to the rafters creates a dramatic effect and expands the space.

Adding beams

Beams add line, direction, and pattern to ceilings. Different kinds of beams are used traditionally in various styles of architecture. Heavy rough beams are characteristic of rustic Colonial American, as in Figure 14-2, and certain Old World European interiors. Lighter, more refined box beams show up in fancier Early American homes (for more information, see Chapter 8). In other interiors, beams are whitewashed, bleached, antiqued, or stenciled.

Adding classical touches

Traditional interiors used fancy, carved plaster trims (called *anaglypta,* a classical Greek term for low-relief decoration) on ceilings, especially on ceiling areas above chandeliers. Many people now have a renewed interest in these ceiling-enhancing decorations. They're available in a lightweight, easy-to-install plastic that looks like the real thing. Ask to see them at your local home center or building supply store.

Creating coffers

A *coffer* is a variation on a beamed ceiling. One difference is that, in beamed ceilings, beams run in one direction, creating repeating lines. When using coffers, you use fewer beams that cross at right angles, creating squares of empty space. Looking up at a coffer ceiling is like looking into the insides of boxes. Coffer ceilings are usually scaled larger and are grander-looking than simpler beams.

Photograph courtesy Rutt Custom Cabinetry

Figure 14-2:
Rustic
beams add
country
charm to
this kitchen.

Painting the inside of this box area a light color and the beam area a darker contrasting color heightens the illusion of depth of space. This is a neat space-expanding trick in a small- or medium-sized room.

Using planks

Planks — especially redwood and teak — add texture, rich color, and a subtle line to ceilings. If you use them in a bathroom, make sure the room is well ventilated and ask your paint dealer about the best coating to protect the wood from moisture. Because planks create lines, make sure they run in the direction you want the eye to travel. Applied lengthwise in a rectangular room, planks make the room look even longer. To make the room seem wider and shorter in length, apply the planks crosswise. If you're handy, you can install the planks yourself. If not, contract a carpenter.

Chapter 15

Wonderful Windows

● ●

In This Chapter

▶ Looking at the roles windows play

▶ Naming different kinds of windows

▶ Leaving windows free of decoration

▶ Using blinds and shades to cover windows

▶ Covering windows with curtains and draperies

▶ Coming up with some special effects for your windows

● ●

*W*indows are natural attention-getters and an easy focal point in any room. But as you plan to dress (or undress) your windows, keep in mind the practical roles they play. Windows provide ventilation, security, and privacy; they open the interior of a room to the views outside; and (particularly in second story rooms) they serve as means of entry and exit in case of fire. Not all windows do all of these jobs. Some, for example, are fixed and don't open. Others, such as awning windows used in basements, offer ventilation but aren't big enough to allow someone to exit through them.

Successful decorative window treatments put function first! Don't be afraid that function will cramp your creative style.

No sooner had windows been invented, than some late sleeper discovered a need for simple shades and blinds. In this chapter, we review different window styles and the functions of each. We also revisit old favorites in window covering and discover new concepts in shades and blinds. Of course, draperies also shut out light and noise, although the tendency is to think of curtains and draperies more as decoration than functional window treatments. In this chapter, you'll discover conventional and unconventional window treatments to inspire you to make all of your windows wonderful.

Leaving Windows Bare and Beautiful

Bare windows (see Figure 15-1) can be beautiful, and a great budget saver.

To make them truly beautiful, treat bare windows to well-designed trims that intrigue the eye. Note that not every window in the same room has to be trimmed identically. You can also add zest by tiling the areas near the window, as shown in Figure 15-2.

Leave windows bare when you don't need light control and privacy is not an issue.

Figure 15-1: Windows and glass doors team up to create a window wall that shows a beautiful face to the world.

Photograph courtesy Pella

Looking at Shades, Blinds, and Shutters

Shades, blinds, and shutters do a great job of blocking out light. Traditionally, they were all installed next to the window and then were topped with a glass or sash curtain, draw curtain, and finally an over-drapery. Today, most windows don't get this much attention, and shades, blinds, and shutters tend to go it alone. Shades, blinds, and shutters are beautiful enough to grab some glory for themselves. But you can use them alone (as in Figure 15-3) or with curtains and/or over-draperies.

Figure 15-2: Extending porcelain tile pavers across a countertop and behind the sink helps transform an oriel into a garden window.

Photograph courtesy Summitville Tile

Name that window

Knowing the names of various types of windows allows you to discuss them with carpenters, drapery makers, blind installers, and designers. Here's the rundown:

✔ **Awning:** Sash cranks that open from the bottom upward (just as an awning is cranked into the open position). Awning windows are often used in basements. They're also used below fixed-pane picture windows in modern rooms. (A hopper window is similar to an awning, but cranks open from the top — like an upside-down awning window.)

✔ **Bay:** Extends floor-to-ceiling and projects beyond the plane of the wall.

✔ **Bow:** A curved window similar to a bay in that it projects out from the facade, but with sashes that may or may not extend to the floor.

✔ **Casement:** Sashes that crank open from the sides or outward from the center.

✔ **Circlehead:** A semicircle window that usually doesn't open (called *fixed*) and that is often placed over a window or a door (see Figure 15-1).

✔ **Double-hung:** Stacked windows that open by sliding up or down past each other.

✔ **Fixed frame:** An immovable window.

✔ **Oriel:** Projects away from the plane of the facade — like a bay — but extends only half- or part-way to the floor (refer to Figure 15-2).

✔ **Palladian:** A particular configuration of two double-hung windows flanking a central same-height, double-hung window, topped with a semi-circular fixed window.

✔ **Window walls or windowscapes:** Collections of various windows and doors that make up a whole wall of glass.

Photograph courtesy Pella

Figure 15-3:
Casement windows with shades sandwiched between layers of insulated glass.

The words *shades* and *blind*s may bring back memories of old-fashioned roller shades from the five-and-dime. But they're not so old-fashioned anymore. Today they're among many favorite window treatments. Looking for the best shade, blind, or shutter for a particular job? Consider the following possibilities:

- ✔ **Shutters** add visual interest and a sense of architecture to otherwise boring windows or bad views. Whether natural wood or painted, shutters supply excellent energy efficiency and good looks. Super wide Plantation width or traditional narrow slats provide privacy and variable light control. They come with fixed or moveable louvers (for flexible light handling) and with solid panels.

- ✔ **Roller shades** are still similar to the ones your grandmother may have used. However, they now come in a wide variety of materials, colors, and textures. Some roller shades block more light than others. You can paint, stencil, trim, and gussy them up in a number of ways. They're especially good for fun areas like kitchens, garden rooms, kid's rooms, and anywhere that your artwork (and your kids') will be appreciated.

Measuring up

If you decide to forgo the bare window look and add some window coverings, you need to know how to measure your windows properly. Measuring windows is not brain surgery, but correct measurements are vital when you're ordering things such as inside-mount blinds and so on. We suggest that you follow these guidelines when measuring and estimating yardage and cost.

If you're the least bit uncomfortable with your measuring prowess, check with a professional before ordering.

✔ **Use a steel measuring tape for accuracy.** Rulers are less accurate, and cloth tape measures stretch and may not give precise results.

✔ **Take exact measurements.** Round up to the nearest $1/8$ inch.

✔ **Measure height, and then width.** Be sure to make note of which measurement is height and which is width, and measure all four sides because windows can be irregularly shaped.

✔ **Measure every window.** Just because windows appear the same to your eye doesn't mean they actually are.

✔ **Decide whether you want mounting inside the frame or outside the frame and measure appropriately.**

Use inside-mounting if you want a clean, Contemporary look — and determine if the space between the window and the face-side of frame is deep enough to hold the hardware.

Use outside-mounting if the window openings are small and you want them to look larger, or if the window is imperfect and you want to hide it.

✔ **For measuring inside-mounting window treatments, make sure the opening has enough clear space for the mounting hardware.** The manufacturer usually recommends the minimum depth possible for inside-mounting.

✔ **For inside-mounting treatments that are completely flush within the window opening, make sure you have the minimum depth for flush inside-mounting.**

✔ **To allow for clearance of operating hardware on blinds and shades on inside mounts only, deduct the amount recommended by the manufacturer for that model (commonly anywhere from $1/16$ to $3/8$ of an inch).**

Various types of blinds and shapes require unique measurements for hardware, operational equipment, or cornices. Check with your supplier for more detailed information before committing yourself.

✔ **Wood blinds** insulate, control light, and provide handsome looks. They're the contemporary equivalent of shutters. Energy-efficient wood keeps rooms cooler in summer and warmer in winter.

✔ **Metal blinds** provide light control and privacy. You can use them in almost any style interior from Traditional and formal to Contemporary and casual. Metal blinds range from a skinny $1/2$ inch to 3 inches wide and with either horizontal or vertical vanes. Use them alone or in combination with other types of window treatments that are more decorative than functional.

- **Perforated metal blinds** let you see outside while maintaining light and glare control. But they don't offer as much privacy as the solid type. Choose perforated blinds if your only concerns are reducing (but not eliminating) the sun's light and heat.

- **Vinyl blinds** — like wood and metal — come with wide and thin slats. Less expensive than wood or metal, they're durable and practical, especially for heavily used windows.

- **Matchstick blinds** (originally made of split bamboo or other tropical materials) add the spirit of the tropics, energy efficiency, and some privacy to a room. But they won't totally block out the sun or create a sense of privacy unless they're backed with light-absorbing material.

- **Natural fiber shades** made from mesh add rusticity. Just like matchstick blinds, you have to have natural fiber shades backed if you want total privacy.

- **Cellular fabric shades** offer energy efficiency, UV light control (although they won't *totally* block out light), sound control, and a unified look (the cords and controls are hidden).

- **Roman shades** come in various degrees of fullness from almost flat to very full and are very decorative. Light control and privacy depend on how much they are let down. For more flexibility consider installing an inside mount metal blind. Roman shades work well with a wide range of styles.

- **Balloon or Austrian shades,** with extra volumes of material, are great choices for Romantic interiors. These kinds of shades are more than beautiful: They provide energy efficiency, light control, and sound absorption.

- **Vertical blinds,** a must for sliding doors, come in metal, vinyl, and fabric and can be coordinated with other types of shades, throughout your home, for complete harmony.

Using Curtains and Draperies

Curtains and draperies are chameleons. They work hard at blocking light and sound, heat and cold. They're also extraordinarily decorative and add enormous personality to a room.

What's the difference between curtains and draperies — and does it even matter? Traditionally, windows were treated to three types of *curtains:* a sash curtain (to filter light), a draw curtain (to block out light), and an over-drapery (which was purely decorative and is now just called a drapery). In very formal rooms (with sufficiently high ceilings), all of this was topped with a cornice or valance (to hide the hardware). This traditional treatment carries on today in period or very formal or dressy rooms.

The modern tendency is to think of curtains as sash curtains (often unlined and in a variety of lengths), and *draperies* (never *drapes*) as those that draw, completely closing off the window.

Another modern move is to drape and swag fabric loosely over a decorative rod or pole, in a nod to conventional valances and swags. Often, swags serve no function, but earn their keep by looking dramatic (see Figure 15-4).

Figure 15-4:
A Con-
temporary
swagged
window
treatment
adds to the
air of
elegant
formality
already
begun by a
Traditional
faux-carved
ceiling
medallion
and ornate
molding.

Photograph courtesy Focal Point

Options

Don't waste time getting hung up on the terminology. Consider the tremendous number of window treatment options you may choose from:

- Hang just curtains of lace, cotton, nylon, silk, or some other sheer fabric.
- Place a curtain over a blind.
- Hang a curtain beneath a chintz, silk, velvet, linen, or other draw drapery.
- Hang draw draperies over blinds or some other shade.
- Hang draw draperies alone on a decorative pole.
- Top curtains with short, purely decorative over-draperies known as *swags* and *jabots*.
- Top a blind or shade with swags, which drape over just the top of the window and long or short jabots, which hang on the sides of windows.
- Top any or all of these window treatments with a cornice or valance.

You can see that the variations are practically endless, especially when you combine these elements with more contemporary window blinds and shades that look like accordion-pleated curtains.

If you're designing your own window treatments, don't hesitate to do up Country-casual fabrics in a fancy, three-curtain and valance window treatment in a formal Country room. The surprise works magic.

And, just to be fair, don't be shy about using a lustrous silk fabric for simple, tie-back curtains. This look is especially terrific when the silk is in a pink-and-white gingham check.

Lengths

How long should curtains or draperies be? Generally, the longer the curtain or drapery, the more dignified, dressy, and formal the look. Shorter lengths always imply a casual, relaxed, and informal mood. The decision is up to you. Take a look at Figure 15-5 and then read the following guidelines to find the style that's right for you.

- In formal or dressy rooms, curtains should just touch the floor.
- A romantic room deserves elegant, extra-long curtains that pool or puddle on the floor.

Figure 15-5:
Dressy or casual, curtain lengths add to the mood of any room.

Going to Great Curtain Lengths

formal, floor length
to the sill
to the bottom of the apron
romantic, puddles on the floor...

✔ Curtains to the sill, or to the bottom of the window trim (called the *apron*), look great and are practical in a kitchen.

   Never hang curtains of any length near a stove!

✔ Dens or family rooms gain dignity from draw draperies or curtains that reach to the floor.

✔ Curtains that stop short of the floor, ending at the top of floor moldings, look awkward. If curtains are hung too high, simply lower them (if possible) to solve the problem.

Not all windows are beautiful. Fortunately, draperies can help hide flaws. Here are some ways to make windows more wonderful:

✔ **Window too short?** Attaching rods just below the ceiling molding and hanging long, to-the-floor curtains make the window look longer and more elegant.

✔ **Window awkwardly long?** Add a deep cornice or valance above draperies with a bold horizontal pattern. Create further distraction by adding a horizontal line in the form of a strongly contrasting louvered shutter.

✔ **Window too narrow?** Extend curtain rods beyond the window and hang draperies so that they barely cover the frame, leaving as much glass exposed as possible, all of which makes a narrow window seem wider.

✔ **Window too wide?** A huge window wall can overpower a room. Break up the space by hanging several panels across the window. They can hang straight, or be tied back in pairs. If draperies must be drawn for privacy, let the panels hang straight and rig drawstrings so that the panels close as though they are separate pairs of draperies.

Creating Special Effects

If you want privacy, but you don't want to cover up your windows, consider the following alternatives to traditional window treatments:

- **Install stained glass.** Stained glass, provides a sense of privacy, hides ugly views, and gives you something beautiful to look at.

- **Consider etched or frosted glass.** This provides a degree of privacy but lets in lots of light.

- **Think about using glass block.** The Contemporary alternative to stained, etched, or frosted glass, glass block hides unsightly views and filters light beautifully, while providing a bit of privacy.

If privacy is not a problem and all your window needs to do is let the sunshine in, simply hang a grapevine wreath or silk flower garland above it.

Instant window treatments

Need a window treatment quickly? Try some of the following ideas.

- **Napkin topper:** Fold colorful dinner-size napkins in half on the diagonal and drape them, pointed side down, over a fat, stained or painted, wooden pole. (Use enough napkins to cover the width of the pole.) This is a great technique for a kitchen or breakfast nook.

- **Faux balloon:** Drape a rectangular table-cloth (folded in half lengthwise) over a fat, decorated pole. Six or more inches from one side of the pole, drape a long folded length of ribbon across the pole with loose ends hanging below the cloth. Gather the ribbon ends and pull them up until the cloth begins to swag, and then tie the ribbon

into a bow. Repeat on the opposite side. The result looks like a balloon shade.

- **Lodge-look draperies:** Add grommets to one end of a wool plaid blanket. Then run lengths of grosgrain ribbon (long enough to finish in a bow) through the grommets and tie them to a wooden pole or tree branch.

- **Paper cafes:** Fold butcher's paper (which looks like a paper bag) into accordion pleats, punch holes through the pleats (on one end only), and push a curtain rod through, gathering it gracefully as you create a café curtain. (You need a length of paper two to three times the width of your window.)

Chapter 16

Lively Lighting

· ·

· ·

Good lighting provides illumination that boosts productivity, improves safety, directs traffic flow, creates interest, and establishes ambiance. Lighting is both functional and decorative — and in many cases is both. Good lighting schemes call for both functional and decorative lighting. And careful planning guarantees you'll get the best results.

Too little light, poor distribution, or faulty color temperature cause eye-strain and headaches. You don't have to know everything about lighting or spend a lot of money in order to make rooms look light and lively. You *do* need to know the basics about functional and decorative lighting.

This chapter explains the differences between functional and decorative lighting. Here you'll find all the information you need to plan appropriately for your lighting needs, on a room-by-room basis. In addition, we help you figure out which types of fixtures you should use, and which kinds of controls you need for the lights. Whatever your lighting needs, you can find answers to your questions here.

Functional versus Decorative Lighting: The Best of Both Worlds

When Thomas Edison invented the first light bulb in 1879, function was what he had in mind. Today, though, we use lighting not only for practical pur-poses, but also as a form of decoration. Before you begin planning the sources of light for your house, you should keep in mind that lighting can, and should, serve multiple purposes.

Functional lighting

Functional lighting indicates where activities take place and controls the flow of people. Lamps placed near seating arrangements help to create conversation areas; chandeliers signify where major events take place; sconces in hallways indicate a safe passageway.

Lighting schemes should address both functional and decorative aspects of each room. A kitchen needs different lighting from a living room, a master bedroom, a family room, an entry, or a dining room. The level, type, and color temperature of light, as well as how the light is delivered, all play an important role in a lighting scheme.

A functional lighting plan provides the right light for every task, as well as general or ambient lighting. Demands change from room to room, as shown in Figure 16-1.

Figure 16-1a:
Functional, flexible light consists of a recessed halogen (1), accent lights (2, 3), a ceiling fixture (4), and a task light (5).

Figure 16-1b: Halogen lights (1) balance fluorescents (2), and under-counter strips produce task light.

Figure 16-1c: Glamorous grooming is made possible by recessed lights (1), Hollywood-style vanity lights (2), and vapor-proof shower/tub fixtures (3).

Decorative lighting

Decorative lighting (as opposed to just bringing in megawatts of fluorescent bulbs) creates mood, meaning, and ambiance in a room. Flat, functional lighting (the kind found in your office) puts people on the alert with hot spots and we-have-ways-to-make-you-talk glare. What's great for an office building is not so great for your home office — and not at all that great for your home. Decorative lighting, on the other hand, brings out the shape of objects, the "feel" of texture, and important key notes.

Mood is partly the result of the natural law of physiology. Bright light stimulates; dim light relaxes. The stronger the light, the busier a room feels. The softer the light, the cozier a room feels.

Using light levels and locations

A decorative lighting scheme has variation in light levels and sources which establishes mood and meaning. By placing the light source at the right height and location, interest is focused, which in turn, creates focal areas.

Meaning is formed by highlighting spaces or objects, emphasizing them against the backdrop of lower level ambient light. In a dining room, for example, a chandelier placed over a table draws attention with its soft upward-cast light. The effect is a soft highlight and is very traditional. A pendant light used over a table, however, casts light downward, then out. The effect is a more concentrated light and is very modern.

Designing decorative lighting

Good lighting results from good planning. To create a plan, you need to first consider which activities take place in the area and the times of day or night when these activities occur. Function dictates lighting needs, but don't forget about being able to vary intensity of lighting according to need.

When considering how and when you use each room, you can see that rooms have multiple functions. Your kitchen may be your favorite place to cook as well as read, do your hobbies, watch TV, and entertain. Would you want the same level of light for a party that you would want for mopping the floor? Of course not! So you want a variety of lighting fixtures that let you play with the effects needed for casual entertaining.

Your bedroom, to look at another example, is where you sleep at night. But, for reading in bed or getting dressed in the morning, you don't want the same level of light you use for undressing at night. When designing lighting, remember that flexibility is key.

Lighting stores and home remodeling centers have trained personnel who can steer you toward your best possible lighting choices. They can't, however, know what it is you like or need unless you have a solid idea and can communicate it effectively. Bring your floor plans and other decorating notes with you when you consult a lighting expert. Even the kind of wall coverings you have will influence your choices.

Lighting Basics

Design can be a solution to a common problem: how to safely, effectively, and beautifully illuminate a room. Lighting design is broken down into three kinds of illumination: general lighting, task lighting, and accent lighting. You need a mix of all three types to achieve *decorative* lighting. Figure 16-2 shows you some of the many lighting choices.

General lighting

General, or *ambient,* lighting illuminates an entire space for visibility and safety. Light is bounced off walls and ceilings to cover as much area as possible.

General lighting can come from up-lights or down-lights:

- ✔ Up-lights point illumination toward the ceiling. Up-light fixtures include torchieres and wall sconces.
- ✔ Down-lights cast light down from the ceiling or wall. Popular down-lights include recessed lights *(cans)* and track lights. Some lights, such as table and floor lamps are both up- and down-lights because they cast light toward both the ceiling and the floor.

Task lighting

Task, or *work,* lighting illuminates smaller areas where more intense light is needed. (The term *work* is used to include even pleasurable activities such as reading a novel or knitting, as well as all necessary functions like slicing and dicing vegetables.)

Bright enough to accomplish tasks, task lighting must be balanced with the surrounding area in a ratio of 3 to 1. In other words, task light should be three times as bright as the ambient light. Focused light beams should allow for detail resolution and minimize eye strain. Overly bright work lamps won't make up for a dimly lit room (instead, you may develop eyestrain). Using higher light per watt (LPW) bulbs in fixtures or increasing the number of fixtures to increase the ambient light fixes this problem.

Good task lighting fixture choices are well-positioned recessed lights, track lighting, pendants, table or floor lamps, and under-cabinet lighting strips.

Figure 16-2:
Types of lighting fixtures include (a) traditional table lamps, (b) wall sconces, (c) pendants, (d) floor lamps, (e) torchieres, (f) chandeliers, (g) theme table lamps, (h) swing-arm lamps, and (i) desk lamps.

Accent lighting

Accent lighting highlights significant objects. It adds brilliant shimmer to make your precious objects, such as knickknacks or that autographed football, look stunning. Paintings, sculptures, and outstanding architectural features can also be enhanced by a focused beam of light. Use a bulb that is no more than three times as bright as the surrounding ambient light. Position the fixture so that the light doesn't block your line of sight. No glaring reflections should bounce back from the surface.

Halogen, in the opinion of many lighting experts, makes the best accent light because of its intensity and brilliance.

Start Smart — Making a Floor Plan

Start with a floor plan that has all the information you need in order to make wise choices. Chart information on your floor plan (for more information on how to make a floor plan, see Chapter 2). Include windows, doors, furniture placement, location of electrical outlets and switches, and any installed fixtures. Record any relevant information on your activities and special needs. Make several copies of your room grid to explore options.

Applying logic

Lighting involves logic and science as well as art and finesse. You should have enough fixtures to cast adequate light leaving no large areas of dark shadow or glaring hot spots. Where do you need overall light? Where do you need stronger light? How many fixtures do you need? What types of lighting fixtures are required? Where do you want the light coming from — down from the ceiling? Up from a lamp? Or both? Finally, what can you afford?

Thinking artistically

The aesthetic aspect of lighting is involved when choosing which fixtures throw the light in the most desirable fashion and from what kind of bulbs (halogens, fluorescent, and incandescent all produce different lights). The beauty of the fixtures themselves is also important (see "Choosing Fixture Types" later in this chapter).

Ask yourself the following questions:

- Do I want to highlight the texture of my walls?
- Do I want to spotlight certain objects?
- Do I want to focus on a specific location in the room?
- Do I want to raise, lower, or create flexible lighting patterns?

Only you can answer these questions. Note all your ideas down on your floor plan. Then take all of this information to your lighting store. The more information you have, the better job a salesperson can do in helping you find the lighting you need.

Getting professional help

If you want top-notch assistance in planning and buying lighting, consult with a Certified Lighting Consultant or visit your local American Lighting Association (ALA) showroom. For more information, check the Yellow Pages under Lighting Consultants, or telephone the ALA at 800-274-4484.

One aspect of lighting that you may appreciate getting help on is planning the electricity. Do you have adequate outlets and switches for the lighting you're planning? How many outlets and control panels are needed? The location of outlets and switches depends upon furniture placement and room function.

If a room has too few outlets, plugging in lamps can be impossible. Long extension cords are unsightly and can cause fire and electric shock. Don't think tucking them under a rug will bury the problem either. Cords, when walked on repeatedly, can fray and start a fire. Be smart about safety! Install extra outlets if needed.

Talk with your electrician about estimates and recommendations. Do this *before* you paint or wallpaper. If the job is big, you may want to bring in three different licensed electricians to give estimates. Have all hardwiring and any behind-the-walls work done *first*. (Calling an electrician back several times to make changes can be expensive.)

Planning General Lighting

Figure out general lighting first, because all other lighting (task and accent) must be in balance with it. The exact amount of general lighting you need depends on some variables. Some rooms require strong lighting — kitchens, baths, and workshops are typical examples. Other rooms — including bedrooms, media rooms, living rooms, and other social rooms — won't need as bright a level of general light.

Planning contrast

The contrast of light and shadow is the key to understanding how to light a room. Reasonable contrast is desirable for two reasons:

✔ Differing levels of light let the eye rest as it moves from bright to dark.

✔ Contrasting of light creates visual interest and mood.

Plan for two to three areas of stronger light to generate a focal point in a room.

AMERICAN OLEAN TILE, "CORALLIN"

Don't forget to add interest underfoot with unforgettable flooring by combining standard tiles (top left), resorting to simple wood planks topped by a beautiful rug (bottom), or spreading an area rug over carpeting (top right).

BLONDER WALLCOVERINGS

HARTCO FLOORING COMPANY

Bright and sunny or creamy and dreamy, yellow is a cheerful color in any kitchen (top left), bath (top right), or living room (bottom).

Make full use of natural sunlight with walls and ceilings of windows (top), a single expansive window (bottom left), or combined wIndows and doors in a variety of fascinating shapes (bottom right).

Natural floral patterns on slipcovers (top) and in stylish scroll work (bottom left and right), in soft and subtle hues lend drama to neutralized color schemes.

Liven up a room with a dash of bright color and one interesting pattern! A dash of metallic gold (top) and a touch of leopard print make the entry hall welcoming. Bright green (bottom left) repeats the leafy print and sparks two adjoining rooms. Warm rosy pink rugs (bottom right) add contrast to a bedroom whose walls are covered in a cool printed paper.

Strong hits of vibrant and unexpected hues enhance a folksy bedroom (top), sprightly garden room (bottom right), and smart contemporary kitchen (bottom left).

Personal style expresses itself in these very individualistic baths. The strong green and red color scheme sets one bath (top) apart. Lots of pattern cozies up the traditional bath (bottom right). Glass-block walls and eccentrically shaped in-floor tub creates a radically different bath (bottom left).

Please your eye by adding cozy comfort with luxuriously patterned throws tossed casually and handily over a chair (bottom right), sofa (bottom left), or ottoman (top).

Avoiding glare

Ambient lighting fixtures should produce glare-free light. Glare is the result of too much contrast of light, which causes the eye to cope with two levels of light. This results in eyestrain, headache, and inability to see. Sometimes glare is called a *hot spot* when you can see a bright spot of light reflected onto an object. Direct glare is not only ugly, it can also be dangerous. If your fixture has exposed bulbs, use coated bulbs. Another kind of glare, *veiled glare,* happens when a light is placed above a flat, glossy horizontal surface (such as a table) and the light bounces up. If this happens at your dining room table, replace the bulb with a coated bulb or an antiglare bulb.

Balancing light

The chief problem created by windows is a misbalance of light. The portion of the room where the sunlight floods in will be bright. Some people mistakenly believe that they don't need additional lighting in a sunny room because the sunlight will somehow distribute itself equally around the room. Laws of physics tell us that this just doesn't happen. The contrast between the light and dark areas of the room will be uncomfortable. Because the eye needs time to adjust to lower light levels, you may feel blinded or confused when moving from dark to bright areas.

Match the level of brightness throughout the room. Walls that consist mostly of large windows call for more, not less, lighting in the room. Your lighting system should emulate the sunlight in two ways: in the way that sunlight falls into the room and in the color of the light. Check the bulb package for more information. Control excess sunlight with shades (see Chapter 14 for more information).

Depending on the space you're lighting, mixing incandescent, halogen, and fluorescent bulbs may best simulate sunlight. Different types of bulbs emit different wavelengths of light, and some bulbs, like fluorescent bulbs, tend to emit narrower spectrums of light rather than a broad array. As a result, certain colors may not be true, skin tones may look dull, and the room may look unnatural. If you're using predominately fluorescent light for your general lighting, you'll definitely want to fill in with table lamps or desk lights fitted with incandescent or halogen bulbs. When picking fluorescent bulbs, check to make sure the Color Rendering Index (CRI) is between 80 and 100. ***Remember:*** The closer a bulb's CRI is to 100, the more it appears like sunlight.

How do you know you'll like the light produced by the beautiful fixture you just bought? Most lighting stores have every fixture wired to show how the light is cast from the fixture. Notice how the lighted fixture looks during the day, how the light spreads out from the source, how intense it is, and how much area it actually covers. Is the effect you're seeing what you want in your interior? Or will you need special bulbs or dimmer switches to create the desired effect? These special features cost only a few dollars extra and provide excellent aesthetic and functional benefits.

Table 16-1 provides direction for choosing the right kind of light bulb. And Figure 16-3 illustrates the many different types of bulbs available.

Table 16-1	Picking the Right Bulb		
Bulb Type	*Emits Light That Is*	*Brightens*	*Mutes*
Incandescent	Yellow-white	Warm colors	Cool colors
Halogen	Brilliant white	All colors	None
Cool White Fluorescent	Blue-white	Cool colors	Warm colors
Cool White Deluxe Fluorescent	White	Most colors	Almost none
Warm White Fluorescent	Light amber	Skin tones	Red, blue, warm colors
Warm White Deluxe Fluorescent	White	Warm colors	Blue, green

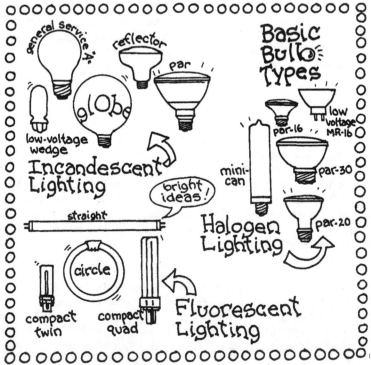

Figure 16-3: Bulbs come in many different varieties, but these are the basic bulb types.

Choosing Fixture Types

Light fixtures can throw light in any number of ways — up, down, to the sides, and all over. Some lights are designed for specific roles and will function only as general, task, or accent lighting. Some fixtures are more flexible depending on the wattage of the bulb.

When deciding which fixture to buy, keep in mind both how the light is cast and what function light must perform. Most light fixture types are available in incandescent, fluorescent, compact fluorescent, or halogen. Many can be adapted to use an alternate bulb as well.

Ceiling fixtures

Obviously, ceiling fixtures are mounted on the ceiling. They primarily throw light down toward the walls and floor. Some fixtures let light bounce up toward the ceiling as well. Practical for illuminating wide areas of space efficiently, these general lighting fixtures are available in incandescent, halogen, fluorescent, and compact fluorescent models.

Chandeliers

Chandeliers generally direct light upward to bounce off the ceiling. The chandelier is actually a special type of pendant (see the next section, "Pendants"), based on a candle. Chandeliers look as though they're holding candles, but are actually wired and fitted with flame-shaped lights (either incandescent or halogen). Chandeliers are traditionally used in dining rooms, living rooms, and entry areas. (We put a beautiful, small one in a tiny, gem-like kitchen in a Chicago high rise. It created quite a sensation!) Chandeliers come in a wide variety of styles.

Pendants

If a so-called chandelier doesn't have make-believe candles, then it is simply a *pendant* light, or light fixture suspended from the ceiling over a table or work area. Pendants usually cast light downward. They can provide either general or task lighting. Pendants come in a wide variety of styles, and can vary from a single halogen bulb to a multi-bulb creation.

Portables

Portable lighting is a great big category that encompasses any light that can be moved at will. Types of portable lighting include torchieres; table, floor, and clamp-on lights; and any other moveable light. Depending on the type and watt of bulb, portable lamps can furnish general, task, or accent light. Upright cans, minireflector spotlights, desk lights, piano lights, and painting lights provide only accent or task lighting.

Recessed lighting

Recessed fixtures can provide general, task, or accent lighting. The actual light is set into the ceiling and is virtually inconspicuous, because only the trim shows at the surface. If you have a low-ceiling area, recessed lighting is a better choice than a ceiling fixture. Recessed lights are sometimes referred to as can lights because they look like tin cans. They're available as downlights, adjustable accent lights, and wall washers. If you're using them for accent lighting, make sure that the bulb position is adjustable.

Tracks

Track lighting provides general, task, and/or accent lighting. It can even do all three functions at the same time, if you have enough lights with high enough wattage. Incandescent, halogen, and compact fluorescent models are available. Very flexible and modern, these lights can be moved, swiveled, rotated, and aimed at individual points along the track. Need more light? Hang pendants or chandeliers from the track.

TIP

Stay on track!

Track lighting is wonderfully flexible and ideal as accent lighting. Any time you change artwork, or simply want to make a new lighting statement, the fixtures can be repositioned somewhere along the track. Track lighting can illuminate art, wash non-textured surfaces with light (called *wall washing*), or enhance dramatic textured walls (called *wall grazing*).

Here are the rules for getting the most out of track lighting:

✔ Affix the track in the right place. For ceilings up to 9 feet high, mount the track 2 to 3 feet from the point where the wall and

ceiling meet. For ceiling heights between 9 and 11 feet, place the track lighting 4 feet away from the wall.

✔ To light art, use one fixture per object. Place fixtures at equal distance from each other, if possible. Aim fixtures at a 30 degree angle to prevent hot spots and glare.

✔ For wall grazing (creating dramatic shadows on textured walls), mount the track closer to the wall (at a distance of 6 to 12 inches) than you would for wall washing, and aim the lights downward. Wall grazing brings out the best in brick or stone.

Under-cabinet and under-shelf fixtures

These fixtures should be used as task and accent lighting. They're great under kitchen cabinets to light the countertop or work area. They're also good for curio cabinets, bookshelves, or any other spot that needs a high-light. These lights are available in incandescent, halogen, and fluorescent, in miniature track, and in strips of low-voltage mini-lights.

Wall-mounted fixtures

Use wall-mounted fixtures to furnish general, task, or accent lighting. They come in a variety of designs and range from swinging arm lamps to wall sconces. Wall-mounted lights are terrific when floor or table space is too limited for lamps. They can also emphasize pretty wall surfaces with up- or down-light.

Vanity lighting strips

Task lighting for grooming is provided by these gently glowing incandescent globes. Great for applying makeup, they create a professional Hollywood makeup studio look.

Lighting Room-by-Room

Think of lighting your entire house adequately: Plan room-by-room. As you move through the house, you should see no dark places — especially in hallways and stairwells. The eye needs time to adjust when moving from a light area to a dark one (eyes need about five minutes to adjust to total darkness). For safety, keep light consistent or plan transitional stages to reduce shock. Light controls should be stationed at all entry and exit points, particularly in hallways. You should be able to turn lights on or off as you move into a new area. Think safety first! Most areas have updated building codes that require a switch for every entry or exit area.

Hallway

Safe hallway lighting should be a happy medium between the most softly and brightly lit rooms in the house. Moving from a darkened room or a bright one into the hallway should not be uncomfortable. Hallways are almost always without natural light. Typically, therefore, they're under-lighted. Do not try to make do with too little light.

Hallway and entryway lighting may simply consist of some up-lights that cast indirect light. If an up-light isn't enough, use a stronger bulb or install extra lights.

Wall sconces placed at regular intervals look dramatic, create a pleasant sense of rhythm, and seem to furnish what is usually a sparsely furnished space.

A nice chandelier isn't a bad option, either. If you opt for a higher-watt ceiling light, make sure to install a dimmer switch so that you won't blind yourself if you have to get up in the middle of the night.

A dim hallway is dreary, especially if it's painted white in an effort to make it look light. Too-dim light makes white paint seem dingy, because there aren't enough light waves to see this noncolor.

Stairways

To safely light stairways, avoid flat light. At the foot of the stairs, use a strong directional light to increase the contrast between risers and treads. At the top of the stairwell, use a down-light. Strip lights can also be placed at each riser for 24-hour illumination. Concealing lighting at the handrail is another way to keep stairs safe. Controls should be at the foot and head of the stairs.

Bathrooms

Two key issues for lighting bathrooms are safety and function. General lighting should be bright, as should task lighting (for grooming). Balance overhead down-lights with up-lights. Fixtures and bulbs shouldn't interfere with splashing water or wet hands.

Small bathrooms may only need up-lights positioned over a mirror or strip lights around the mirror. Mount decorative wall brackets at both sides of the mirror, add one at top if additional light is needed. Wall brackets should be 60 inches off the floor. Use warm white fluorescent for energy-efficient lighting. Install theatrical globe lights around the mirror.

Larger bathrooms may require ceiling fixtures — use warm white fluorescent or incandescent. Don't forget to include a night-light that can be left on 24 hours a day for maximum safety. (The most common cause of broken foot bones is stumbling into the toilet. Ouch!)

In both small and large bathrooms, use mirrors freely to help bounce light around the room. For making-up and grooming, use shadow-free lights around the mirror.

Tub and shower enclosures need an enclosed damp-location, recessed down-light in the ceiling. The shower light should be a wet-location recessed fixture or surface-mounted wet-location fixture that helps prevent shock. Fixtures above the shower must be sealed against moisture. These shower-proof fixtures come in specially marked packaging. (A shower light is a must, to prevent everything from shaving nicks to stumbles.) Use enclosed damp-location recessed down-lights over whirlpools and saunas for added safety. For added heat, install an infrared heat lamp.

Bedrooms

Bedrooms need both general and task lighting. Ceiling fixtures, fan lights, recessed down-lights, or wall sconces provide sufficient general lighting that need not be overly bright — and be sure to include dimmers. Task lights and accent lights can do more of the lighting work.

Many tasks call for high levels of light that you must balance with the ambient light. Reading, for example, whether it is done in bed (many of us love to read late into the night) or in a comfy chair, calls for relatively bright light. Lamps placed on tables or nightstands cast nice light, but make sure the lamp is tall enough to keep light from glaring directly at the level of your eye. Make certain that the lamp shade keeps light from piercing straight into your eyes. If glare is a problem, simple solutions include placing a stack of coffee table books under the light or buying a taller shade. Table lamps or strips of light also work well for vanity areas.

In a bedroom shared by a couple, plan for separate task lighting areas for reading, with separate controls. Position controls on either side of the bed. This makes it possible for one person to read while the other sleeps. Turning lights on and off is also easier when there is more than one control panel. Swivel-arm wall lamps used on each side of the bed save valuable nightstand space. If space in general is at a premium, use recessed lights or pendant lights.

Light the interior of closets with recessed or surface-mounted lighting to make early morning dressing easier.

Children's bedrooms

When it comes to lighting for young children's bedrooms, decorate for fun, but think safety first. Here are some tips:

  ✔ Lamps and other lighting fixtures can be playful and fun. Just make sure that they're not breakable.

- ✔ Make it easy for children to turn on overhead lights by placing controls at their reach level — about 30 inches from the floor — and by using easy-to-operate rocker or slide controls.

- ✔ Track lights are great sources of light for task and accent lighting. (Install them with a dimmer switch.)

- ✔ Install light bulbs with a built-in backup filament. If the main filament burns out, the second filament lights up. Specialty light bulb stores carry these bulbs.

- ✔ Use smart light bulbs with programmable microchips that gradually dim the bulb over a period of time. Check your local specialty light bulb store.

- ✔ Provide a night-light with a built-in sensor that turns on when light levels are low. Place these in hallways and bathrooms as well.

- ✔ Keep a wall-mounted flashlight that children can reach for emergencies.

- ✔ For bunk beds, provide individual lamps with independent switches.

- ✔ Throughout the room, take extra precautions with wires. Make sure that lamp cords are neat and out of the traffic flow (but, for safety reasons, don't tuck them under carpeting).

- ✔ For children who work at computers, make sure lighting is adequate, but not so bright that there is glare.

- ✔ Use only bulbs recommended by the manufacturer of the fixture. Make sure halogen fixtures, which get hot to the touch, are surrounded by a guard.

Living rooms

If yours is a live-in living room, make lighting a decorating priority. Here are some ways in which lighting can make big differences in the way you see and are seen in this important space:

- ✔ Bring out the beautiful textures in stone or brick fireplaces or walls in your living room with recessed lights.

- ✔ Add interest to a long, boring wall by creating a scalloped effect of light, with wall-washing lights placed so that their arcs of light gently overlap.

- ✔ Place a reading lamp behind every reader's shoulder (40 to 42 inches above the floor). To avoid glare, the bottom of the shade should be a little lower than eye level.

- ✔ Highlight a pretty painting with halogen track lighting.

- ✔ Accent handsome house plants with an up-light can fixture. Place it between the wall and the plant to create a dramatic silhouette.

Dining rooms

You'd think those fast food places would catch on — nothing kills the appetite like a too-bright light. On the other hand, ever been afraid to taste food because you couldn't see it! Here are some ideas for adding just the right lighting to your dining room:

- ✔ Create a focal point and add glamour to the dining room. Hang a chandelier in the center of the room. If the dining table is in the center of the room (traditionally, it is), hang the fixture 30 inches above the tabletop (allow a clearance on each side of 6 inches).

- ✔ Tout any table, whether in the center of the room or not, by suspending a pendant light that is 12 inches narrower than the table top 30 inches above the table. Or position a ring of four track lights or recessed halogen lights over a table to make table settings sparkle.

- ✔ Play up your buffet. Hang wall sconces on either side and then place recessed lights 24 to 36 inches apart from the ceiling above it.

- ✔ Focus on the china cabinet. Install strips of halogen mini-lights under the shelves in a china cabinet or hutch to highlight your china and collectibles.

- ✔ Accent artwork. Put a soft focus on it with recessed adjustable fixtures or halogen track lights.

Kitchens

With all those knives, open flames, hot pots, and so forth, kitchens are dangerous places. Let there be lots of light where you need it! Here are some pointers for picking lights and placing them where they will do the best job:

- ✔ General lighting from overhead — with energy-efficient fluorescent tubes — is the easiest way to supply diffuse light.

- ✔ For kitchens with lots of natural light, the fluorescent light should be as bright as sunlight in areas that are far away from the windows.

- ✔ Center halogen pendants over bars and counters.

- ✔ At the sink and range, install individual recessed down-lights (use a compact fluorescent) as task lighting.

- ✔ Islands also need task lighting. Suspend pendant lighting 30 inches above the surface.

- ✔ Under-cabinet lighting is a must. Mount fluorescent strips (12 to 48 inches long) close to the front edge of cabinetry to avoid glare. Lighting should cover two-thirds the length of the counter.

- Kitchen cabinets that have glass panes benefit from low-voltage mini-lights over, under, or inside cabinets.

- Place additional strips of mini-incandescent lights in soffits and other concealed locations to highlight cabinetry and add a warm atmosphere to the kitchen.

Home offices

Home offices are workplaces, despite the fact that they're a part of your home. Effective lighting is a must. First, think of glare-free lighting strategies. Next, be careful to eliminate harsh contrast. To achieve these lighting designs, follow these tips:

- Place two or more large, energy-efficient fluorescents to the front and back of the desk area for well-diffused general lighting that eliminates shadows.

- Illuminate credenzas that have a cabinet above them with under-cabinet lighting. Use fluorescent bulbs and place them close to the front of the cabinet to prevent glare. If your credenza has no cabinet above it, add a pair of table lamps. If this is a heavy work area, augment table lamps with wall sconces or flanking torchieres.

- Position adjustable portable lamps to the side and rear of computer screens to reduce glare.

- Use accent lighting to create pleasant, homey areas in the office.

Green lighting

Go green and think of the environment when you choose your lighting. While we'll all be reaping clean air benefits, you'll be saving on bulbs and electricity. Replacing a single incandescent with a replacement compact fluorescent bulb could mean that 500 pounds of coal won't be burned and the air will be much cleaner! Switching several light fixtures in heavy-use areas such as kitchens and baths can mean big savings over the long haul.

Compact fluorescent bulbs (CFB) come in a variety of shapes and sizes, which allows them to be used as replacements in almost any light fixture. CFB Fluorescent lighting is available in a range of cool and warm color temperatures. Pick a cooler bulb to intensify greens. Pick a warmer bulb to bring out reds and yellows. For the most naturalistic lighting, choose a bulb with a Color Rendering Index between 80 and 100.

To make CFBs even better for home use, newer dimmer-switch technology lets you vary light levels, a must for areas like living rooms and bedrooms.

Taking Control

Planning how to control lighting is crucial for convenience and safety. The location of switches is not only a safety issue, but also an aesthetic one. Consider the height of the controls and the logic of their location. Make sure _everyone_ can reach light switches, including your 4-year-old.

Minor inconveniences can cause major tragedies. To prevent that, here are three important don'ts to consider when you plan lighting:

- While in your house, don't leave yourself in the dark.
- Make sure you don't have to backtrack to turn off and on lights as you move through a room.
- Make sure you don't have to get up out of bed to turn on or off the lights.

The following are the basic types of light controls:

- **Wall switches:** On-off toggle, rocker, slide, and touch-sensitive are the most common ways to control light. For children, older people, or the physically challenged, choose a touch or slide control switch. Most are available in illuminated models. If a room has more than one door, install a three-way switch (a switch at each door) or a four-way switch (conveniently positioned to control lights from three to four locations). Face plates come in lots of styles and prices, but usually whatever matches the wall surface is the best choice. Plates can also be covered with wallpaper to create a seamless match.

- **Dimmer switches:** These inexpensive, install-it-yourself controls reduce the flow of current, which, in turn, adjusts the level of illumination from dim to bright. Dimmers cut down on electricity consumption and increase the life of bulbs. Integrated dimming systems — a sophisticated computerized means of controlling light — lets you preset to lighting _scenes._ These preset light levels can be recalled by the touch of a button from a control pad or hand-held wireless remote control.

- **Infrared or sound and motion controls:** Infrared or sound and motion controls turn lights on as soon as they sense the presence of a moving or warm body, and they turn the lights off after anywhere from 5 to 15 minutes or more. These controls save electricity consumption because they turn off the light when no one is in the room.

Light, color, and lighting

You may have noticed that things appear differently under dim or fluorescent light than they do under sunlight. That's because there are fewer of whatever wavelengths are needed to perceive color correctly. How much reflected light makes it back to your eyes depends on the value of the object's color. This simple fact dictates how much light you'll need anywhere in any room.

The lighter the room, the more light is reflected. White sends back 80 percent of the light striking its surface; black soaks up 95 percent. The lighter the room, the less light is needed, and the darker the room, the more light is needed. (If you change a room from beige to navy, for example, you need to double the amount of light just to equal the previous level of perceived illumination.)

Texture also absorbs light. You'll need more light for heavier textured wall coverings, and less light for matte-finished painted walls.

For best light planning, take note of the size of the room, the number and position of the windows, and the type of furnishings (for example, large, dark pieces soak up light).

Part V
Tackling the Three Tough Rooms: Kitchen, Bath, and Home Office

The 5th Wave   By Rich Tennant

"I like the marble vanity and the wall sconces, but I think the Eurostyle fixtures on the whirlpool take away some of its simple country charm."

In this part . . .

Why are the kitchen, bath, and home office the three toughest rooms in a house? Because they involve the newest technology and, therefore, demand more thoughtful planning and larger budgets than other rooms. Before you decorate any of these areas, check out the technical stuff we cover in these chapters — just to be on the safe side.

Chapter 17

Creating Your Dream Kitchen

· ·

· ·

*W*hether you're an enthusiastic cook who spends lots of time in the kitchen or you opt for eat-and-run meals from the microwave, you want your kitchen to look great. After all, the kitchen is the heart of the home. And restaurant owners aren't the only ones who know that environment affects your appetite and your sense of well-being!

Naturally, you want your kitchen decor to reflect your personal style. But before you pick out paint, remember that your kitchen has to be more than just a pretty face. One of the two most heavily used rooms in the house, above all else, your kitchen has to work.

In this chapter, we take you step-by-step through the process of assessing your kitchen as it is now and deciding what you would like it to be. Because the kitchen is the heart of your home, the thought of changing it may send chills down your spine. But in this chapter you'll find all the answers you need to put your mind at ease.

Furnishings Info

So many things go into decorating and furnishing a kitchen — flooring, wall coverings, furniture, and accessories. Thanks to new technology, so much is available that choosing can seem overwhelming. The following sections provide a short refresher course on key elements.

Cabinets

There are two types of kitchen cabinetry: *face frame* and *frameless*. In the face frame type, a solid wood frame is visible between doors and a structural support. Usually, exterior hinges are mounted on the frame which is exposed around doors and drawers. (A more modern way calls for concealing hinges under a full "overlay" door simulating a frameless effect.) The face frame type of construction is most commonly used for Traditional designs.

The frameless cabinet is sometimes called the *European style* and is commonly associated with Contemporary design. In frameless cabinets, the doors are hinged directly to the sides of the cabinet "box," leaving little or no reveal.

Sturdily built cabinets, like furniture, have mortise-and-tendon joints, the strongest joinery. Look also for cross rails or corner braces that hold cabinets square and tight.

Materials affect appearance, performance, and price. Cabinets in the low-to-middle price range may be made of particleboard. Higher-priced cabinets use plywood substrates laminated with vinyl foil, Melamine, or high-pressure laminate. High-priced, custom-made cabinets are usually made of wood but can also be made of a laminate material. Before you decide on cabinets, do your homework — read the specifications and comparison shop at two or three different sources.

You can easily detect quality features by looking at a drawer. If the drawer is well made, it has solid hardwood sides and a plywood bottom. It is also well sanded, smooth to the touch, and fitted with heavy-duty slides that offer almost no side-to-side movement. Drawers should be full-drawer extension, so you can get into the back of the drawer easily. If drawers are well made, you can usually rest assured that the cabinets are also.

Finishes tell a quality tale, too. Laminates should be bubble-free. Painted finishes should be perfectly smooth and ripple-free. Some new high-tech varnishes protect like a urethane coating. Another durable kind of coating — synthetic resins — are heat-cured. Not even nail-polish remover affects that finish!

Countertops

Countertops have a big influence on your kitchen's appearance. Just changing one can work decorating wonders. Choose from the following materials that let you make a personal statement (and perhaps still stay within your budget):

- **Butcher block:** This surface is generally used for *small* cutting and chopping areas because it requires care and wears down. Butcher block has not been considered the most sanitary surfaces available, but it can be sanded down to renew the surface and remove bacteria.

- **Ceramic tile:** Ceramic tile (which is decorative and heat-resistant) can chip, providing an uneven work surface if it isn't carefully installed. The grout between tiles is more difficult to keep clean than other smooth surfaces and eventually may need to be replaced over time.

- **Laminate (Formica, Wilsonart, and others):** Laminate comes in more colors and finishes than any other countertop material and is among the most affordable. Different edge treatments and profiles (curved, right-angle, and so on) provide style options. Some laminates have color all through that eliminates the old (undesirable) black line edge.

- **Solid surface materials:** Usually a blend of acrylic and other materials, these are a popular choice because they wear well and are available in many colors and patterns (some look like natural stone). Sinks of the same material are often integrated into the countertop, eliminating unsightly crumb and dirt-catching trims. Before you decide on a particular brand, be sure to compare.

- **Stone:** Granite and marble are increasingly popular countertop surfaces. Granite is all but indestructible and costs about the same as solid surface materials. Marble is not as durable as granite and not a good material for use in all counter areas. However, its cool, non-stick surface makes it popular for use in bake centers.

Islands

Islands and peninsulas make excellent use of limited or unorthodox space. They can be easily built, using stock cabinets as the base. If you're adding an island to an existing kitchen and cannot match existing cabinets, paint the island cabinets a contrasting color. (In a pinch, a butcher block or other work table can act like an island and add convenience. What you'll miss is below-worktop storage.)

Both islands and peninsulas are usually 36 inches high — the same as a kitchen counter. If you prefer, build yours at table height and use an ordinary kitchen chair instead of an uncomfortable, high stool. Or make it taller (for a tall cook) or multilevel (if space allows) to suit several cooks' needs.

The minimum width for any countertop is 15 to 18 inches; but make countertops that are extensions of the kitchen counter 24 inches wide. A table-like peninsula can be 30 to 42 inches wide (the same as a café or standard table) or as wide as space permits.

Match surfaces with the same height as the adjoining kitchen countertop; or, if your peninsula is a snack counter and lower than the kitchen counter or is higher than the regular counter, use a contrasting surface.

Counter attacks

Countertop work surfaces usually take up large areas and have a big effect on a kitchen's appearance and function. If you're updating your kitchen by changing the counter, consider these tips for improving both the way your counter looks and works.

↙ So you don't shell peas? Lower the height of a counter anyway so that you can sit down to do some other jobs.

↙ Eliminate sharp corners. Round or dog-ear (cut on a slant) countertop edges to reduce the chance of injury.

↙ Make the countertop edge obvious for safety's sake: Add a contrasting edge.

↙ For those with special needs, install a grab bar at the countertop edge or end.

Don't be shy about using more than one type of countertop material (marble for the bake center, laminate elsewhere, for example). Try to separate different counters by changing the height, interrupting them with an appliance, or using a contrasting material on an island. Blend colors and patterns in small kitchens. Larger kitchens allow for more contrast.

Provide a place for sipping and snacking — whether it's an island, peninsula, countertop, or table (see Figure 17-1). For a welcoming, comfortable kitchen — no matter how small — you have to have a place to sit down for a cup of morning coffee or a late-night snack.

Figure 17-1:
Adding just a few inches to the width of an island countertop provides a place to sit.

Floors

The kitchen is a place for practical and pretty flooring. No matter what the style, kitchen floors have to stand up to hard wear, be easy to clean, and skidproof. Popular flooring options include synthetic (vinyl or other) sheet or rolled flooring, vinyl tiles, and carpeting made especially for kitchens. Hard flooring includes wood, ceramic tile, brick, and stone.

All these substances are reasonably durable. However, you may expect hard surfaces to wear longer than soft flooring. To increase the life of a wood floor (especially if it has a painted surface like the one shown in Figure 17-2), protect it with several topcoats of polyurethane. Expect to renew it every three to five years. Top glazes may wear away from ceramic tile and if that's a concern, consider porcelain tile, which has color throughout that will not wear off. Brick and stone will also need renewable protective finishes to prevent them from absorbing grease and stains and to make them easier to clean.

Hard floors are considered hard on the feet, legs, and back, but if you wear sneakers, that may not be an important consideration.

Figure 17-2:
Heavy-duty oil-based deck paint topped with several topcoats of protective, long-wearing polyurethane make painted wood floors practical for kitchens. For interest, paint on a checkerboard pattern.

Photograph courtesy Stanley Furniture Co.

Faucet facts

Faucets come with either single- or double-handled controls (and holes in your sink have to match!). Single levers are the easiest to operate and come in all sorts of styles ranging from old-fashioned to ultra modern. Lab-look faucets with high-crook neck spouts make filling a deep pot easier. Euro-style spray pull-outs with a one-finger control button on the handle are also easier to use. With these, you can fill and refill deep pots on a nearby stove (eliminating lifting hot pots).

Make sure your pull-out spray faucet has an integrated vacuum breaker to prevent contaminating backflow.

Walls

The kitchen is the number one place for spills and splatters. So even if cleanliness is not an obsession, cover your kitchen walls with something washable, because at one time or another you'll need to wash at least a part of it. The following sections provide some options for kitchen wall materials (And be sure to check out Chapter 12 for more information about wall coverings.)

Keep an open mind and think creatively — you may want to mix two or more of these materials.

Ceramic tile

Ceramic tile isn't your ordinary material for complete kitchen walls, but it's very popular when used as a backsplash for countertops, stoves, and hoods. An endless variety of styles, colors, shapes, patterns, and textures is available to suit every taste. Ceramic tile, of course, is synonymous with Old World charm, but nothing says Modern more than new large-format Italian tiles in a zillion different looks.

Don't use heavily textured tiles directly behind a stove, where hard-to-remove grease may accumulate.

Paint

Use a washable semi-gloss or high gloss paint in your kitchen. Decorative paint techniques and faux finishes that add interesting depth and hints of pattern and texture are great, especially if you're using paint alone (with no wall covering). Your kitchen ceiling doesn't have to be white. Consider spreading the same color as the wall across the ceiling of a large room. The ceiling in a small room looks good in a lighter tint than the wall. Don't hesitate to paint ceilings a contrasting color.

Just remember: light tints for small rooms; darker, more contrasting tints for larger rooms.

Paneling and planks

Wood is a very comforting surface and shows up in kitchens in various guises, including knotty pine, barn board, bead board, and paneling of all kinds. Choose the one that underscores your decorating theme or style and a finish that can be cleaned. Remember color guidelines: Lighter colors keep small rooms from looking claustrophobic; darker colors tend to make spaces look smaller but work well in large rooms.

Wall coverings

In the old days, the term was wallpaper. Today it's *wall covering,* which refers to old-fashioned wallpaper or vinyl coated paper or fabric. Most popularly priced wall coverings are actually vinyl. High priced, multi-screened designer patterns are printed on a high quality paper. Vinyl-coated wall coverings are a favorite surface for kitchen walls because they are hard wearing and washable.

Wall coverings add color and distinctive pattern to establish a decorating theme. This color and pattern adds interest to rooms where so many surfaces — cabinets, appliances, and ceiling — are plain solids.

If you choose wall coverings, follow these guidelines:

- Choose a pattern that hides fingerprints, especially if small children are around.
- Use big patterns, if you have large expanses of uninterrupted wall space.
- Stick to a small, all-over pattern that doesn't require much matching, if space is broken up by architectural features like doors and windows and by kitchen cabinets and appliances.
- Use bold, distinctive patterns in bright colors as room identifiers for young children and those with low lines of vision who have difficulty seeing.

Decorating Do's

After you've decided on your furnishings and backgrounds, it's time to get down to the nitty gritty. If you need a boost getting started, read on.

Select a style, theme, or look

Answer this question in 25 words or less: What do I want my kitchen to look like? Not sure? Read on.

What's your style?

If you think that you may prefer a period style, but you're not sure which style or exactly what's involved, look to the myriad kitchen and bath remodeling magazines available. Clip the photographs of the rooms you like, then zero in on the various elements that create that look. Check the sources listed for each article. Many have telephone and fax numbers for consumer information that you can request.

If period styles are not your thing, think of a theme that appeals to you. You'll be surprised how many wall-covering patterns and accessories address the theme of your choice.

 Still not sure? Rip photographs from decorating magazines, collect brochures, copy photos from a kitchen design book that have special appeal. Don't be surprised to discover that you've collected a variety of different looks. Compare the pictures to see what the common denominator is. Perhaps they're all white, have lots of natural woods, use stainless steel appliances, or are Modern (or Country). Make a list of your likes and dislikes about each. You'll discover your own personal style.

Let cabinets be your guide

Cabinets are the main furniture and natural star of the kitchen. Cabinet costs are also a major part of any remodeling or redecorating budget. If you must replace old cabinets, buy a style and color that will be the basis for your new scheme (French, English, Country, Victorian, Euro-Modern, and so on). If possible, reuse existing cabinets.

Using your old cabinets will save a bundle of money and a lot of time. Ask yourself the following questions:

- ✔ Are my cabinets sturdy and in good working condition?
- ✔ Do they provide adequate storage?
- ✔ Is the color of the cabinets okay? If not, can the color be easily changed?
- ✔ Are the cabinets simple square boxes that can be resurfaced?
- ✔ Can old doors be exchanged for new?
- ✔ Can outdated hardware be exchanged for a new style?

If your answers to these questions are "yes," cosmetic changes will undoubtedly save the day. See the nearby sidebar "Fabulous facelifts for kitchen cabinets" for ideas on how to redeem your old cabinets.

Fabulous facelifts for kitchen cabinets

If your cabinets provide enough storage and work space where you want it and they're in good working shape, cosmetic changes can work wonders. Here are some ideas and options:

✔ Clean or refinish handsome wood.

✔ Paint simple cabinets with a high gloss lacquer-look finish in the color (or colors) of your choice for a new Modern look. A new trend is to paint wall-hung cabinets one color and base cabinets another, or cabinets around the wall one color and an island cabinet a contrasting color.

✔ Finish French style or carved cabinets in an antique color for an Old World or Country Cottage look.

✔ Paint bead board cabinets high-gloss white for a Country look or stain them a natural wood color in the Victorian style.

✔ Re-laminate all cabinets in one solid color. Or, for a more Contemporary or Eclectic look, mix and match colors and interesting patterns. For example, keep the cabinet "boxes" plain and add different colored or patterned doors or vice versa.

✔ Exchange old doors on plain cabinets for new fancy doors in the style of your choice.

✔ Add classic architectural trims to plain cases: fluted pilasters at corners, pediments and crown moldings on top, deep base moldings at the bottom.

✔ Change and update your hardware in your new chosen style. For unity, match cabinet hardware and faucet finishes (all brass, copper, steel, iron, or so on).

Create the background

Cabinets should star against a background chosen to show them off. Contrast is important here.

If cabinets are fancy, the background (walls, floor, and ceiling) should be plainer. Using this principle, choose either a simple paint or paneling or a small-patterned wall covering for walls. The ceiling may have beams or other architectural interest but should be painted simply in a light color that coordinates with the cabinet color. The flooring should be a material in a darker value than the walls, but should not be too colorful or patterned. If, for example, you use ceramic tile, you'll probably choose a plain color tile. You may or may not add a decorative diamond inset tile, which may be too busy, depending on the color, the amount used, and the size of the room.

If you use a very plain cabinet, you may use boldly contrasting colors, patterns, and textures for walls, floor, and ceiling to show it off. Generally, the larger the space, the more of everything you can use. A small space demands some discretion.

How much is enough, too much, or just right? The rule is that the less contrast you use, the quieter and more serene your room. (Just don't put yourself to sleep, unless that's your goal!)

Don't overlook the ceiling in your kitchen. Most of the time, ceilings get short shrift when it comes to decorating. Kitchens are great places for beams, coffers, beautiful paint colors, wall coverings, stenciling, and trellises. The larger the kitchen, the more obvious the ceiling and the more it demands that some visual interest be added.

Furniture do's and don'ts

Great kitchens (or any room, for that matter) call for upholstered pieces that introduce color, pattern, and texture into a room. Decide whether you want your furniture fabrics to play a starring role or second fiddle to an exotic floor or wall pattern. If upholstery's the star, patterns can be big and bold. If it's second fiddle, choose a pattern that's on the small side (such as a small woven check, plaid, or stripe). For kitchen chairs, make fabric pads in coordinating fabrics, keeping in mind that using lots of fabric in the kitchen helps to absorb and muffle sound.

Be sure the upholstery and other fabrics you select for your kitchen are easy to clean. You may even want to consider using washable slipcovers over any upholstery.

Dining chairs should be comfortable and well built so as not to tip over easily. Watch out for table and chair legs that splay out — they're accidents waiting to happen, because it's so easy to trip over them. If your decorating style is Eclectic, don't hesitate to pit antique chairs against a modern table, or vice versa. This sort of visual opposition can be a lot of fun and it's never boring.

Free-standing or *unfitted* cabinetry is a current trend that encourages adding antique or just plain storage units to kitchens with standard built-in cabinets. Baker's racks, old medical cabinets from dentists' and doctors' offices, gym lockers — anything goes as long as it goes well. You be the judge!

Window treatments

Usually, the kitchen needs all the light it can get. The kitchen is one place where a handsome window with no treatment at all is most desirable. In any case, less is better. However, you may need to control sunlight or want privacy at night. Thick-slat aluminum or vinyl window blinds are almost standard where fabric is not desired. But dozens of alternative style draperies, curtains, swags, and jabots are available. And this is one place where creativity is especially welcome.

So go ahead and hang that bamboo fishing rod that adds to your beach house or fishing lodge look. Or cut and hang a slender tree limb cum curtain rod to enhance the log cabin flavor. A host of ready-made balloon swags, headers, and so forth is available. When it comes to kitchen window treatments, the world's your oyster, because almost any window treatment for use in any other room can be adapted to the kitchen. Want draw draperies under an elegant valance? Brocade would do for the dining room. Just switch to a handsome cotton for the kitchen.

Skylights can be tricky. You can get too much of a good thing, especially when that good thing is mega-watt sunshine hitting your eyes at the breakfast table. Avoid the problem by selecting skylights with built-in blinds for the kitchen (and throughout the house).

Accessories add eye appeal

A recent trend has been to leave cabinet tops open for stashing big, hard-to-store items such as platters, bowls, baskets, brass pots, and plants. A bonus is that these useful items have a lot of eye appeal and make great decorative accessories.

Items on open shelves also become accessories and should be carefully arranged. Painting the wall behind an open shelf a decorative color to better show off displayed items may be a good idea. This technique works well when the items themselves are not especially colorful (like white plates) and when they're small (like a collection of egg cups).

Almost anything used in the kitchen can double as an accessory (see Figure 17-3), especially when you've got a collection of things such as wooden bowls, spoons, or rolling pins; interesting pottery or porcelain; colorful trays; woven baskets; old painted tins, cookie cutters, copper pots, tole ware (decoratively painted tin objects); and so forth. Just arrange them artfully, for all the world to see.

A lovely touch is to use an antique cruet, pretty decanter, or another capped bottle as a dish-soap dispenser. Just fill the vessel with a bright liquid detergent, and set it on your counter for all to see!

Two accessories you can't forget are those that aid in fire prevention. Keep a fire extinguisher near the cooktop and a smoke alarm just outside the kitchen.

Figure 17-3:
Almost
anything
you use in
the kitchen
can be
displayed
as though it
were an
accessory.
Here,
baskets
even double
as a
window
treatment!

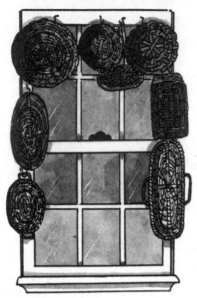

Chapter 18
Making Your Bathroom Beautiful

The bathroom is obviously an essential room in any home. But because of its smaller size, many people pay less attention to bathrooms when decorating. This chapter helps turn your attention to the smallest room in your house.

Personalizing your bathroom is just as important as personalizing the rest of your house — and it can even play a part in your mood and sense of well-being. Cosmetic changes can give an unappealing bath a facelift without the need for heavy remodeling. In this chapter, we also share some tried-and-true decorating secrets for transforming ugly or outdated cabinets or ceramic tile into something beautiful. We also provide ideas for accessories, which add the finishing touches to complement the walls, floor, and ceiling. Finally, we turn our attention specifically to master baths, guest baths, and bathrooms for kids. Whatever questions you have about decorating your bathroom, you can find the answers you need in this chapter.

Looking at Long-Term versus Short-Term Strategies

Before you redecorate, ask yourself how long you'll be using your new bathroom. If you'll be staying indefinitely, feel free to create the bathroom you want. But if you'll be moving soon, and if a potential new owner may be turned off by that outrageous wall covering that you like, perhaps you'd better stick to a tried-and-true style that most people prefer.

The following is a list of things that please most people most of the time (which is your goal when selling your house):

- ✔ Decorative lighting fixtures, especially around the vanity mirror
- ✔ Large mirrored medicine cabinets
- ✔ Ceramic tile floor and walls (a *must* in the tub/shower area)
- ✔ Neutral colored walls, floors, and fixtures
- ✔ A few important, simple accessories
- ✔ Light-penetrating window treatments that also allow privacy

Considering Budget-Stretching Strategies

Does it surprise you to hear that everyone — no matter how rich or poor — has a budget? As decorators, we've never met a client whose budget didn't need to be carefully managed. Even if the sky's the limit, why not consider up front as many ways to stretch your decorating dollar as possible? You don't have to sacrifice style in order to save. If your budget's tight or you just get a kick out of spending less, consider these suggestions:

- ✔ **Choose classic white fixtures.** They're less expensive than colored ones, and they never go out of style.

- ✔ **Use chrome faucets, fittings, and accessories.** They look very classy, but cost less — and, in certain climates, hold up better — than brass. (Just changing faucets can give your bath a lift!)

- ✔ **Opt for plain vanilla ceramic tiles.** They form a classic, stylish background that allows you to substitute creative imagination for more expensive decorator tiles.

- ✔ **Use large ceramic tiles for walls and floors.** Even in small bathrooms, these large tiles look terrific and cost less to install than smaller tiles, which require more grout, installation time, and maintenance.

- ✔ **Find vinyl flooring in ceramic tile or stone patterns.** A stylish substitute for more expensive ceramic tile, vinyl flooring gives you the look for less, is easy on the feet and legs, and is simple to maintain.

- ✔ **Shop kitchen and bath design centers or showrooms for custom-order cabinets, faucets, and fixtures that clients may have refused on delivery.** In these cases, shop owners are more interested in recouping their costs than making a profit, and they may sell these items to you for less than their original price.

Personalizing Your Bathroom

The truly personal bathroom works the way you need it to work — so function comes first. But looks do matter, so walls, flooring, ceiling, lighting, and accessories should all underscore the style or mood that you're aiming for.

Decorating surfaces

Walls, floors, windows, and ceilings create backgrounds against which cabinets, fixtures, faucets, and accessories shine. So what's your style? Chapters 8, 9, and 10 help you determine your style. And, although you can read about walls, floors, ceilings, and windows in general in Chapters 12, 13, 14, and 15, here are some things to keep in mind about these surfaces in bathrooms.

Walls

Bathroom walls should be easy to clean. Ceramic tile and vinyl surface materials are popular for walls. Of the two, the more expensive ceramic tile is more durable. Ceramic tile is almost always used in shower stalls (on walls and on ceilings). Many bathrooms make use of ceramic tile for tub and shower surrounds, too. You can extend the tile around the remaining walls to at least chair rail height (about 30 inches). Marble and granite are more expensive, but are also very popular because they look great and are easy to maintain.

Ceramic tile is available in an extraordinary range of styles, patterns, and colors as background tile, decorative inserts, and charming borders. Ceramic tile lends itself to endless design experimentation. Consider mixing various tile colors and patterns for unique walls. Be careful to use tiles of the same thickness when you mix tiles from various collections and companies.

Wall covering adds distinct pattern and color to the bathroom. Be sure to install vinyl wall covering (not wallpaper), which can be washed. Choose a pattern that underscores the look you want. For unity's sake, choose a background color that blends with other wall surfaces in the room.

Figure 18-1 shows a bathroom in which the background of the striped wall covering above a raised whirlpool bathtub blends with neutral colored surfaces throughout the room. Contrasting-colored slender stripes in the wall covering create a sense of rhythm and make the wall area look taller than it really is. The large-scaled floral wall covering in Figure 18-2, however, has a different feel: it turns this master bath into a garden room. The dark green background contrasts smartly with crisp white cabinets.

Figure 18-1:
The wall
covering
you choose
can
transform
your room.

Make sure that your wall-covered bathroom has ample ventilation to prevent moisture damage to your wall covering.

Floors

Bathroom floors must stand up to continual wear and frequent cleaning. Ceramic tile and less expensive vinyl flooring are popular choices. For ceramic tile floors, tile sizes range from 1-inch square mosaics to large-format tiles up to 24 inches on a side. Generally, the smaller the bath, the smaller the tile you should use.

However, you may want to use a light-colored large tile and light-colored grout in a 5-x-9-foot bathroom. Designers say that using large tiles and fewer grout lines make these typical bathrooms look larger. Set them on the diagonal for a sense of motion, which also helps make the room seem bigger.

Vinyl floor covering is less expensive than ceramic tile. Although it won't last as long, it's easier and less expensive to change.

Wood flooring is not generally recommended for use in the bathroom. However, certain hardwoods, covered in protective polyurethane, may stand up to the wear and tear. Afraid to try it? Then substitute laminate flooring that looks like wood.

Figure 18-2:
A large-scaled floral wall covering works its decorating magic.

Photograph courtesy American Woodmark

A quick and easy solution to a really ugly floor is wall-to-wall, washable, bathroom carpeting that you can cut with shears (to fit around fixtures) and lay in place. Secure the carpeting temporarily with double-faced tape (so that you can pull it up and toss it in the washing machine whenever you like). You can usually find this carpeting sold in 5-x-9-foot bundles in bed and bath shops. It's relatively inexpensive — and attractive, too!

Whether you decorate with a brand new floor or just want to dress up an old one, remember that you can add extra pattern and color with washable throw rugs. But be sure to buy the non-skid kind!

Ceilings

Ceilings in bathrooms are often just painted white to reflect the most light. However, ceilings in tiny and large bathrooms are very visible and often cry out for decoration. Here are some tips:

- Keep contrast to a low level in small bathrooms and in large bathrooms with low ceilings.

- In a large bathroom with a high ceiling, a strongly contrasting color or pattern on the ceiling adds interest.

- ✔ In a wall-covered small bathroom, treat the ceiling to either the same or a coordinating wall covering. Just choose either a small-scaled pattern or a three-dimensional one (such as a trellis or landscape) that makes the room seem larger.

- ✔ If you're using a directional patterned wall covering in a small bath, use a small-scaled coordinate on the ceiling.

- ✔ If you're using a tiny, non-directional geometric pattern, continue it on a small bathroom ceiling. For the tiniest bath, use a light background; for a slightly larger bath, use a slightly darker background.

- ✔ Ceilings may be wood plank, as shown in Figure 18-3; just make sure the wood is properly treated and that your room is adequately ventilated.

Windows

Windows are another important background feature in the bathroom area. Most of us want the bathroom to allow daylight to stream through, but we also want to temper this with a feeling of privacy. Following are a few tips on how you can accomplish both:

- ✔ Consider installing frosted glass windows. This allows light to filter through, while also providing some privacy.

Figure 18-3:
A roof window (a skylight that opens) adds functionality by providing ventilation to prevent moisture buildup and damage to this wood-plank ceiling.

Photograph courtesy National Kitchen & Bath Association

✔ Install roll-shades on windows. If you like the look of undecorated, no-nonsense windows, these can be rolled up and out of sight when not needed and can be drawn for extra privacy.

Other types of blinds are also available if you want semi-privacy some of the time.

Most folks like to keep their bathrooms light and airy. Light cotton curtains and/or lace toppers seem to work well in most bathrooms. For more information on window coverings, skip back to Chapter 15.

Accessories

Accessories are the finishing touch to any room. They can and should underscore the mood you've set by your choice of background materials and fixtures. Accessorizing any room is the fun part of decorating and you should never hesitate to experiment and try new ideas, but here are some things to keep in mind:

✔ Match, don't mix, metals. If the faucets are brass, keep towel bars and rings, curtain rods, wastebaskets, and other metal surfaces brass as well.

✔ If the faucets in your home mix metals — using brass as a trim for chrome or chrome as a trim for brass faucets — let all other metals you use in your room match the faucet, not the trim.

✔ Protect pictures for the wall by not hanging them near splashing water.

✔ Keep gilded picture frames away from direct water sources, which will damage the finish.

✔ Keep accessories related but not too repetitious. If you really want a personalized bathroom, avoid ensembles that look as though you'd just come from a bed and bath shop. Instead, take some time to select your own grouping of things that especially appeal to you (see Figure 18-4).

✔ Consider live plants to be accessories — just make sure they have a realistic setting (that usually means plenty of sunlight) and place them out of harm's way (where they can't fall into the tub or cause someone to stumble, for example).

If you use fake (or faux) plants made of silk or plastic, pretend they're real and don't place them where a real plant couldn't survive!

✔ Don't try to match beige towels or a shower curtain to your beige wall. Instead, buy white towels and a white shower curtain and monogram them in a matching beige thread.

If you already have beige towels, however, and you want to repaint your trim, paint stores can custom-match paint to your towels!

✔ Consider a unique wall-hung mosaic sink and a matching mirror to be major accessories. Build your color scheme around them.

Photograph courtesy Kohler Co.

Figure 18-4:
Note how accessories — a toy ship, a ship's lantern, and the porthole mirror — add to the nautical theme.

Decorating Special Bathrooms

Certain bathrooms require special decorating tactics. Master bathrooms, guest bathrooms, and bathrooms for children have different needs. Customizing a bathroom for the needs of those who will be using it just takes a little thought and creativity. And the following sections will get you on the right track.

Making master baths magical

Master bathrooms are usually, but not always, meant to be used by two people. When that's the case, having two of each important fixture makes for greater convenience and efficiency. Whether there are two people or just one person using the master bathroom, consider adding personal comforts and conveniences — such as photographs, plants, and potpourri — that will make the hour or more that you spend there each day more delightful. Even a tight budget can allow for a few luxuries — scented soaps and candles, a silk flower arrangement, bath salts in your favorite fragrance — to enhance the ritual of the bath. Here are a few tips for creating magic in your master bath:

✔ Install wall-mounted adjustable magnifying mirrors for each person.

✔ Add a standing screen (easily made by hinging louvered shutters together) to create privacy for the toilet, if there's enough room.

✔ For optimal storage and greater convenience, customize cabinets with compartments for drawers and pullout shelves.

✔ What's luxury without soothing sounds? Add a radio (positioned where it cannot fall into the tub or sink) so that you can listen to your favorite music station as you soak in the tub.

✔ For visual comfort, add a television/VCR (either wall-mounted or concealed in a cabinet on a pull-out shelf) that lets you keep up with the news or watch your favorite tape as you soak. (A remote control is the safe way to channel surf. Store the unit in a special holder that sticks to the tub or wall to keep it out of the water.)

✔ Add a luxurious decorative touch such as a mosaic border or a mosaic mural for the wall, or a medallion for the floor.

✔ Tuck a padded bench under the vanity. They're great for relaxing while doing makeup or hair.

✔ Add a heated towel rack that serves up warm towels on cold days and adds additional heat to a chilly bathroom.

✔ Install a telephone for emergencies or for use when not in the water. (Don't talk on the phone while soaking in the tub.)

✔ Create luxurious comfort with furnishings just for the bath: A terry-covered chaise lounge or comfy chair is useful for everything from relaxing after a bath to sitting while you blow-dry your hair. We brought in an inexpensive white plastic chair (the patio kind). Most of the time it holds a stack of folded towels — much handier than the hall closet — and it looks great, too!

✔ Let the light in with skylights, windows, or glass block walls wherever you can. And, because your master bath is private, consider exchanging the solid door for a glass French door that lets more light into the bath (and keeps steam and noise in). Our carpenter put one in by mistake, and we liked it so much it stayed!

✔ Bring the garden inside by adding favorite plants and flowers throughout. Many plants, such as ferns, love the steamy setting.

✔ If you have the room, expand the uses of your master bath by creating a mini-gym area with exercise equipment, such as a stationary bike or treadmill.

✔ Customize your new glass-enclosed bath/shower with glass etched in a personal design.

✔ Whether your bath is large or small, add pretty area rugs for color, pattern, and warmth for cool feet.

✔ And don't forget the little things — scented candles, potpourri, fresh flowers from your own garden, sachet packets for drawers, a display of pretty bottles. These all add up to comfort in the bath.

Strategizing for small baths

Smart layouts and small-scale fixtures can be combined to make small, full baths a reality and powder rooms (guest bathrooms with only a toilet and lavatory) more gracious. If you need to make a small powder room seem grand, check out the following suggestions:

✔ Make a bathroom look larger and lighter by creating walls or panels of transparent glass between fixtures. Use glass tub and shower doors. (Expect to pay at least $200 for frameless glass doors.) A custom glass enclosure (walls and doors) may cost more. But these are luxuries that pay back big time in physical and emotional comfort, as well as when you put your house on the market.

✔ Generally, light colors make small spaces seem larger; but, there's a limit to how big a tiny room can look. Sometimes you're better off creating a three-dimensional effect with a trellis or other patterned wall covering that directs the eye out of the room, making it seem less confining and larger.

✔ Mirrors are great space expanders, especially when used on opposite walls — and even more so when used on all four walls. Mirrors also expand light, which is a real bonus. You may want to save the four walls of mirrors for a very fancy guest powder room. Actually, you don't have to extend the mirror from the floor to the ceiling. Just use it above a chair rail (and save money). We've seen this done, and the effect is magical.

✔ Light itself seems to expand space. So use windows wherever possible. Keep window treatments simple and blend blind and fabric colors with the background color of the wall. (Contrast reduces the sense of space.)

✔ If the need for privacy doesn't allow for a window (even with a frosted pane), substitute light-transmitting glass block. The filtered light coming through the glass block lends a magical quality to a room.

✔ Consider a light-transmitting, glass block wall between a tiny private bath and adjoining bedroom, even in a Traditional setting.

✔ Substitute French doors for hinged solid wood doors between a small private bathroom and an adjoining bedroom. French doors control sound, odors, and moisture vapors, but visually expand both rooms. Continue the bedroom style and color scheme into the bath for the greatest continuity.

- If possible, replace a hinged door with a *pocket door* (one that slides back into the wall), which requires no swing space.

- Create storage by building shelves between wall studs, so that no shelves extend into the room or intrude into the space. If you must have a shelf, use glass or some other transparent shelving that seems weightless and takes up no visual space.

- Store only the essentials in a tiny bathroom. Keep refills and replacements handy in an adjoining room or hallway.

- Keep accent colors and accessories to a minimum to avoid any sense of clutter and space-consuming confusion.

Getting guest bathrooms in shape

Sharing your bathroom with guests is inconvenient and awkward. When a couple we knew grew tired of sharing the only bathroom in their house, they figured out a way to divide and conquer. They lopped a few feet off the rear of the hall bath to create a tiny, fully equipped, master bath, leaving enough space up front for an adequate hall bath.

Obviously, it's not whether a guest bathroom is big or small, but whether it *works* that counts. So, the first thing to consider is whether your guest bathroom has the three essential fixtures — a toilet, a sink, and either a shower or a bathtub. (Don't forget ventilation to remove odors and moisture!) If your guest bath has these essentials, you're on your way to creating a great bathroom.

- Relate the color scheme of your guest bath to that of the adjoining bedroom. This technique creates a sense of continuity, unity, and harmony. But what if the adjoining bedroom is large, airy, and has dark walls and light accents? Won't this *negative* (dark background) scheme make the small bathroom look even smaller? Definitely. So flop the color scheme to a *positive* one, with light walls and the same dark color in the bedroom scheme as an accent.

- Store paper, linens, a new toothbrush, and other necessary supplies inside the bathroom, for easy access. If your guest bathroom doesn't have a linen closet inside, consider placing a shelf on the wall.

A shelf over the toilet should not be wider than the top of the tank. If the bathroom is small, keep the shelf light — use glass or open wire mesh, or paint a dark shelf white.

- If you don't have room for a wall-hung shelf, you can store rolled towels in a wicker basket, and perhaps add in some new bathing sponges and shower gels. Provide a magazine rack, pretty soaps, and maybe even a radio or tiny TV.

Choosing the right look for your children's bathroom

Think of children's bathrooms and you may automatically think of primary colors, clown motifs, and wild and crazy accessories. If that's what your child likes, that's fine. But your child may surprise you. So, ask before you decorate.

Of course, there's another reason for not rushing out to buy fire engine red ceramic tile and red, white, and blue fixtures: resale. Resale value is a real and valid reason for taking it easy on wild, weird, and way out schemes, even if they do bring out the kid in you.

Potential buyers may be turned off by anything extreme. Does that mean you can't have any fun decorating your child's bathroom? Absolutely not. Here's what we suggest. Consider a neutral background — white, beige, or light gray — and introduce colorful accents and fun motifs in towels, bath mats, framed art, soaps, and so on. You can easily change accents and accessories in strong colors that your children love now, when their tastes change as they grow.

With neutral-colored ceramic tiles, you can still use a decorative ceramic tile border with special appeal to your youngster. A host of colorful and imaginative art tiles are available. Some tiles are sculptural, with dimensional frogs, dragonflies, butterflies, and other flora and fauna that even an adult can love!

Vinyl wall covering is not permanent and can easily be changed, so you may want to be adventurous here. To save time and money, choosing a neutral texture and adding pattern and color in pictures and fabrics makes sense.

What probably concerns everyone most is creating a kid-friendly, safe bath. Here are some suggestions:

- Prevent scalding by installing hot stop valves that prevent a child from turning water on to the highest, hottest temperature.

- Round corners on countertops to prevent injury to tots whose heads may be near the same height.

- Prevent a child from locking himself in the bathroom. Be sure the exterior door can be unlocked from the outside.

- Be sure the shower door opens out so that no child (or adult) can become wedged in.

- Provide a stool that won't tip over for small children to use at the sink.

- Install easy-to-maneuver lever faucet handles and mount them on one side of the sink, near the front edge of the counter, so that a child can reach them without having to climb on top of the vanity.

✔ Lock doors of medicine and cleaning supply cabinets.

✔ Avoid using slippery area rugs and make sure the flooring is skid-proof.

✔ Be sure that glass for the shower or tub doors is tempered so that it won't shatter.

✔ Place a rubber non-skid mat in the tub so that children won't slip.

✔ Place lever handles on all doors at a child's height.

✔ Install rocker-type light switches low enough for a child to reach.

✔ Remove radios, hair dryers, and any other small appliances that could be dropped into the tub or sink.

✔ Use freestanding shelves that can't be tipped over.

✔ Keep a night-light on around-the-clock.

Decorating Quick-Fix Ideas

Transforming something ugly (like old cabinets or a sad-looking sink) into something attractive with imagination, a little elbow grease and perhaps a coat of paint, is real decorating magic. Plus, it's fun and can save money if it means that you don't have to replace a big-ticket item. Here are some suggestions for transforming certain things that usually bug us most about bathrooms in older houses.

Improving vanity cabinets

Bathroom vanity cabinets (the cabinet that holds the bathroom sink or lavatory) are sometimes less than beautiful, even when they're brand-new. Age certainly doesn't improve them. Before you give yours the old heave-ho, consider these possibilities:

✔ **Paint it.** If your vanity cabinet is metal, ask an automobile painter about repainting it. If it's wood, paint the cabinet the same color as the wall, and it will fade into the background.

✔ **"Antique" a carved and fancy cabinet.** Use an antique paint kit to highlight raised carvings, fancy moldings, and trims, and turn a sows ear into a silk purse.

✔ **Relaminate a laminate.** We asked our carpenter to relaminate a dirt-cheap, white, bathroom cabinet with a beautiful, but not expensive, almond-colored laminate. Then we accessorized the cabinet with solid brass, egg-shaped knobs and splurged just a little on a new solid-surface (faux granite) countertop.

✔ **Change the hardware.** Maybe there's nothing really wrong with the dark wood Early American base that new hardware can't fix. So take off the cheap hardware and upgrade with brass and ceramic handles and knobs.

✔ **Add pizzazz.** Create an Old World look by outlining cabinet doors with a row of decorative brass upholsterer's nail heads. They're usually used to trim the fronts of leather chairs, but furniture designers are beginning to use them on doors of furniture and cabinets. (Nail heads are available from an upholsterer, home center, hardware store, or crafts shop.) Before you nail, remove the door and place it on a firm surface. Lay out the nails in a pattern that suits you.

✔ **Cover a simple vanity with wall covering.** Use the same wall covering as you use on the walls, and the old eyesore will blend right in.

Working with unattractive ceramic tile

Ceramic tile on the floor or halfway up the wall is expensive to replace. If you've inherited any one of a half dozen unappealing color schemes, don't despair. We have the remedies for you:

✔ Wall covering that combines the offending colors with some unexpected tints and shades can save the day. You may have to look at a lot of wall covering books, but trust us — inevitably, you'll find a pattern that will work. Apply the wall covering on wall areas not covered by the tile, and the tile suddenly seems less obvious and offensive.

✔ Faux paint by dabbing paint (unevenly and in an interesting way) onto the wall area above the tile, using the colors of the tile that you don't like, plus an unexpected accent color. Not sure what the accent color should be? Look to wall coverings, fabrics, and even gift wrap for inspiration.

✔ After you've completed your wall treatments, underscore your scheme with an area rug that picks up and plays back the colors. (Rugs are also great for covering offending flooring colors and patterns.)

Chapter 19

Having a Homey Home Office

*W*orking in home offices is becoming more popular all the time. But sometimes finding the right kind of environment to work in can be a challenge. In this chapter, we guide you through the process of striking just the right balance between home and office, all in one room.

What will it take to make your home office work for you? You have to figure out where to locate your home office, measure the space you have to work with, and design a floor plan that meets your needs. In this chapter, we show you how to do those things. We also show you what kind of lighting works best and help you determine how much electrical power you need. You discover what kind of furniture your home office requires, and you top it all off with just the right accessories to make your home office the kind of place you love to work in. The perfect home office has everything you need for comfort (see Figure 19-1).

Figure 19-1:
All the comforts of home and the efficiencies of a real office make this a highly productive home office.

Photograph courtesy Sauder Woodworking Co.

Finding the Right Location for Your Office

Realtors are fond of saying that the three most important things in real estate are location, location, location. We say the same thing about your home office. The ideal location should provide easy access to the people who use it. The location should also provide adequate privacy, comfort, and space. Your productivity is directly related to all these factors, but how much you need of any one of these things is an individual preference. So be honest about *your* needs as you plan. Knowing yourself and your priorities helps you make any necessary compromises between the ideal and the real.

When you're deciding where to put your home office, you need to take into consideration some key issues. Ask yourself the following questions:

✔ **Who will use your home office?** If you are the only one using the office, then you could easily put it in a converted garage across an open driveway. If other family members will occasionally use your computer or equipment, you may want it to be in a room that is attached to, or a part of, the house. If you have an assistant working with you, a larger and maybe more professional-looking office (away from the private areas of your home) may be necessary.

✔ **What kind of work will you do in your office?** What you need varies greatly according to the job you plan to do. For example, if you're an interior designer, you need storage space for fabric swatches and samples, catalogs, drawings, and client correspondences. If you use your office to do research, you need shelving space for books, files, and directories. If you're an accountant, you need plenty of work surface for ledgers and maybe room for visiting clients. Think about your requirements for work surface and storage space, as well as any special equipment you may need.

↙ **Will you see clients or colleagues in your home office?** Visitors are usually more comfortable using an entry directly into your office from the outside rather than having to walk through private living areas of your house. If you plan to meet with other people, you also need space for extra seating and maybe even a conference table.

↙ **What kind of environment do you prefer working in?** Where you locate your home office depends on the environment you like. Do you need privacy? Or do you want to be near the rest of your house? Do you need total silence? Or do you like background noise? Think about the times you've felt most productive, and write down the kind of environment you were in. Then try to find a location for your home office that comes as close to your perfect environment as possible.

Ideally, your home office should be a room of its own. When your home office is a separate room, you can close the door during working hours and keep outside distractions at a distance. If a closed, solid wood door makes you feel claustrophobic in a particularly small office, you can substitute a glass French door that shuts out sound but makes the room seem larger.

If you prefer working in the middle of all the action or if space doesn't allow you to put your office in a separate room, a computer work center, like the one shown in Figure 19-2, is a great solution. When you finish working, simply close the doors, and the office disappears.

Figure 19-2:
A work center provides room for a home office in a small amount of space.

Photograph courtesy Sauder Woodworking Co.

Measuring Your Space and Planning Furniture Layout

As you decide where to locate your home office, space should definitely be a consideration. But most people, because of the nature of their houses, can't find the perfect space for an office. Perfection isn't as important as function when it comes to where you work, so after you've found a place to put your office, you need to turn your thoughts to measuring the space you have and figuring out how to fit all the furniture and equipment you need in that space.

Before you can plan the layout of your office, you need to know how much space you have and how much space your furniture will take up. Make a floor plan of the room (check out Chapter 2 for more information on creating a floor plan), and measure each piece of furniture and equipment (including your computer, printer, fax machine, desk, and chair) so that you can experiment with different layouts. Note on your floor plan the location of windows, doors, and electrical outlets. Experiment with several possible layouts. Imagine yourself walking through a typical workday — reaching for one item, filing another — until you find the plan that best suits you and what you'll be doing in your office.

Keep in mind that storage space may be at a premium in your home office, and plan on needing space to store things like paper, which takes up a great deal of room.

If you have a beautiful view from the windows in your home office, don't block the view with furniture. Instead, build cabinets, shelves, or window-seat storage below and around the windows.

Lighting Your Office

In any home office, you need three kinds of lighting: natural, general, and task. When you plan the kinds of lighting you need, take a critical look at the natural light sources in the room. Does the room have plenty of windows? If not, can you add them before you set up shop, or would that require more remodeling than you want to do? Think also about which direction the windows face. Do you get the morning light? Or is it bright in the late afternoon? When will you be working in the room? The answers you have to all of these questions help you decide what kind of lighting you need to bring in, as well as how much.

Pay attention to the direction of natural light coming into your office, and place computers and other equipment at right angles to the light source so that the monitor screen is out of the glare. Don't position your computer so that when you face the screen, you are also facing a window. Constantly adjusting your eyes to these two different light sources causes fatigue and, eventually, eye strain. Use blinds to control the levels of natural light. Make sure that ambient lighting in the room is no brighter than the light level of your computer monitor.

As important as natural light is, it can't replace artificial lighting, even in the daytime. You may need more artificial light to serve as general lighting in the areas of the room that are opposite walls with windows. If your room is large, you may want to use two or more controls for the ceiling lights, so that you can light only the side of the room where you're working.

In a home office, task lighting is especially important, particularly if you do a lot of reading or focusing on small objects. Make sure that task lights are flexible and adjustable so that you can change the angles and heights when you need to. Check out halogen lights, which produce as much light as an incandescent bulb ten times larger in size. Consider the new long-life and special-function fluorescent task lights that use 60 percent less energy than a standard bulb and last ten times longer.

Don't hesitate to ask for advice from a lighting consultant. Be prepared to install a variety of light sources, including general overall illumination and specific task lights, as well as different kinds of bulbs. Chapter 16 provides even more information on the different kinds of lighting available.

Powering Up for Performance

After you decide where each piece of electronic equipment and furniture will go, check to see whether outlets are available or you need to add them. Some older homes have badly placed outlets. Only newer homes have a certain number of outlets per feet as required by code. Also check the kind and condition of the wiring, especially if you own an older home. Some wiring can't handle the load of all the equipment you'll need. Other homes don't have adequate electricity running into the house. You may need to double-check with your electricity company for more precise information. Experts recommend 20-amp dedicated circuits for computers, printers, and fax machines. If your home was built prior to the 1990s, you may want to call in an electrician to determine your needs. Nothing is more frustrating than having your work disrupted by a total blackout. You should safely be able to run your microwave at the same time you're running Windows — without a power crash.

Add wall-hung, strip outlets above the height, and within reach, of your desk. These outlets are easily accessible for your computer, printer, and other equipment.

Upgrade telephone wiring from the normal CAT 3 wire to faster CAT 4 or 5, especially if you plan on using the Internet.

Use surge-protector extension cords to protect all your electrical equipment.

Equipping Your Office

The nature of your work and the way in which you do it influence the kind, quantity, and arrangement of the furniture, as well as the kind of equipment that you need in your home office.

Electronic equipment

Communication is increasingly important, and most people who work out of home offices find that staying connected is essential. Two telephone lines are considered minimal for home offices, but three phone lines are best (one each for telephone, fax, and modem). Machines that combine more than one communications function are available, so instead of installing a phone and answering machine, you may want to invest in a more versatile combination of fax, phone, answering machine, and copier. Cordless phones free you to move around while you talk, and cellular phones keep you in touch at all times. You may find that you need one or both of these kinds of phones, depending on your work. No matter what equipment you need, investing in the highest quality you can afford is essential. Up-to-date, efficient equipment keeps you competitive in the marketplace — and it lasts longer, too.

Computers (including keyboards, monitors, and printers) have become the focal point of most home offices. Again, buy the best computer you can afford and get equipment that can be upgraded. Consider investing in a laptop (which goes where you go) and a docking station (which transforms your laptop back into a big screen model), complete with a standard keyboard and mouse. If children and other family members plan to use your computer, look into adding workstations (which keep your own desk area off-limits to them).

Furniture

Forget about the idea of using a quaint kitchen table and a straight-back chair as your office furniture. You won't find carpal tunnel syndrome, a stiff neck, or other environmentally-induced discomforts very quaint when they keep you from doing your job. Ergonomically designed work surfaces and chairs, which are made to support your body, are available in many different, affordable price ranges, and they should be at the top of your list when you go to buy furniture (see Figure 19-3).

Figure 19-3:
Choosing
ergonomically
correct
furniture
can make
the
difference
between a
comfortable
work
environment
and one you
dread.

Ergonomically Incorrect   Ergonomically Correct !

Desks

A desk is usually the most important piece of furniture in a home office, so be sure to spend some time looking at different desks and finding the one that's right for you. To determine how big a desk you need, choose a position for your computer (dead center, on the right, or on the left of the desk). Then figure in enough extra work surface to accommodate the different jobs you may do during the day.

Any desk should be at least 24 inches deep. The standard height of desks is 29 inches. A computer keyboard should be between $24^1/_2$ and 28 inches off the floor. (You can install an adjustable, retractable keyboard tray under the work surface if you want to leave your desk space free.)

L-shaped and U-shaped desks provide a wraparound work surface that's easy to use. A P-shaped desk (which is a variation of the L-shaped desk) flares out into a wider semicircle at one end, and it allows for comfortable desktop conferencing. Work surfaces of between 32 and 36 inches wide, flaring to 42- to 48-inch-wide conference table ends, are very popular. Either end of the desk can be attached to a matching, standard 6-foot-long wall unit consisting of a desk with a file-drawer pedestal and optional bookcase hutch. These units are available in all price ranges and come in a wide variety of materials, including fancy wood veneers and easily-cleaned laminates.

Allow a 5-foot square floor space for a P-shaped, U-shaped, or L-shaped desk. Add another two feet to each side of the square if you augment these work surfaces with a freestanding credenza.

Whenever you draw in a desk on your floor plan, add a minimum of two feet for your office chair, plus another two feet in which to push back your chair when you stand up.

Custom-built furniture is generally more expensive, but it often makes the most efficient use of space. If space is tight, you may be able to build in an adequate desktop that's less than the standard 32 inches wide. Or even build a desk with a space-saving breakfront (which is wider in the middle and narrower on the sides) or banjo shape (wide on one side and much narrower on the other). Some rooms have such odd-shaped nooks and crannies that custom furniture is the only way to make use of the space efficiently.

You may need more than one desk in different locations, just for your own use. If you spend a lot of time conceptualizing, treat this desk and your-self to a view. For putting your concepts into writing, switch over to your computer work surface (and a desk that *doesn't* allow you to look directly out the window).

Chairs

What kind of chair do you need for your home office? A swivel chair with five legs for stability and casters for mobility is probably your best bet. Choose a model that's easily adjustable — one that can be raised and lowered, tilted forward and backward. Be sure that the seat is well-padded and firm for comfortable support. Upholstery fabric should be either leather (which is cool in the summer and warm in the winter), a high-quality vinyl, or a tightly-woven fabric that doesn't attract lint or dirt. The fabric should be easy to clean (especially if you drink coffee and snack at your desk like the rest of us do at ours). Your chair should have open, not confining, adjustable arm rests. And before you buy it, try it!

Guest chairs for your home office can be anything you like, as long as they're comfortable. A rocking chair is a natural. Wing chairs are another favorite. Place a chair by your desk for a guest and put another beside a small table where you can read. The kinds of guest chairs you need depends upon the number of visitors you have and what they do while they're in your office.

Storage

Don't forget bookshelves, filing cabinets, and other storage areas. Allow for storage on your floor plan layout if you have room. But if you can't find space for storage in the room, consider taking over a nearby hall closet. You can put filing cabinets in the closet and add shelving above them. You can create shelving in many great places, and although orange crates may not work for you, consider using armoires, baker's racks, gym lockers, and many other pieces that can (with a coat of paint) double as storage units.

Not all ready-to-assemble bookshelves are quick and easy! We ended up paying a carpenter as much to assemble some complicated shelves as we had paid for the shelves, doubling the cost and creating a very unattractive bottom line! Ask to see a parts list and assembly directions before you buy.

Save decorating dollars by painting inexpensive white laminate bookshelves a richer, more dramatic color. To paint a bookshelf, follow these easy steps:

1. **Cover the bookshelf with primer and let it dry.**

2. **Lightly sand the bookshelf. Gently wipe away excess debris.**

3. **Coat the shelf again with primer and let it dry.**

4. **Cover the bookshelf with two coats of an oil-based, semi-gloss, enamel paint, sanding it well between each coat of paint.**

   Use a sponge brush, which leaves no brush strokes. Add Penetrol, (which improves your paint and is available at your local supply store) to the paint to make a smoother surface. (You can substitute latex enamel paint for the oil-based paint if you want, but the oil-based version makes the laminate look more like real wood.)

Let the paint dry for 10 days before you stack anything on your bookshelves.

Coming Up with a Color Scheme

If you're having trouble deciding whether your office furniture should be dark or light, take into consideration the following guidelines:

- ✔ Dark furniture (such as cherry, mahogany, or fruit wood) usually appears Traditional, more formal, and more serious than furniture in light finishes.

- ✔ Light woods (such as oak, maple, or birch) work better in Modern, casual, rustic, and less formal styles than dark finishes.

- ✔ Light laminates (such as white, beige, or gray) work well in Contemporary styles.

Furniture color influences your choice of color schemes for your office, so keep in mind what colors you want to use for your walls, too. *Remember:* Strong contrasts make spaces seem smaller.

Keep in mind the following guidelines:

- ✔ To make a room appear smaller, use dark furniture in a light-colored room or light furniture in a dark-colored room.

- ✔ To make a room appear larger, use light furniture in light-colored rooms or dark furniture in dark-colored rooms.

Accessorizing for Fun

When you work at home, you don't have to think about the corporate taste police — you can decorate the way *you* want. Take a look at the following ideas to get your creativity going:

- ✔ For wall art, group diplomas, certificates, awards, photos of family and friends, old maps from favorite vacations, framed book dust jackets, framed magazine covers, or other favorite things.

- ✔ Decorate open shelves with basket trays that can hold magazines, brochures, or papers.

- ✔ Stand rolled architectural drawings or rolls of colorful wallpaper on end in a decorative brass or ceramic umbrella stand.

- ✔ Hang a decorative mirror somewhere handy so that you can check your appearance before you answer the door.

- ✔ Stencil inspirational quotes on one or more of the walls just below the cove molding.

- ✔ Cover a wall in corkboard. Check home centers for cork tiles that you can glue to the wall.

- ✔ Add a big blackboard or dry-erase board for notes and messages.

- ✔ Hang a large, decorative, easy-to-read calendar within sight of your telephone.

Part VI
Fixing Up the Four Easy Rooms: Bedroom, Living Room, Dining Room, and Bonus Areas

The 5th Wave   By Rich Tennant

"We had it in the guest bedroom, and then in the hallway, but for now we're leaving it in here until we figure out which room it seems to want to be in."

In this part . . .

The chapters in this part cover the four areas of your home that are fun and easy to decorate. We provide all the information you need on decorating your bedrooms, living room, and dining room. And we even include a chapter on decorating bonus areas, like the attic and basement. So, go to it!

Chapter 20

Designing Dreamy Bedrooms

• •

In This Chapter

▶ Determining your bedroom's purpose

▶ Figuring out how much room you have to work with

▶ Choosing the right bed

▶ Making the most of your storage space

▶ Creating the look you want with bedding

▶ Arranging your bedroom furniture effectively

▶ Planning according to the needs of those who'll use the bedroom

• •

Many people use bedrooms for reading, watching TV, listening to music, being alone, exercising, recouping, conversing, dressing and undressing, and even working. Meeting all the many functions of a bedroom can be tough in limited spaces (most bedrooms average a modest 10 x 12 feet).

In this chapter, you'll figure out what purposes your bedroom will actually serve — and how to customize it to suit your personal preferences and style. You'll also see how to make the most of the space you have. We guide you through the process of selecting a mattress, a bed, bed coverings, and pillows. You'll also discover ways to maximize your storage space. Finally, this chapter provides great suggestions for ways to tailor a bedroom for the people who will be using it.

Bedroom Basics

Every bedroom requires certain essentials, including the right bed, storage space for clothing, a nightstand, and task lighting. Beyond the basics, you may want to include some other conveniences of contemporary life, such as a TV and VCR, stereo, storage space for videos and CDs, a desk for reading and writing, and a chair or two. Answer the following questions to determine exactly what you need and want in your bedroom:

✔ Who will occupy the bedroom?

✔ What is your personal style? (See Chapter 10 for more information.)

✔ What will you and your family or guests use the bedroom for?

- Nighttime sleeping
- Daytime sleeping
- Resting
- Working
- Napping
- Reading
- Studying or doing homework
- Watching television
- Listening to music
- Grooming
- Getting dressed
- Talking
- Exercising
- Playing
- Entertaining

✔ What size and how many beds will you have in the room?

- Twin
- Full/Double
- Queen
- King
- California King
- Custom

✔ What style or type of bed will you have?

✔ What additional furnishings do you need in the room?

- Nightstand
- Table
- Sofa or love seat
- Easy chair
- Reclining chair
- Chaise lounge
- Convertible sofa bed
- Vanity table
- Hope chest
- Desk and chair
- Armoire
- Bureau
- Dresser
- Footlocker
- Mirrors
- Media cabinet

✔ Where do you need task lighting?

- Bedsides
- Tables
- Desk
- Vanity table

✔ **What equipment do you need for the room?**

- Television
- VCR
- Computer
- Stereo

- Intercom
- Telephone
- Fax machine
- Answering machine

Keeping your answers to the preceding questions in mind, take a look at the sections in this chapter that pertain to your specific decorating needs.

Finding the right bed

The bed is the key piece of furniture in any bedroom. To figure out which bed suits your decorating needs, you need to think about the size, the comfort of the mattress, and the style. Each of these factors plays a part not only in the function of the bed (how well you sleep at night), but also in the way the bed complements the style of the entire room.

Size

Before you go shopping for a bed, you need to know the maximum amount of space your bed can take up. Many people choose a bed that's too big for their bedroom, making it nearly impossible to move around the bed.

Remember that you have to be able to get the bed through the door. Measure all the door openings and hallways to make sure the mattress can be moved into the room. You may have to take the doors off the frames in order to squeeze the bed through.

The mattress you choose should be at least 3 inches longer than the height of the tallest person sleeping on it. The standard mattress sizes are as follows:

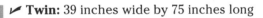

✔ **Twin:** 39 inches wide by 75 inches long

> If you plan to use two twin beds, allow a minimum of 24 inches between them, adding the bedcover width to each bed. You may find that you want a nightstand between the two twin beds, in which case the width of the nightstand will determine how far apart you place the beds. Just remember to take all of these measurements into consideration and be sure the room is big enough for the furniture.

✔ **Extra-Long Twin:** 38 inches wide by 80 inches long

✔ **Double:** 54 inches wide by 75 inches long

✔ **Queen:** 60 inches wide by 80 inches long

✔ **King:** 76 to 78 inches wide by 80 inches long

✔ **California King:** 72 inches wide by 84 inches long

To find out how much floor space a bed will take up, consider the following elements of a bed and add the appropriate measurements to the basic mattress size:

- **Bedcovering:** Add 3 inches to both the width and the length of the bed.
- **Changing the bedcovers:** In order to confortably change the bed-coverings, add 15 inches of clear space around the bed.
- **Headboard:** Add 3 to 4 inches to the length of the bed.
- **Footboard:** Add another 3 to 4 inches to the length of the bed.

Also keep in mind the height of the bed. You may want a higher or lower bed for decorative reasons or for physical comfort. Here are some examples:

- Adding an extra box spring to a bed set can raise a bed high enough for you to have a better view out of your window.
- A simple low metal frame may be all that's needed to raise a bed to the exact height of a window sill, so that the window and the view out of it aren't obstructed.

Comfort

Mattresses don't have any objective industry standards for labeling, which means that the quality of firmness and support varies from maker to maker. Ultimately, you have to let your body be your guide. When you go mattress shopping, wear comfortable clothing. Then test out the mattresses by getting into the positions you actually sleep in — and expect to take a few minutes to fully relax. Getting a feel — literally — for a mattress is the best way to tell if it's right for you.

Before you invest oodles of time road-testing every mattress at the bedding store, read the labels for specific information. Examine specifically the number of layers, the kinds of layers, the number of coils, the type and construction of the coils, and any special features (some manufacturers have patented construction techniques). Also, look carefully at the cutaway sample that demonstrates the mattress's construction — you're looking for good, solid construction. The most common type of mattress is the innerspring, which features tempered spring coils covered by layers of upholstery. The more coils, the better. So compare the number of coils from one brand to the next. A good guideline for any size mattress is a minimum of 400 tempered steel coils, topped by several layers of upholstery, one or more layers of foam, and finished with a quilted pillow top. Some bedding retailers recommend coils numbering at least 600. More coils tend to make for a longer lasting mattress. The sizes of the coils are in proportion to the size of the mattress, so these figures hold true for twins as well as kings.

Buy the best mattress you can afford. Always ask about construction, and try it before you buy it.

When you buy a mattress, always buy the matching box spring. Innerspring mattresses come paired with box springs — they're designed to work together, as a system. Don't combine a new mattress with old box springs, because your mattress won't get the support it needs.

If you need a hypoallergenic mattress, a good alternative is a foam mattress made of natural latex rubber. The foam density should measure at least two pounds per cubic foot. The higher the density, the better the foam. But remember: You'll still need a box spring or foundation to support a foam mattress.

Another great alternative to traditional mattresses and box springs is a waterbed. Soft-side waterbeds look like an innerspring mattress, but inside the upholstered cover are vinyl-covered, easy-to-fill cylinders. Hard-side models have a vinyl, water-filled mattress and heater encased in a wooden frame. Test the waterbed to make sure its degree of motion — ranging anywhere from waveless to full-flotation — works for you.

Style

Add personal style instantly with a dramatic bed. Many styles of bed are available, and they range from dramatically over-scaled to unobtrusively minimal. The choice is yours. Because your bed is the dominant piece of furnishing in your bedroom, choose a style that suits your taste. ***Remember:*** You spend one-third of your life sleeping, so make your dream time as beautiful as it is restful. Beds come in a variety of styles, so you can always find one that complements your decorating scheme. Here are some of the most common styles of beds:

- **Captain's bed:** Inspired by the beds made for ships, captain's beds feature a drawer beneath the mattress for storage. These beds are often used in children's and teenagers' rooms, because they hold lots of stuff and are easy to get in and out of. The captain's bed comes in a range of sizes and in a variety of styles. For safety reasons, the top edge of the frame should be lower than the top of the mattress to prevent those who sleep in it from banging their knees as they crawl into bed. Captain's beds are especially good for rooms that require extra storage space.

- **Four-poster bed:** This bed features four vertical posts and usually a headboard and footboard. Four-poster beds come in a variety of styles, from Traditional to Contemporary. Four-posters are good choices for rooms with high ceilings or large rooms where anything else would seem proportionately too small.

- **Tester (canopy) bed:** A tester (or canopy) bed, is a draped four-poster bed. Originally designed for warmth and comfort, a canopy bed has draped fabric covering the top and sides. Most people choose canopy beds today for a romantic sense of luxury and privacy, especially in spacious rooms.

✔ **Daybed:** These beds, shown in Figure 20-1, are intended for napping — or even sitting — during the day. They're usually more compactly sized than standard beds and typically are placed sideways along a wall to save space.

✔ **Hollywood bed:** A Hollywood bed is a very low bed, with or without a headboard. Sleek and contemporary, this style doesn't take up much space visually. The headboard of a Hollywood bed is very tailored, with straight lines.

✔ **Platform bed:** Sleek and contemporary, a platform bed is essentially just a mattress "floating" on a stage-like box that raises the bed anywhere from one to two (or more) feet off the floor. This bed is a simplified design idea derived from the elevated beds of European kings. Modern and streamlined, the platform bed adds a sophisticated sense of drama and is especially good for large, open spaces.

If the platform is more than one step high, include a handrail and allow an 8-inch toe kick (like those beneath kitchen cabinets) to prevent stubbed toes.

✔ **Sleigh bed:** Sleigh beds are usually very high, with slightly curved headboards and somewhat lower, curved footboards, drawing on the design of 19th century sleighs. Sleigh beds may feature heavy carving or simple, plain wood surfaces. Sleigh beds generally are not for very small spaces, because they're heavy in appearance.

Figure 20-1: Stylish and functional, a daybed lets you catnap beautifully.

Photograph courtesy Century

CHEAP CHIC

Creating your own headboard

Headboards can help create the style you want in a bedroom. But you don't need to spend a lot of money to get the look you want. Check out the following suggestions for quick, easy, and inexpensive headboards:

✔ **Pillowcases:** Above the bed, firmly install a drapery rod that extends the width of the bed. Add grosgrain ribbon tabs at intervals along one side of the pillowcases. Insert pillows into the pillowcases, and hang them on the rod as a headboard.

✔ **Antique shutters:** Attach shutters to the wall at the head of your bed. (Antique ones from the local salvage yard add a true cottage flavor.)

✔ **Standing screen:** Place a standing screen between your bed and the wall. If the screen is in need of stability, you can secure it to the wall.

✔ **Tapestry or quilt:** Hang a tapestry or quilt on the wall behind the head of your bed. Make sure it's fastened securely by drilling hooks into the wall or by installing a rod supported by brackets. Make sure that your hanging is not so fragile that rubbing against it will damage the tapestry.

✔ **Wrought iron gate:** Check out the salvage yard for an old iron gate that you can secure to the wall for a headboard. These gates add lots of Old World charm to any bedroom.

✔ **Wagon wheel:** Old wagon wheels make natural headboards for a boy's twin bed. Fasten one wheel securely at the height that you like.

✔ **Demi-canopy:** Attach a curtain rod that is shaped like a semicircle on the wall near the ceiling, leaving a space of about two to three inches for the top of the curtain (sometimes called a curtain heading). These special rods are available at craft stores, decorating shops, and drapery makers. Then hang ready-made curtains long enough to reach the floor.

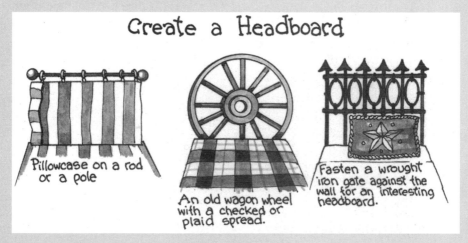

Create a Headboard

Pillowcase on a rod or a pole

An old wagon wheel with a checked or plaid spread.

Fasten a wrought iron gate against the wall for an interesting headboard.

Maximizing storage space

Storage space — for clothing, shoes, accessories, and myriad other things — is a necessity in any bedroom. The first step in tackling the issue of storage is to analyze what you already have and compare it to what you need. Then you can figure out how to make the most of your bedroom storage space. With just a few simple steps, your bedroom can accommodate virtually all your storage needs.

Taking an inventory

Before tackling the storage space in your bedroom, you need to determine how much space you have and figure out how much space you need. The following questions will help you do just that:

✔ **How many of the following storage facilities do you need?**

- Armoire
- Media center
- Cabinets
- Shelves
- Drawers
- Closets
- Walk-in closets

✔ **How much hanging storage do you need for the following items? (Measure in linear feet.)**

- Pants
- Skirts
- Suits
- Shirts/blouses
- Dresses
- Coats

✔ **How much shelving space do you need? (Measure the height and width of folded garments.)**

✔ **How many of the following do you need**

- Shallow drawers (2 inches deep)
- Deep drawers (4 or more inches deep)

✔ **How many pairs of the following do you need room for?**

- Shoes
- Boots
- Sandals
- Sneakers

Increasing storage space

After you've determined your storage needs, you can start thinking about ways to get the most out of the space you have. Here are a few suggestions for maximizing storage space:

✔ Use wire shelving systems, rods hung at various heights, hooks, and shoe racks in your closets to use the space efficiently.

- ✔ Use an oversized armoire, like one shown in Figure 20-2, as a media cabinet. The drawers and shelves allow you to store clothing and other things, and your TV is out of the way and at an optimum height for viewing.

- ✔ Stack a smaller chest of drawers on top of a larger chest of drawers or two. Make them look spiffy by painting them the same color and adding decorative stenciling. (Fasten the units together in the back with simple hardware and secure to the wall or floor to prevent them from tipping over, especially if you have small children.) This technique allows you to store a large amount in a small space — and it looks great, too!

Choosing the right nightstand and task lighting

Nightstands and task lighting are essential to any bedroom, but many people tend to forget about them and view them as accessories. The following two sections provide information on the importance of nightstands and lighting, and guide you toward choosing the right ones for your room.

Figure 20-2:
An armoire
adds
storage and
stature
to the
bedroom.

Photograph courtesy Milling Road

Tables and nightstands

Tables and nightstands provide surface space for lamps, necessities, and accessories. Nightstands, as an added benefit, have drawers that let you keep medicines, personal items, and supplies out of sight. No one, it seems, ever has enough storage and surface space, and a nightstand can help you store more things in an out-of-the-way place.

Tables of various heights can be used inventively for function and decoration. Place an armless "slipper" chair next to a low table for a cozy reading spot. Nestle two wing chairs around a higher table for an intimate coffee and conversation spot. Place nightstands on both sides of the bed to store items for two people. For a touch of personal style, drape a round table (you can buy very inexpensive ready-to-assemble ones) with a favorite sheet or coverlet.

Task lighting

Good, flexible lighting is a must for the bedroom. With so many people reading and working in bed, bright task lighting is a must. Table lamps are a natural on top of a nightstand, dresser, or other surface. But if your room is small, or you don't have room on your nightstands, consider pendant lights positioned on both sides of the bed or arm-mounted swinging lights. Additional task lights such as table lamps, torchieres, standing lamps, and desk lamps can be used next to seating areas to provide bright reading or working light.

For ambience and function, install dimmer switches for general lighting. Place additional controls within easy reach of the bed so you won't have to jump up to shut off lights and then stumble back in the dark. Think mood, function, and safety when lighting the bedroom. For specific information on lighting, see Chapter 15.

Accessorizing with Bedding

Dressing a bed is an art. Your sheets, pillows, and bedspread reflect your style, and they're every bit as important as the furniture you choose. The way your bed looks and feels plays a huge part in your comfort, so spend some time thinking about what you want, and have fun planning!

Bedcoverings

Sheets are an easy way to add style and comfort to your bed. When you buy sheets, read the label carefully for information on the materials they're made of and the way they were made. Check the feel, or *hand,* of the sheet to make sure it's the level of softness you want. Sometimes the printing process can stiffen sheets, although changes in technology have dramatically improved the softness and the look of the print.

Start by picking out sheets that coordinate with your color scheme and personal style. Pick solids, patterns, or prints that match the mood of the bedroom. If you enjoy variety, select three sheet sets that work with each other, and then mix and match. Floral patterns can easily mix with both solids and stripes to create interesting, varied effects.

Buy at least one white or ivory set of sheets. Also, have on hand a minimum of three sets of sheets in the linen closet — that way one set can be on the bed, one in the closet, and one in the laundry, at any given time.

A dust ruffle or bed skirt is great for hiding the ugly box spring and the frame legs. If you don't like dust ruffles or more tailored bed skirts, cover the box spring with a fitted sheet — an inexpensive and tasteful solution (as long as the bed's legs don't show).

Top the bed with a bedspread that flows to the floor or a coverlet, comforter, or duvet that simply tops the mattress area. A *coverlet* is thin like a bedspread (both are traditional ways to cover a bed). A comforter or quilt, is generally decorative and is a more contemporary bed dressing. A *duvet* is a European, down-filled comforter that comes in a very plain casing and is designed to be inserted into a *duvet cover,* which is like a giant pillowcase. A duvet cover can also go over a comforter for a quick change.

The traditional bedspread generally covers the pillows to create a seamless top. But if you like more romance, add decorative little pillows, pile on your favorite dolls or stuffed animals, or drape throws or extra quilts over the top.

Draping a bed adds lots of drama, pattern, texture, and interest to what could otherwise be an uninteresting room. If you have high ceilings, a tester (canopy) bed makes the most of a lot of volume. For Traditional bedrooms, use traditional fabrics (toile, chintz, and classic florals are good choices) and pick a Traditional style bed of your choice. Use cleaner, simpler draperies with tailored pleats to drape a simple, Contemporary bed frame. Mosquito netting (available already attached to a frame and ready for hanging) adds sheer mystery to Traditional or Contemporary bedrooms.

Pillow talk

For more Contemporary appeal, arrange pillows on the top of the bed, propping them artfully against the headboard. For a stylish mix, use two or more European-sized pillows, which are large square shapes that show nicely behind a rectangular pillow. Stack pillows covered with dramatic pillow shams and regular pillows. Add drama to the entire look by choosing shams with *flanges,* and deep edges that are either tailored or ruffled. You can add dimension with round neck pillows or bolsters and small accent pillows. Or add texture by mixing weaves, finishes, laces, and tapestry.

Arranging Your Furniture

The bed is the key piece of furniture in any bedroom, and it naturally becomes the focal point. Bedroom furniture is traditionally arranged according to a few general rules. For the most part based on common sense, here are some general guidelines for you to follow:

- ✔ **Traditionally, folks tend to place a double, queen, or king size bed against the center of the wall opposite the main door to the room.** With this arrangement, the headboard is the center of attention as you enter the room.

  If the dimensions of your room prevent you from positioning your bed on the wall across from the door, other possible choices depend on which walls are long enough to accommodate the bed. Diagonal placement works well when you have the space.

- ✔ **Do not place a bed under a window, if the window will frequently be open.** Open windows can create uncomfortable drafts. Positioning a bed between two windows, however, works well.

  If your home is air-conditioned or heated year-round and the windows are seldom open, you may be able to ignore this rule.

- ✔ **Do not place the bed where it obstructs a door into the room or a walkway through the room.**

- ✔ **Consider nontraditional furniture arrangements if doing so will free up space or use space in a more interesting way.**

  For example, a bed may look dramatic placed in front of a secure window; on a diagonal, which takes up extra space; sideways along a wall, to maximize floor space; or in an alcove (a technique called *lit clos*).

- ✔ **If your closet is large enough and you'd like to free-up floor space, put your chest of drawers inside your walk-in closet.** Doing this will let you add additional pieces of furniture, such as a writing desk, a seating group, or a big screen TV, to transform any bedroom into a luxury suite.

Tackling Specific Bedrooms

Bedrooms used by a specific group of people have unique needs. Whether you're decorating a master bedroom, a guest room, or a room for children, the following sections provide you with the tips you need.

Bright and cheerful colors on walls,
upholstery, and floor coverings make
a formal room more welcoming.

Plants — real and faux — add a special decorative note to any room. Greenery in a dramatic vase fills a niche (top left). A trailing vine brightens up a study (top right). Flowers in a pitcher and live plants in the window and on a table are cheerful spots of color in the family room (bottom).

Checks like those found in the kitchen curtains (left) and stripes like those on the three-drawer chest (bottom left) and wallpaper dado (bottom right) are simple geometric patterns that add interesting contrast to floral patterns used throughout any room.

Red, the warmest color in the color wheel, is equally at home in an elegant living room (top left), dining room (top right) and country kitchen (bottom).

Architectural features, including freestanding columns (bottom left), built-in cabinetry with arched tops (top), and the handsome stairway (bottom right) create great backgrounds for furnishings.

Exterior light is valuable, whether it comes from small, minimally dressed transparent windows (bottom left and right) or is transmitted through translucent glass blocks like those in the kitchen (top).

Today's windows may be left bare, like those in the living room (bottom), dressed in a dramatic swag like the one in the home office (top left), or be simply shuttered, like the window in the bedroom, (top right).

Classic shapes like those in vases and vase-shaped lamp bases (top right and left) and in classic contemporary furniture (bottom) provide timeless touches that are always in style.

Chairs come in so many distinct designs, be sure to select a style that expresses your own personality.

Pattern has power! Use it in wall coverings in an entry (top),
paneling (bottom left), or ceramic tile flooring (bottom right).

Bring in the outdoors with green plants (top left), and glass doors (top right), and bring out the indoors in gaily colored, waterproof floor cloth (bottom).

More is better in casual Country-style rooms. Avoid a sense
of chaos by carefully organizing displays of accessories.

Nature is an important part of any decorating scheme. In the formal living room (top left), ceiling lights look like stars. In the Country-style kitchen (top right), the countertop is of slate, a natural stone. Fern prints, plants, and French doors that open easily bring the out-of-doors into the Traditional dining room (bottom).

Bright colors and bold schemes with touches of dramatic black make rooms in all styles seem vital and up-to-date. Black and white enlarged photographs in the living room (bottom) are not only dramatic accents, but seem like windows.

Cabinetry (top), a strong wall covering border (bottom left), and a ceramic tile dado capped with chair-rail-type trim (bottom right) add restful horizontal lines.

Inventive use of light and lighting brings these rooms into strong focus. An offbeat space brightens up with a dormer window (top). Brightly hued pendant lights supplement kitchen sunlight (bottom left) and an inviting chandelier over a small dining table makes a small space important (bottom right).

Master bedrooms

A master bedroom doesn't have to be huge, but it does need to offer the amenities you need. If your space is less masterful than you'd like, take a look at some of the following suggestions for decorating your bedroom:

- ✔ **Make the bedroom look larger by eliminating clutter.**

- ✔ **Use only necessary furniture.** If you can, push a chest of drawers into a walk-in closet to free up floor space.

- ✔ **Keep the bed visually low.** Use a headboard, but don't use a footboard, and opt for something other than a four-poster bed, all of which tend to take up space visually, making the room seem smaller.

- ✔ **Keep all your furniture — like the rest of your color scheme — light.** Light colored furniture, walls, floors, window treatments, and bedding make a room seem bigger.

Regardless of the size of your master bedroom, the following tips can help you to make it as comfortable as possible:

- ✔ **Add bedside tables that are as big as space will allow.** If you read or watch TV in bed, you'll find these tables helpful.

  You can buy restaurant café tables for very little money and drape them with quilts.

- ✔ **Try to make room for at least one comfortable chair.** Chairs are great for company on a sick day, for daytime resting, or for reading.

- ✔ **Consider carpeting all bedroom floors to reduce noise in the room.**

- ✔ **Add a lady's desk — a small, delicately proportioned furnishing for writing letters and so forth — if you have room.**

Teen bedrooms

Teenagers usually know what they want in a bedroom and aren't slow to tell you that they need storage for books and music and space for their collections of just about anything you can name. They have firm ideas about style and colors, so ask! And when your son or daughter requests a wild color, do your best to persuade him or her to use it as an accent.

More and more activities from surfing the Net to entertaining take place in a teen's room. Extra seating and small tables provide space for visitors. Keep furnishings practical and easy to care for.

Children's bedrooms

Nurseries must be planned with the child's future years in mind. But from the beginning, make room for a changing table near the crib. As always, keep safety in mind. The following tips will help you do all of these things:

- ✔ **Keep cribs away from windows and window blind cords.**
- ✔ **Make sure cribs and bunk beds meet federal safety standards.** Check to see that mattresses fit snugly against the crib's sides. Slats, spindles, rods, and corner posts should be no more than $2^3/8$ inches apart from each other. Make sure a child can't release the drop side of a crib.
- ✔ **Choose chests and cabinets that can't be tipped over (even when drawers are opened and a child crawls up and into them).** This may call for fastening them to the wall for security.
- ✔ **Find hardware that's rounded, sanded, and has no sharp edges.**
- ✔ **Equip all electrical outlets with plastic safeguard plugs.**
- ✔ **Eliminate any small throw rugs on slippery floors.**
- ✔ **Make sure all flooring is skidproof.**
- ✔ **Eliminate dangling cords on window blinds.**
- ✔ **Choose bunk beds with sturdy ladders, handrails, and safety rails.**

Make sure you have a guest bed for occasional sleepovers. A trundle bed, which neatly stores a second bed beneath a regular one, is the ideal solution for children's rooms.

Guest bedrooms

Setting aside a room for guests makes their stay more comfortable not only for them, but also for you. You can furnish the guest room with a marvelous bed and all the necessary furnishings and forget about it. Check out the following suggestions for ways to make your guest room comfortable:

- ✔ **Buy a handsome, space-saving daybed or sofa bed that fits smartly against the wall and out of the way.**

  The versatility of these beds makes them a delightful option in a home office or other double-duty room. You may even consider installing a Murphy bed that hides away in a closet.
- ✔ **Make sure that your guest has plenty of closet space.**
- ✔ **Dedicate two sets of sheets, a comforter, special pillows, a duvet cover, and pillow shams to your guest room.**

Chapter 21

Decorating Your Living Room

- -

In This Chapter

▶ Figuring out the function of your living room

▶ Positioning the furniture to meet your needs

▶ Using paint, wall coverings, and paneling to cover your walls

▶ Dressing up your floors, ceilings, and windows

▶ Adding accessories

- -

Style is an individual choice and the options before you are numerous. You may be fortunate enough to have two living rooms — one formal and the other for family. But whether you're decorating one or more living rooms, the planning process is the same — one just becomes finer and fancier, and perhaps less used.

In this chapter, we show you how to recognize the many functions your living space performs. You'll discover the tried and true techniques for stylishly furnishing your living room from bottom to top and side to side to meet the demands of function and home fashion. The best ways to arrange your furniture; cover your floors, walls, and ceiling; and dress your windows are mapped out within this chapter. Finally, you'll discover little bits of decorating magic — the niftiest ways to accessorize your living room to achieve the look you want.

Determining the Function of the Room

Before you even think about decorating any room, you need to determine which functions the room performs: what activities take place within those walls? (Yes, being a couch potato is considered an activity!) Understanding what activities you will use your living room for helps you figure out what you need. A living room — even a formal one — should be flexible enough to handle multiple activities. If your living room also serves as a den or family room, you probably expect more of the room. And if you have a family room in addition to your living room, you can probably leave your living room for more formal occasions.

Start your plan by listing all the activities that may take place in your living room. Ask yourself if you will be using the room for any of the following purposes:

- ✔ Gathering with friends and family?
- ✔ Playing board games or card games?
- ✔ Watching television?
- ✔ Reading?

- ✔ Writing letters?
- ✔ Knitting or sewing?
- ✔ Playing the piano?
- ✔ Listening to music?

Leave out no activity, no matter how trivial it seems. Next, list the furniture you need to make each function possible. Determine which of the following items you need:

- ✔ Sofa or couch?
- ✔ Love seat?
- ✔ Lounge chair?
- ✔ Occasional chairs?
- ✔ Ottomans?
- ✔ Coffee table?

- ✔ End table?
- ✔ TV/VCR?
- ✔ Stereo system?
- ✔ Desk?
- ✔ Floor lamp?
- ✔ Piano?

As you figure out what you plan to use your living room for and what furniture you need, you may think of possible places in the room where some of these activities can take place. For example, the sofa may work well near the fireplace, the reclining chair could face the TV, the piano could fit on an inside wall, and your rocking chair may be perfect near the window. If you're not quite sure where each piece of furniture works best, read the next section to find lots of great suggestions.

Arranging the Furniture

Furniture arrangement is the art of establishing relationships among individual pieces of furniture — all within the context of the room. If your placement of furnishings is going to be successful, not only do the furnishings have to look appealing but they must also function effectively. You may have many unexplored options for arranging furnishings. You may be able to think of only one way that the furniture will fit, because that's the way you arranged it years ago. Or you may have the opposite problem: You simply can't choose the one best arrangement because of all the tempting possibilities.

The best way to decide on a furniture arrangement — and to see the many possibilities in *any* room — is by laying out various floor plans on paper. You can buy ready-to-use layout kits, with graph paper and to-scale furniture templates, in craft and decorating shops. You can also make your own template by using graph paper and a measuring tape. Just measure the dimensions of the room and each piece of furniture, and use the length of each square of graph paper to represent one foot in length. After you draw the room and the furniture to scale on the graph paper, you can easily move the templates of the furniture around and experiment with different locations. Or use a nifty computer program (for more information see Chapter 2). The more you experiment, the more options may occur to you. And this technique is much easier than shoving a sofa or a grand piano around a room!

Looking at different layouts

Solutions to furniture placement can sometimes be easy to find. But in other rooms, because of the location of architectural elements, such as windows, doors, a fireplace, and so on, an answer doesn't come easily. Most of the difficulties people have with arranging furniture arise in rooms that have two different *focal points,* or areas that draw attention. For instance, many people have trouble trying to situate seating in rooms with both a television and a fireplace, or a television and a picture window. Occasionally, you may figure out a way to take advantage of both focal points; but sometimes you just have to choose one over the other. Take a look at the next section, "Playing up a focal point," for more information.

We prepared four different layouts for a client's living room, just to demonstrate that there's more than one way to arrange a room. The one the client chose was not the one *we* would have chosen, but that's the point of drawing several layouts — you can choose *your* personal favorite, not one that a friend or home decorator suggests. These layouts demonstrate that choices are subjective.

The arrangements we came up with (shown in Figures 21-1 through 21-4) take into consideration many functions of our client's living room. We allow extra seating room for big family gatherings, space for a crowd of people to watch television, areas for conversations among a large group of people, as well as intimate conversations between two or three people. Each layout also provides room for reading, letter writing, scenery watching, piano playing, and group sing-alongs.

In the first layout (shown in Figure 21-1), seating is arranged according to tradition, with the large fireplace as the center of attention. The baby grand piano and chaise lounge make the bay window a second strong focal point, while the television, placed in front of picture windows, is incidental.

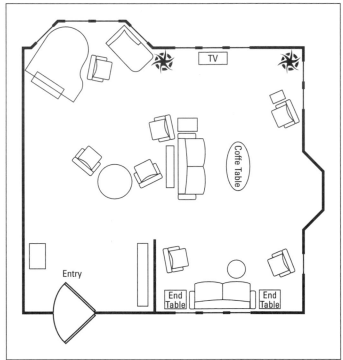

Figure 21-1:
A Traditional
living room
layout.

In another plan (shown in Figure 21-2), back-to-back love seats create two living areas. The imposing fireplace draws the most attention, while the bay window and the grand piano play a supporting role. The television can be seen from the love seat and lounge chairs placed at an angle.

In the third layout (shown in Figure 21-3), a Contemporary, L-shaped couch on a diagonal faces away from the windows. The fireplace is the strong focal point of the room, but this layout makes the television more important. A necessary traffic path to the couch creates a separation between it and the lounge chairs. The grand piano sits in the bay window.

Finally, in the fourth layout (shown in Figure 21-4), two separate seating areas create a sharp distinction between indoor and outdoor focus, allowing room for both. The main seating area focuses on the fireplace, but has a clear view of the television. The secondary seating area makes the most of the bay and outdoor scenery. And the grand piano, tucked behind the sofa, fits nicely with both seating areas.

When arranging your furniture, take architectural features into consideration. We followed some basic guidelines when we created the layouts in Figures 21-1 through 21-4. Check out the following suggestions for devising your own layout:

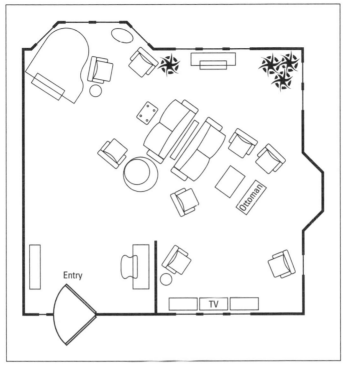

Figure 21-2:
Two living
areas in one
room, with
the focus
on the
fireplace.

- Let the fireplace, a prominent element in any room, be the natural focal point that it is. Create major seating areas around the fireplace.
- Place a large amount of seating around the television set, if you want it to be another focal point.
- Nestle some furniture near the windows that have a beautiful view. This technique balances the seating in the primary area of the room.
- Keep a piano in the background, so it doesn't obstruct the traffic flow. If you have both a piano and a fireplace, place the piano opposite the fireplace wall, to balance the room.

Playing up a focal point

Every living room should have a focal point. But what should you do with a room that doesn't have a natural attention-grabber like a fireplace or a large window? You can create a focal point with an imposing piece of furniture. Secretaries, armoires, wall units, and media centers fill the bill. So do big buffets and handsome dressers and chests (who said they have to remain in

Figure 21-3:
An L-
shaped
couch, with
the focus
on the
television.

the dining room or bedroom?). Make a dresser or chest even more important by hanging a big mirror or painting above it. Underscore this arrangement with a pair of decorative lamps and a super floral or fruit arrangement.
Go even farther, if you want, by adding small, decorative items in a
tablescape, an artful arrangement of objects.

Discovering some basic furniture arranging guidelines

Although you can arrange your furniture in a multitude of ways, some
general guidelines do exist to help you narrow down the possibilities.
Before you decide how to arrange your room, keep in mind the following
suggestions:

  ✔ If the front door to your house opens directly into your living room,
    shield the room by placing a standing, folding screen at right angles to
    the wall.

  ✔ Keep conversations going by grouping chairs a comfortable three to
    four feet apart.

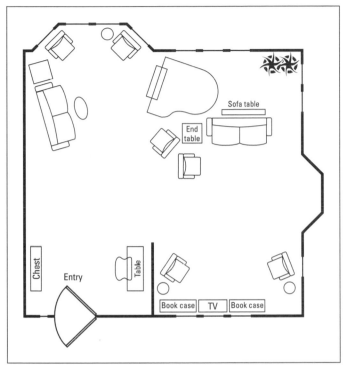

Figure 21-4:
Two seating
areas,
focusing
attention on
both the
indoor and
outdoor
scenery.

A foolproof and very comfortable seating arrangement is a sofa or love seat flanked by two comfortable, upholstered chairs.

✔ Place a table near each chair for holding refreshments, reading glasses, a book, and so on.

✔ Treat a large room as though it were several small ones, breaking it up into various seating and activity areas.

✔ If possible, arrange for traffic *not* to pass between people and the television set.

✔ Don't be afraid to leave a wall free of furniture (especially when the wall flanks a walkway).

✔ Make the most of unusual space by building furniture (shelves, consoles, and so on) into the room. The only negative (you can't take it with you) may not be all bad.

✔ Do not place furniture where it will interfere with the operation of doors and windows.

✔ Furniture placed with lines parallel to the wall creates a greater sense of unity than pieces placed on the diagonal.

Creating Great Backgrounds

Walls, floors, ceilings, and windows create a background not only for your furniture, but also for *you*. Choosing the materials to use for each of these elements involves practical, aesthetic, and budget considerations. Make a clear distinction between what you want and what you need, especially if you don't necessarily *need* everything you *want*. For example, if your house is home to small children and pets, you need something more practical than a white rug and sofa. Of course, with today's technology, most surfaces are stain-resistant and easy to clean. Just make sure you know what you're buying.

For unity, plan adjoining rooms that are openly visible to each other as though they were one space. Treat them both positively (with the same backgrounds) or as positives and negatives (using a dark background and light furnishings in one and a light background and dark furnishings in the other).

Focusing on the walls

Walls, the greatest background area of any room, do a great deal to determine the mood. You can choose from many different materials to cover your walls. Some popular choices include paint in plain or faux finishes, wall covering, and paneling (see Chapter 12 for more information on walls). Keep in mind that each material offers qualities not matched by the other. If you're having trouble choosing between these choices, remember that your house has many rooms, so you can use a different wall covering in each one!

Before you choose a particular material for the living room, consider two things: the room's architecture and your color scheme. Will you use color as a tool to visually reshape the room? (Chapter 4 includes some great tips on determining a color scheme.) Is the room too long, short, square, small, big, or broken up by doors and openings? Is the room more Traditional or Contemporary?

Relying on color to visually alter space may influence your choice of materials. Paint, for example, may offer the widest selection of colors and be easiest to apply. On the other hand, a complex wall covering pattern, such as a trellis may make the space much more dimensional and larger than even faux paint could. Or perhaps a combination of materials (paint and wall covering, wall covering and paneling) could provide the best solution and help you achieve your goals.

Keep in mind that texture also affects space in the following ways:

- The lighter, smoother, and silkier the texture of all surfaces (walls, floors, and ceiling), the airier the space.

- The rougher, coarser, and furrier the background textures, the smaller (and perhaps cozier) the room will seem.

Texture is particularly important to neutral color schemes, which are especially popular in conservative living rooms and other public areas. (Unless you're a very brave soul, save wild, weird, and way-out colors for the laundry room or a basement playroom.) Neutrals please most people most of the time, but they can become boring. To prevent boredom, add texture.

Paint

Keep in mind that while many people choose neutral colors for living rooms, yours can be any color you like. Paint offers infinite color options, is relatively inexpensive, and can easily be applied by amateurs. Generally, a matte (nonshiny) finish is good for walls and ceilings, while trims should be treated with a high gloss (shiny) finish. The matte (or eggshell) finish hides minor flaws, looks rich, and wears well. (It can be washed lightly, but not scrubbed.) Use a semigloss if you like some sheen or shimmer, but beware that it reflects imperfections. More faux finishes (resembling marble, wood grains, and striped fabric) appear all the time. For the most part, they're easy for even a klutz to apply with amazing results.

Special finishes are not expensive, but they're not exactly dirt cheap either. So if you're not sure whether you'll like it, buy a small quantity and try it out on a small wall area. If you like the results, you can always branch out. If not, you haven't spent much money, time, or energy.

Wall coverings

Wall coverings are minor miracles of color and pattern. Nothing can do for a wall what just the right wall covering can. Finding the right pattern or texture is sometimes a hunt, but it's well worth the time and energy invested. And with all the patterns, textures, and colors available, the right one for you is just waiting to be discovered.

Don't overlook textured wall coverings for neutral living room walls. Textured wall coverings such as suedes, brocades, velvets, linens, burlaps, and metallics add a special quality of richness and depth that a more one-dimensional paint (even when *fauxed*) cannot achieve. Take a look at the following tips for decorating your living room with wall coverings:

- Use textured wall coverings with contemporary furnishings.
- Marry traditional colors and patterns (such as stripes) with traditional furniture.
- Many popularly-priced wall coverings are vinyl and can be scrubbed.
- Use a small amount of handscreened wall coverings (vinyl or paper) for an accent, if your budget doesn't allow for an entire room done in this expensive material. Consider adding the wall covering to borders, wainscot effects, or panels bordered by moldings — three places to get big impact.

To order wall coverings, measure your walls (height and length) and give those measurements to your wall covering dealer. Don't deduct the space used by windows and doors. If you leave a little extra room in your dimensions, you'll never run out of paper. And having a couple of extra rolls is a lot better than running short. Use any extra paper to cover a wastebasket or lampshade.

Paneling

Paneling ranges from extraordinarily expensive, solid wood, traditional, English-style paneling (and French *boiserie,* which is fancy wood paneling), to knotty pine planks and more familiar, less expensive, 4-x-8-foot sheets in a wide variety of woods and wood looks. Paneling is available in a huge variety of natural wood colors and textures, painted finishes, and antique colors.

Shop around for the paneling that adds the look you want for your room. Generally, those with raised grounds and trims, which look like boxes, are dressier. Plank styles, with vertical grooves, tend to look casual and are at home in informal rooms. You may like paneling used as wainscot, usually about 30 inches high in Early American, Victorian, and Country style rooms and even higher in Arts and Crafts interiors.

Wood paneling adds a certain richness to walls. But actually, paneling is probably the quickest and least expensive way to repair damaged walls.

Dealing with ceilings

As a guideline, the more obvious the ceiling, the more it needs decorating. If the ceiling is unobtrusive (out of sight and out of mind), you may want to save time, money, and effort by just painting it a pleasant white (to reflect maximum light). If you want your ceiling to stand out, take a look at Chapter 14 for information on the different options for creating a sensational living room ceiling.

Adding interest underfoot

When it comes to floors, the options are numerous (see Chapter 13 for complete information). Choose warm and friendly floorings, such as wood, carpeting, or rugs, for casual living. Choose cooler, more distant floorings, such as marble or ceramic tile, for formal rooms. And for rooms that fall somewhere in the middle, consider options like wood, carpeting, ceramic tile, and resilient and laminate floorings. You may even want to combine some of these different floorings — especially in large rooms.

If you combine two different flooring materials (carpeting and wood, carpeting and ceramic tile, wood and ceramic tile, and so on), be sure that the finished surfaces are the same height, in order to prevent someone from tripping.

The following are some guidelines for decorating your living room floor:

- ✔ Quiet a marble, ceramic tile, or wood floor with a well-padded room-size rug.

- ✔ The gentler the wall (in a soft color with little or no pattern), the louder the rug pattern and color can be. Let upholstery play second fiddle to an extravagant rug.

- ✔ In Traditional rooms, the flooring is usually the darkest of three color values (dark floor, medium walls, light ceiling).

- ✔ In a Contemporary room, the floor is usually the lightest color in the room (turning the tables on Traditional color distribution).

- ✔ Match the scale of a patterned floor to that of the room. In a small room, choose a small pattern; in a big room, a big pattern.

Jazzing up the windows

Window treatments may either carry on the particular style of the room (Traditional or Contemporary, for example) or offer a witty, eclectic contrast.

Traditional window treatment designs abound. Decorating magazines offer up a feast of window treatments which you're free to copy. Pattern books of beautiful designs of *over-draperies* (a draw drapery over sheers over window blinds, valances, and cornices) are plentiful. Drapery shops can create custom designs (or perhaps you're talented and can make your own). Many stores offer both custom and ready-made window treatments.

Contemporary treatments are generally simple. They run the gamut from no-treatment to simple blinds or shades to draw draperies.

If you choose to make a witty statement and go eclectic — by using a Contemporary treatment in a Traditional room or a Traditional treatment in a Contemporary room — be sure your audience appreciates the joke.

Accessorizing

Accessories should contribute to the overall design of the living room. If in doubt, take it out! No matter how much you love a particular vase or painting, if it doesn't add to the room, subtract it. Put it in another room where it will make a real contribution. Otherwise, it will only confuse the eye and you'll end up with a hodgepodge. Chapters 24 and 25 offer more information on art and accessories, so check them out.

The following are some general tips for adding accessories to your living room:

- Use lamps and light fixtures as accessories. In addition to providing lighting for specific tasks and contributing to overall ambient lighting, they're great sources of added color, pattern, and texture.

- Use a variety of lamps throughout a room. Using the identical lamp repeatedly is unimaginative and looks as though you discovered them at a garage sale.

- Keep lamps flanking a sofa similar in size, shape, and color, though not necessarily identical.

- Include torchieres for style and soft, indirect light.

- The more is better rule applies in Cottage-type interiors. The dressier or more contemporary the room, the fewer but more important and higher quality the accessories.

- Hang an ancestor oil portrait over the mantel, but it's generally not a good idea to hang family photographs in the living room or entry hall. Family photographs are too intimate and informal for the living room. Instead, put framed photographs of family and friends in intimate areas, such as dens, libraries, and bedrooms.

- Add flowers, but not fruit, to the living room. Keep edibles in the kitchen or dining room.

- Accessorize according to the season, helping yourself to budding blossoms or turning leaves. This timeliness is fresh and caring.

- Hang any artwork at eye level — where it can be seen with the least effort.

- Avoid any sense of clutter — it's unnerving even in Country-style rooms.

- Add accents to break up large expanses of overbearing solid color, such as big sofas and large upholstered chairs. Add pillows, an afghan, or a quilt for relief.

- Avoid lavishly tablescaping a much-used table. Accessories should delight, not get in the way.

- Don't load a sofa with so many pillows that there's no space for sitting. Make pillows available by piling them into a handy basket.

- Don't clutter up the room with too many little lamps. Vary lamp shapes and sizes, and reserve mini-lamps for secretaries, china closets, and etageres.

- Place a stack of colorful books beneath the base of a lamp that's too short. This technique looks great and works well.

Chapter 22
Designing Dining Rooms

• •

In This Chapter

▶ Determining how many people your table seats

▶ Deciding on a style for the room

▶ Creating a formal dining room

▶ Making room for dining throughout the house

▶ Transforming small spaces into great dining areas

▶ Decorating quickly, with what you have on hand

• •

*W*hat's the difference between eating and dining? Today's lifestyles are very casual, so any time you add a napkin (even if it's paper), consider yourself dining!

In this chapter, we show you how to figure out how many people your table seats and help you decide on an overarching style for your dining room. We look at decorating a formal dining room. And then we get real, showing you how to make eating in other rooms in your house a pleasant experience. We also give you tips on making small spaces work well, and we show you how to decorate your dining room quickly with the materials you have available. This chapter has everything you ever wanted to know about dining — in your dining room or throughout your house.

Planning Your Table

The dining room table is often the setting for important family gatherings, on special occasions and holidays. So you want to make sure your family and friends are comfortable when they gather around your table. If you're not sure how much space you need for each place setting or how many guests your table can seat, take a look at the following guidelines:

- ✔ **Plan a minimum of 24 inches for each place setting.** If you have the room, 30 inches is ideal.

- ✔ **Make sure the table you use doesn't have a low *apron* (the wood panel below the tabletop).** A low apron may prevent your guests from crossing their legs at the table.

  If your table does have a low apron, try to find chairs that sit at a comfortable height for both eating and sitting.

- ✔ **If you plan to use a sofa (or bench) for seating at a long table, choose one with long enough legs so that the seat is high enough.** Add casters to the sofa legs if you need to raise the seat height.

- ✔ **Be sure that the arms of the chairs around your table are low enough to slide beneath, and not bump into, the table.**

- ✔ **Provide at least 24 inches of space behind each chair when someone is sitting in it.**

  You're better off setting up an additional table in another room than crowding a dining room with a table that's too big and other furniture that doesn't really fit.

If you're in the market for a new dining room table, or you're just not sure how many people the table you have can comfortably seat, check out Table 22-1 for the lowdown on table shapes, sizes, and seating capacity.

Table 22-1	Table Sizes	
Shape	*Dimensions*	*Seating Capacity*
Round	36-inch diameter	Four for drinks, two for dining
Round	40-inch diameter	Four
Round	56-inch diameter	Eight
Square	38-inch square	Four
Rectangular	60 x 36 inches	Six
Rectangular	72 x 36 inches	Six to eight
Rectangular	84 x 36 inches	Six to eight
Rectangular	96 x 48 inches	Eight to ten
Rectangular	132 x 48 inches	Twelve

Determining the Style of Your Dining Room

The dining room is one of the easiest rooms in the house to decorate, because it serves a very definite purpose. When you decorate your dining room, you need to take into consideration not only the style you prefer but also how you plan to use the room. Your best bet is to continue the style you've used throughout the rest of your house in your dining room. You want your dining room to be a natural extension of the rest of your home so that your guests feel comfortable in the room and don't have to deal with the chaos that a completely out-of-place dining room can create.

Before you can plan the mood of your dining room, you need to think about how formal or informal you want the room to be. Be honest with yourself — many people whose houses lean toward the casual maintain a very formal dining room and then never have the occasion to use it. If you want the room to be reserved for very special occasions, you decorate differently than you do if you want to use the room on a daily basis.

After you determine the mood that you want to achieve, take a look at the following suggestions to get some ideas for ways to decorate your dining room:

✔ **Formal:** If you have a formal dining room, you have several options.

- You can be a purist and keep your furniture, walls, tableware, and linens all the same style, like the Traditional room shown in Figure 22-1.

Figure 22-1:
A Traditional formal dining room.

Photograph courtesy Focal Point

- You can relax a little but still keep your dining room dressy. Mix furnishings from various periods, mix and match patterns, and warm up your walls with wallpaper.

- You can go Modern with glass and chrome furniture, a light background, and plenty of dazzle. Keep all the dining furniture and furnishings modern, too.

- You can be Eclectic and mix some Traditional and Modern elements, but keep them all equally fine, fancy, and formal.

✔ **Informal:** An informal dining room may seem like a contradiction to you, but you can actually achieve it easily. The following are some options if you want an informal look:

- **Dressy:** America's diverse Country style makes room for tons of individuality and is especially good if you want an informal dining room. Dress up a round Country-style table with a to-the-floor tablecloth. Give period chairs a more relaxed look by covering them in a plaid cotton fabric. Light up the room with an extravagant chandelier, like the iron fixture shown in Figure 22-2.

- **Relaxed elegance:** Dining areas needn't be formal, especially if they flow into the kitchen or family room, as they do in many Contemporary open plans. Don't restrict yourself to thinking that meal-taking can only happen at a table — an island or peninsula can offer an off-beat yet elegant eating experience.

Figure 22-2:
An iron light fixture lightens up a dressy, but informal, dining room.

Photograph courtesy Blonder Wallcoverings

• **Casual charm:** An old but charming wood table with drawers for handy storage of flatware and napkins can double as a food preparation and eating area, especially when you have lots of company and several cooks. Including a place for a quick cup of coffee or a light snack also works well in any eating area, and you don't need much space to accomplish this.

Creating the Perfect Formal Dining Room

Formal dining rooms are wonderful places for celebrating. They can make even ordinary menus somehow seem extraordinary. And between dining times, a well-designed dining room can do double duty as a library or home office. But whether your formal dining room is dedicated to dining or doubles as something else, decorating it should be a top priority.

When you decorate a formal dining room, you have to take into consideration things like comfort, furniture, china, and linens. The following sections show you each piece of the puzzle.

Comfort

You and your family *can* be comfortable in a formal dining room. You just need to think about what makes you comfortable and use some common sense to incorporate those things into your room. Take a look at the following suggestions to make your formal dining room especially comfortable:

- ✔ **Opt for comfortable seating.** Padded chair seats fill the bill. Choose between an upholstered chair (which is more expensive) or a thick, tie-on cushion (which is less expensive). For upholstery or cushions, be sure to find a stainproof, wipe-clean fabric or material. Removable cushion covers that can be laundered or sent to the cleaners are also a great idea.

- ✔ **Find the right lighting level.** Make lighting bright enough that diners can see what they're eating, but keep light levels low enough for a relaxed mood. For a lighting level that's just right, control overhead lights with a dimmer switch or use indirect lighting. Candles should be either above or below, but never directly at, eye level.

- ✔ **Control sound in the room.** The noise level in the room should be neither deathly quiet nor too loud. Fabrics (including rugs, tablecloths, and draperies) absorb sound and help quiet a room.

Movement

Freedom of movement in the dining room is very important. Your guests need to be able to move into and out of their chairs without bumping into each other. So leave 1½ to 2 feet between chairs, and add casters to the bottoms of chairs for easier movement. Traffic should be able to flow around the table and the seated guests, so leave at least 2 feet for passage of one person and up to 3 or 4 feet for servers carrying heavy trays.

Color, texture, and pattern

Color influences our emotions, so deciding which colors to include in your dining room is important (for more information on color, see Chapter 4). Warm colors stimulate people, and cool colors calm them. So if you wanted to make people eat faster, you could paint or cover the walls in a warm color, up to and including red. (Have you ever noticed that fast food restaurants frequently use red and orange in their decorating schemes, while fancy uptown restaurants tend toward soothing neutrals, ranging from off-whites to grays, beiges, and taupes?) Your own strategy can call for striking a balance — a cool background spiked with warm and speedy accent colors, or vice versa.

You can also heighten stimulating effects with more sheen in paint (with high gloss), wallpapers (with metallics), fabrics (with silks, metallics, or light-reflecting glazed surfaces), or with mirrors. Tone down and slow down the emotional climate with *matte* (dull) finished surfaces.

The finer and shinier the texture, the dressier the room; the duller, rougher, and coarser the texture, the more rustic, informal, and casual the room.

Pattern also affects our sense of formality. In general, tiny floral and geometric patterns tend to be folksy and informal; whereas larger, more graceful, and symmetrically balanced patterns are dressier and more formal. Choose the patterns for your dining room based on the degree of formality you want to achieve.

Furniture

For the most part, the furniture you need in a dining room is basic — a table and chairs are the main requirements. But if you have room, a china cabinet can be an impressive addition to a dining room. A china cabinet with a lighted, mirrored back and glass shelves adds a sense of depth, sparkle, and glamour — and it also provides practical storage.

Harmonizing mismatched furniture

If you find yourself with tables and chairs that work well but just don't match, don't panic. You can go two ways:

✔ Instead of hiding it, you can flaunt the mismatch. (This strategy works best when the furniture is really interesting.)

✔ Your second choice is to add some sense of unity by painting all the furniture the same color. White works best in light-hearted Country-style interiors. Black works best in sophisticated, uptown settings.

But don't feel limited to painting mismatched furniture white or black. You can definitely try other colors. Cinnabar or Chinese red can transform an assortment of 18th century or Traditional chairs and a big table into a set. How about a smart marine blue for fancy or oddball furniture intended for an updated dining room? Have some fun by painting ill-assorted pieces mint green or melon for a Southern, chintz-filled dining room. And don't forget interesting new faux finish paints such as crackle or stone looks — straight from a spray can! Pit pretty-colored furniture against stark white walls, or match painted furniture to an accent color in an exciting wall covering.

Don't crowd a formal dining room. If your dining room is too small for a china cabinet, table and chairs, and adequate room to walk around the room, you can compensate beautifully with a narrow, wall-hung shelf (which doubles as a buffet) with a large mirror above.

Take a look at the following list of furniture strategies for small rooms:

✔ **Place your china cabinet in a nearby space accessible from the dining room.** Most furniture is designed for flexibility; so it works in more than one room. Putting the cabinet in a hallway or living room nearby where ample room is available can prevent you from having to crowd a small space.

✔ **Build in your buffet.** Custom furniture can be any size you like and smaller than ready-made pieces, so it can conserve space in a smaller room.

✔ **Substitute smaller pieces for a standard china cabinet.** A 10-x-48-inch glass shelf on gold or silver standards above a narrow buffet, a serving piece, or a 30-inch high bookcase all work wonders. Store and display china at the same time by using small easels on glass shelves.

China and glassware

In the past, tradition dictated that all your china, glassware, and silverware match. Life around the formal dining table was not very creative. But today, we're alive to the possibilities of mixing and matching china patterns and glassware to create settings that never repeat themselves.

Take a look at the following suggestions for setting an exciting, mixed up, but far from crazy, dining room table:

- **Match solid-color accent pieces to a color in your china pattern.** If you use solid white accent pieces, pick a china pattern with a white (not ecru, beige, or ivory) background.

- **Mix a geometric china pattern with a floral pattern in the same colors.**

- **Mix a large-scale floral pattern with a tiny, all-over pattern.**

- **Mix glassware by choosing contrasting colors with clear or frosted glasses, plain stems with fancy stems, and undecorated with decorated glasses.** When you add colored glassware to the setting, choose a color that matches or relates to a color in your china, or add a centerpiece of the same color as your glassware, for a sense of unity.

- **Choose highly contrasting silverware.** For example, contrast plain and ornate handles, or silver-handled knives and forks with black-handled spoons. Use gold-tone dessert spoons if the rest of your silverware is silver. (And if you use gold-tone spoons, use some china or glassware with gold trim.)

Linens

Linen is what we call all tablecloths, runners, place mats, and napkins — even though they may be made of cotton, wool, or some synthetic fiber. Old or antique linens were actually made of linen, which required a great deal of care. These true linens fell out of style, but they're now considered collectibles.

Linen tablecloths are still available and are very elegant. But save labor (especially if it's your own) by choosing crease-resistant, wash-and-wear types. Cotton lace is also an easy-care cloth for a formal table. Embroidered and cutwork tablecloths (in which patterns are created by cutting away some of the fabric and finishing cut edges with embroidery) are also good choices for formal tables.

Monograms add a sense of elegance to the formal table. Usually, the tablecloth is not monogrammed, but the napkins are.

A tablecloth for a formal dinner should drop 12 to 15 inches on each side of the table (to cover the apron and add a sense of grace). Using a pad with a tablecloth in order to protect the tabletop from heat and spills is common.

Wide runners and place mats are considered acceptable alternatives to tablecloths for all but the most strictly formal occasions. They're especially appropriate when the tabletop itself is particularly beautiful. Runners and place mats may be quilted for extra protection.

Storage

To store dining items efficiently, put them near the place of food preparation or near the table itself. Older houses have pantries for storing china, crystal, silverware, and linens. In modern houses that have no pantries and kitchens with minimal storage cabinets, these items are usually stored in a china cabinet, buffet, or small dresser in the dining room. If necessary, consider commandeering a handy closet and fitting it with shelves for storing dining room items.

Dining Throughout the House

Most people today eat anything from a light snack to a full meal in a variety of places throughout the house. The trick is knowing what makes you and your family happy and then planning for it. The following sections provide suggestions for eating in various areas of the house.

In the living room

What makes dining in a living room work? A wipe-clean tabletop (ours is a salvaged, glass-topped, wrought iron café table that doubles for games and reading), well-padded chairs, and a rolling cart. The cart transports everything needed to set the table (place mats, napkins, silverware, glassware, and dinnerware) and then returns them in one trip to the kitchen for cleaning and storing. Plug in a lamp with up-lighting on either side of the table for a pleasant setting.

In a wide hallway

Some homes have kitchens too small to eat in, but they may have a wide hallway area just outside the kitchen. Maybe a glass door offers a spectacular outdoor view and lets in radiant light. In this situation, place a narrow table — with drop leaves that can be pulled out at mealtime and lowered during high traffic times — against the wall. Flank the table with chairs that can be pulled into place at mealtime. Or use folding chairs that can be stored out of the way in a nearby closet. If you need extra light, plug one or more lights into a nearby wall socket (soft up-light is pleasant for dining).

In the kitchen

You can also dine in your kitchen. Eating in the kitchen is a good idea because it's the place closest to the food. Adding a few graceful elements — nice place mats and napkins, a bouquet of flowers, and soft lighting — make dining in the kitchen very pleasant. Countertops (islands, peninsulas, or bars) are the handiest of eating spots, if you don't have room for a small dining table. The most comfortable have a 12- to 15-inch overhang so that when you pull a stool or chair close, you have knee room. For greater comfort, lower the countertop to standard dining table height and add upholstered chairs (see Figure 22-3). Make sure that overhead lighting has a dimmer switch, and keep a few candles at the ready.

Figure 22-3:
Lowering the countertop and adding upholstered chairs adds a convenient eating area to any kitchen.

Photograph courtesy Kitchens By Krengel, Inc.; Michael Palkowitschm, CKD,CBD

In a media room

Eating in front of the TV set is so popular that certain furniture manufacturers have created high-low tables that can be raised for dining and let down again to coffee table height. Sitting on most sofas (which are low) and dining at a coffee table forces you to bend over, straining your back. If you plan to eat on the sofa, you're better off choosing a higher sofa and substituting a tea table for a coffee table.

In other rooms

If you eat in other rooms of the house, such as the bedroom, garden room, or screened-in porch, keep collapsible TV trays and folding chairs handy. Store them near where you most often use them. Also, in the kitchen, keep a rolling cart stocked with napkins, salt and pepper shakers, and other items necessary for meals. Then you can add serving plates, glassware, and foodstuffs to the cart and roll it where they're needed. If you have no electric lighting in the room (for example, on a porch or deck), use candles with protective hurricane shades.

Making the Most of Small Spaces

Whether you dine formally or informally, a sense of spaciousness makes any meal more pleasant.

Here are some tips for making small spaces seem more spacious:

- ✔ Keep backgrounds — walls, floors, and ceilings — light and bright.
- ✔ Choose wall coverings with trellis and other dimensional patterns.
- ✔ Keep furniture light-colored.
- ✔ Use light-colored tablecloths, napkins, and plates.
- ✔ Mirror the wall opposite the windows.
- ✔ Mirror the inside back of your china cabinet.
- ✔ Hang landscape paintings or photographs with deep perspective, which provide distant, view-expanding vistas.
- ✔ Use just a few pieces of furniture and keep them small in scale.
- ✔ Select a table with a glass top.
- ✔ Consider a drop-leaf table, which takes up less space when the leaves are dropped.

Creating Instant Dining Decor

You're planning a meal for a dozen or more guests and you have no table-cloth large enough. For that matter, you don't even have a table that *seats* 12 people. Don't panic! You don't have to run out shopping for a big table and a tablecloth — or break the bank in the process. Just take a look at some of the following suggestions:

✔ Use a wash-and-wear flat sheet as an impromptu tablecloth. Usually even an expensive sheet is much less expensive than a similarly-sized tablecloth.

✔ Knot the corners of a big tablecloth for a casual meal at a smaller table. For a fancy table, tie a beautiful ribbon around each corner, gathering them up until the cloth fits.

✔ Use a couple of sawhorses and a 4-x-6-foot sheet of sturdy ³/₄-inch plywood as a table for 10 or more guests. Pad the plywood with a thick blanket and cover it with a cloth (king-sized sheets work well) to hide the legs.

✔ Use a round, glass-topped or mesh outdoor table for indoor dining. Disguise them by padding the top with a blanket or quilt and adding a round tablecloth that drops to the floor. Use a king-sized sheet and tuck the corners underneath so that the cloth looks round, if you don't have time to cut and hem it.

✔ Find charming, patterned, standard pillowcases to make instant slip-covers for unsightly ladder-back or folding side chairs. Gather the top corners and tie each corner with a grosgrain ribbon. Scrunch the bottom where it bunches at the seat.

✔ Create a candelabra by placing a collection of candles (the candlesticks don't need to match) on top of a raised cake stand. (If you're placing the candlesticks on untempered glass, protect the glass from the candle heat with a coaster or other heat-absorbing surface.)

Chapter 23

Making the Most of Bonus Areas

In This Chapter

▶ Transforming attics, basements, porches, and patios into living spaces

▶ Decorating bonus areas

onus areas are those spaces in your house that you may not think of as rooms, such as attics, basements, porches, and patios. These places have enormous potential to expand the living space in your house considerably. But each of these spaces has special decorating considerations. So this chapter helps you prepare these spaces to be lived in, and it provides decorating suggestions as well.

Decorating Attics

Attics often provide plenty of room for additional bedrooms and bathrooms. Few attics are finished, so you probably need to do some remodeling before you can begin decorating.

After your attic is prepared for habitation, decorating it should be fun. The following are some basic considerations to keep in mind:

✔ **Add adequate lighting.** Attics, unless you've added dormers and/or skylights, are usually not very bright spaces. Compensate for low-level natural lighting by using light or sunny colors and adding ample artificial lighting, preferably as in-ceiling, high hat type fixtures that take up no visible space because they are set into the ceiling.

✔ **Consider the angles.** Attics are full of angles that add interesting diversity. But that great amount of diversity requires you to give more attention to unity. Achieve unity by keeping walls and floors relatively light and nearly the same in color. If you want to use a patterned wall covering, keep the background light and the pattern small to medium in scale and relatively open — like a trellis or trailing vine (which has a trellis effect). The see-through quality of a trellis tends to create a three-dimensional effect that makes any space seem spacious.

✔ **Find a way to combat the low ceilings.** No matter how big the floor plan, attics usually look smaller than they actually are because about 50 percent of the space has less than $7\frac{1}{2}$ feet of headroom. To compensate, stick to a light, monochromatic color scheme for floors and walls. An alternative to a trellis or trailing vine is to paper the knee wall (the short wall between the floor and a peaked ceiling) in a vertical stripe with a light background (see Figure 23-1), and paper the ceiling area in a coordinating, small, open-ground geometric or floral.

✔ **Leave windows uncovered.** Why cover usually-small attic windows? You probably only need to install a simple blind that provides light control and privacy when needed. Otherwise, avoid space-taking draperies. If you do feel the need for drapery-added softness, keep the contrast between the drapery and walls minimal, to retain a sense of spaciousness.

✔ **Use flooring to your advantage.** To absorb sound and take up little visual space, use a low-pile carpet with a thick pad.

Pass up noisy, hard-surface floorings, and avoid space-eating, deep-pile rugs such as shags.

✔ **Use furniture to make the space seem bigger.** Keep all furniture low and horizontal, so that it seems to blend into the low knee wall and not encroach on the ceiling height. If you plan to use your attic as a bedroom, consider dispensing with the bed frame and just placing the box springs directly on the floor. Or if the bedroom is for children or young guests, use a futon or camp cot as a bed, as shown in Figure 23-2.

Figure 23-1:
A vertical stripe with a light background works well in the area between the floor and the peaked ceiling of an attic.

Figure 23-2:
Low
furniture
makes
an attic
space seem
bigger.

Beautifying Basements

Basements are one of the first areas that homeowners consider using for additional living space. After your basement is ready for habitation, consider the following decorating basics:

✔ **Ceiling:** Unless you have high ceilings (8 feet or higher), keep ceilings light in color. Avoid dark hues or busy pattern effects on ceiling tiles or other ceiling materials. The simpler, the better — and the higher the ceiling appears.

✔ **Colors:** To counteract the gloomy feeling caused by the too few and too small windows typical of basement spaces, choose light, bright, sunny colors from the warm side of the color wheel.

✔ **Flooring:** Synthetic tile flooring is a popular choice for most basements because small amounts of moisture won't harm the material. If your floor is moisture-proof and you provide an appropriate sub-floor, you may want to carpet. Choose a synthetic fiber designed to withstand moisture. Ask your carpet dealer to help you select a non-organic fiber that permits wicking away of any moisture.

Real wood flooring is not a good idea for basements because of the potential for damage caused by excess moisture. But if you want the look without the problems, consider a wood-look synthetic flooring. Again, consult with your floor covering dealer to be sure that the material you're installing will perform under damp conditions. Also, if you're redecorating more than one room, use the same flooring throughout. The continuity of flooring increases the apparent size of the space by unifying it.

A dehumidifier can help cut back on the dampness that is characteristic of many basements.

- **Furniture:** Virtually any type of furniture may be used in below-grade spaces. The size of the entry to the basement is probably the only limitation to the furniture you can use in a basement. With proper ventilation and humidity control, upholstery is right at home. If you're not using synthetic tile on the floor (which allows wicking away of moisture), you may want to use moisture-protection pads for furniture as a safety precaution.

- **Lights and lighting:** Provide ample ceiling lighting and install warm rather than cool bulbs, because warm bulbs tend to make the space more appealing. This kind of lighting also eliminates the need for table and floor lamps that eat up space physically and visually. If you want extra lighting, choose wall sconces or pendant lamps.

  Mirrors bounce back light and tend to make spaces seem both brighter and bigger, so use them as wall covering or accessories in basements, to accomplish both tasks.

- **Walls:** After you're sure that the walls are moisture-proof, you may finish them with popular wooden paneling or wallboard. Paneling is a one-step installation, so you can apply it quickly. Wallboard needs spackling and either painting or wallpapering, so this process is a little more expensive than paneling. The vertical lines of paneling tend to make walls seem higher, but wallboard (and painting or wallpapering) is more versatile.

- **Window treatments:** Basement windows need privacy. Thin-slat blinds do a great job here.

Sprucing Up Porches and Patios

Perking up a porch or patio requires more than just plunking down a few pieces of furniture. If you want it to be a living space, think of your porch or patio as a real room.

Weather affects your porch and patio furnishings, so don't confuse indoor with outdoor furniture — they aren't the same thing. Outdoor furniture can withstand moisture and extremes of temperature. Indoor furniture will rust, rot, and fade if left outside.

Always check your community and homeowner's associations to find out if any ordinances or bylaws restrict or prohibit porch and patio decorations. Be sure to secure furniture (if possible) to prevent loss to theft or storms.

Here are a few decorating tips to keep in mind:

- **Accessories:** Potted plants — especially those that bloom — are a natural outdoor accessory. Pile a bunch into a child's red wagon (see Figure 23-3), antique wicker pram, or old wooden boxes. Hang paper

Figure 23-3:
Potted
plants in a
child's
wagon are
a great
accessory
for a porch
or patio.

lanterns (which are actually made of weather-resistant plastic) surrounding electric light bulbs or votive candles. Painted wooden fruit and vegetables, dried or painted gourds, and marble fruits and vegetables are also festive for this outdoor environment. Other fun and even practical ideas include gaily-painted watering cans, wooden duck decoys, equipment for outdoor games (such as croquet or badminton), and colorful plastic children's toys in brightly colored plastic crates. Just about anything that says "outdoors" and looks pretty goes well on your porch or patio.

✔ **Flooring:** Stone floors are a natural for the outdoors and usually need nothing more than an occasional hosing down to look great. Porch floors and cement patios, however, usually benefit from a good coat of paint. Choose a color that's compatible with the color of the exterior walls of the house — maybe a color that matches the existing shutters. (Check with your paint dealer to be sure you're using the right kind of paint.) Consider adding a sisal (fiber) rug, a washable cotton area rug, or a painted floor cloth on protected porches. Area rugs create a very desirable indoor ambiance for sheltered areas.

Don't expect a wool area rug to stand up to outdoor use. It will mold, stain, and be eaten by moths. Instead, look for tough, rubber-backed synthetics that look like oriental or other traditional rug designs.

✔ **Furniture for Seating:** Don't put indoor upholstery on the porch, where sun, rain, and dust will damage it. Instead, use wicker (shown in Figure 23-4), teak, aluminum, wrought iron, or any material that can stand up to the elements. For comfort, choose cushions covered in a washable fabric and stuffed with fiberfill designed to stand up to the weather. Arrange seating just as you would indoors, in close conversational proximity.

If your porch or patio is large enough, provide groups of furniture for various functions, such as conversation, games, and dining.

Figure 23-4:
Wicker
furniture is
especially
well suited
for outdoor
seating.

✔ **Lighting:** Porches have protective roofs and most often come equipped with overhead or wall sconce ambient artificial lighting for evening use. If your porch has a wall plug, use it for one or more floor lamps or a string of white (or colored) Christmas-tree or patio lights. Patios may also have outdoor wall lights. Additional lighting sources for porches and patios include glass-globed hurricane lamps and lanterns fitted with candles. Torches with stakes are another temporary lighting source.

✔ **Shelter:** On porches, openings like the ones between porch posts may need to be treated to hangings that block sun and rain. Consider installing louvered shutters, painted to match the walls or other shutters on the house. Custom awnings are another option (but they can be a bit expensive). Or substitute wash-and-wear sheets for awnings. We did this very simply (and inexpensively) by sewing curtain rod pockets into the narrow bottom hem of king-sized sheets and shearing the curtains on spring-tension shower rods between the porch posts. (Find non-directional patterns for the sheets you use. But if your sheet does have a directional pattern, use the wide top hem for the rod pocket.) You can add cotton tie-backs, held by cup hooks, that secure the curtains when you don't need privacy or shelter from mild breezes. When it rains, you can undo the tie-backs and let the sheets blow dry.

Shelter for open patios and terraces may come in the form of umbrella-covered tables, awnings, or freestanding tents to shield the area from sunshine or showers.

✔ **Walls:** Porch and patio walls are the exterior walls of your house, so you probably won't paint them a different color. But you *can* decorate them with hanging planters, ceramic tiles or plates, painted wooden plaques, and other appropriate items that neither sunshine nor rain will damage.

Part VII
Embellishments: Accessorizing with Art and Other Stuff

The 5th Wave   By Rich Tennant

"I just can't figure out how we overshot our decorating budget by $8.4 million already. We haven't even bought the new dining set."

In this part . . .

Embellishments — art and accessories — are like icing on a cake, the finishing touch. So, if you've completed the background — walls, floors, ceiling, and window treatments — and your furniture is in place, but your room looks like an empty, lifeless stage, don't panic. What your room needs is accessories! Just as actors bring life to a decorated stage, accessories bring personality and life to a room.

In this part, we define *art,* which we use as an accessory, and discover the difference between *fine, decorative,* and *fun* art. You'll see how to make the most of each, and get the hang of arranging framed art attractively.

You'll find that *decorative accessories* can be anything from art to books to bric-a-brac. You'll also discover that an accessory may be something as functional as a cup and saucer that's just too pretty to store out of sight. The phrase "a place for everything and everything in its place" can mean letting it all hang out instead of hiding lots of great stuff behind solid cabinet doors.

Chapter 24

All about Art

Art is a favorite accessory. But art is also a big, confusing area that needs some explaining. To begin with, how do we distinguish between the art that goes into museum collections and other interesting, attractive, artfully designed items? What kind of art are we talking about when we think of decorating? One common way to accessorize is with framed art, which we usually think of as "pictures" that we hang on walls. In a nutshell, framed art can be divided into three categories: *fine, decorative,* and what we call *fun* art. As a consumer, you need to know how each of these three categories differ so you have the ability to make smart purchasing decisions. After all, why pay fine art prices for less valuable, purely decorative art? As a decorator-in-training, the more you know about these various kinds of art, the better you'll be able to use them. Of course, there are other kinds of fine, decorative, and fun art in a variety of media — textile art to hang on the wall, sculpture and soft sculpture, and so on. Generally, there's less confusion about these kinds of art, and as interior decorators, we just call them accessories.

Knowing the basics of the three types of frameable art is just the beginning of this crash course in Art Appreciation. You also need to know where to place the art after you find it and how to tastefully mix art with other furnishings for the most pleasing results. Not an easy task. Lucky for you we cover all the bases right here in this chapter.

What Is Art?

Some modern artists argue that anything anyone makes is art. (You may recall controversial art exhibits of toilets, cardboard boxes, and so on.) But, for decorating purposes, we think of art in the traditional sense — as pictures (or other wall hangings) or sculpture (including figurines). These are objects created to please the eye, stir the intellect, and delight the imagination. Art has no practical or functional purpose. In decorating, we use art as an accessory, to complete the decorative scheme. Art adds something to your room's decor by furnishing otherwise boring or empty spaces. (If a space is not boring or empty, it probably doesn't need art!) Because a home is not an art gallery, we think that all art should harmonize with a room's theme, underscore the color scheme, and play up the mood. In other words, although a work of art chosen to hang over the sofa should not *match* the sofa, it definitely should look great with the sofa, and sculpture should look at home, not as though it escaped from a bank lobby.

Fine art

Knowing why some paintings and sculptures make it into museum collections and others do not isn't absolutely necessary. But knowing about all kinds of art will help you decide what you want to buy and where you want to place it in your home. Fine art is made to be looked at and appreciated for its intrinsic value. Like a rose, we buy it for its beauty, not because it will perform any work for us. Art speaks to our aesthetic faculty. (Not to turn this into a philosophy course, but our aesthetic faculty is our ability to experience and judge good, better, and best and to differentiate right from wrong.) Fine art, then, establishes a dialogue with us, and makes us think. It's always interesting, but it's not necessarily beautiful.

You can expect to pay more for fine art because of its aesthetic qualities and the fact that all fine art is *original art* — the only one of its kind. Because original works of art are relatively expensive and are expected to increase in value, they're considered to be an investment. If you decide to invest in a work of art, be sure you know what you're investing in. Following are a couple of important points to remember when considering fine art:

- ✔ **Buy from a reputable source.** This is extremely important in ensuring that you get what you pay for. See the upcoming section "Fine art from fine sources" for some general tips.

- ✔ **Develop an eye for quality.** You can sharpen this skill by participating in museum tours, seminars, and classes; gallery visits; art history and media classes; and reading magazines and books.

If you love the look of fine art, but your budget just won't budge, consider buying reproductions of fine art pieces. You can achieve the same basic look from reproductions — without breaking the bank! (See the upcoming section, "Decorative reproductions" for more information.)

Multiple originals?

In most cases, fine art is unique; that is, only one such oil painting, watercolor, tapestry, or sculpture exists in the whole world. The exception is original graphic art (called *multiples*), largely including woodcuts, etchings, and lithographs. These forms of art are considered originals even if several of the same subject exist, because each is created by the hand of the artist.

These multiples are usually pencil-signed and numbered by the artist who indicates the sequential number in the series that forms a limited edition, followed by a slash and the total number of that particular edition. Knowing that you're buying number 1 of 200 *original* pieces is important because all original art is rare, and therefore more valuable than reproductions — which is nice to know when you decide to sell. No one piece in an edition is considered more valuable than any other. Usually, a small edition with only a limited number of prints (say 100 total pieces) is more valuable than a large or unlimited edition of as many as 1,000 pieces.

Decorative art

Decorative art for the wall is considered *decorative* because it doesn't do battle with your brain cells, it just brightens up your day! Certain original oils, acrylics, and watercolors fall into this category. So do reproductions (copies of originals) in oils, acrylics, watercolors, graphic media, and some *original* photographs.

Just remember that decorative art — no matter what the medium — is meant to entertain, not educate. Therefore, buy decorative art to spice up your room. Don't buy it, however, as though it were an investment, because decorative pieces are never expected to grow much in value. In other words, you're not going to make a killing when you put it in your garage sale.

Our general rule is to never pay more for a piece of purely decorative art than we'd pay if we were buying the frame without the art in it.

Decorative "originals"

Decorative "original" oils, acrylics, and watercolors may be the work of a trained artist who works alone, or be created by teams of artists, each of whom paints only a part of the total picture. (Interior designers facetiously call this "art by the yard.") Purely decorative art isn't intended to contribute to art history; it's meant to hang over your sofa and look nice.

Shutter-bug style

Black-and-white photography, a fine art form, is increasingly popular and makes for striking display, especially when prints are framed simply and hung in groups. Work by certain photographers is considered original, collectible, and investment art. Some, like works by Alfred Stieglitz and Man Ray, have sold at auction for hundreds of thousands of dollars. Works by some lesser known artists from the same period (the 1920s and 1930s) are considered as good, but sell for less. Today, you can order work by noted artists from catalogs such as Ballard Designs, Exposures, Light Impressions, Pottery Barn, and Spiegel.

Don't let an overzealous salesperson convince you that these paintings are great art, and therefore have great resale value — their value is purely decorative. Favorite themes and subjects are usually personal, romantic, sentimental, and popular. Romantic Paris street scenes, moonlit seascapes, autumn woods, snowcapped mountains, gorgeous floral bouquets are pretty and relatively inexpensive (and, of course, there's nothing wrong with that!).

The real rule when buying art is to buy what you like. Buy the art, not a salesperson's ill-informed or unethical spiel.

Decorative reproductions

Reproductions are copies of original fine art that can look amazingly like the real thing — right down to the brush or knife stroke. Traditionally, they were not considered in the best of taste, and were considered fake. But tastes change, and today, when fake is exalted as faux and faux is the way to go, they're plentiful!

We can think of several acceptable reasons for decorating with reproductions:

- ✔ **Cost:** They're affordable, which is extremely important for most people.

- ✔ **Tasteful subject matter:** Oftentimes the subjects, like certain Beatles tunes or operatic arias, are old favorites. The Taste Police won't slap the cuffs on you for the subject matter!

- ✔ **Availability:** Reproductions are readily available. You can't turn around in many home stores without bumping into reproduction art.

- ✔ **Cheap insurance:** Although they may look like quality items, household insurance rates are much lower for reproductions than they are for insuring the real thing.

Many people choose this kind of art for second homes or vacation homes for that very reason. And if you buy reproductions, you don't need to worry that art thieves will break in and steal them!

Posters are a favorite form of decorative art and make great accessories because of their bold graphic design. Some, despite the fact that they're one of a multiple series, even become collectibles. For example, we know a professor of Greek, who is a talented amateur magician, and especially prizes a poster of Thurston, a magician more talented, he says, than Houdini. The poster has become rare and the subject culturally significant. Naturally, this gift from his wife hangs prominently in their living room.

Fun art

Fun "art" — not art in the strictest definition — is just about anything you want to hang on your walls. It speaks to us in purely personal tones. You may decide to frame theater tickets from the concert where you met your mate, a child's first kindergarten art work, your old ballet shoes, the front door key to your first house, or rusty horseshoes. Framers love to rise to the challenge of showcasing these unusual objects. Often, the framing itself is artful!

From a decorating point of view, fun art is a real conversation-starter and definitely helps make our homes our very own castles.

When it comes to fun art, we, not the gallery owner or art world, decide what it's worth. And, although it may not increase in monetary value, it will undoubtedly grow in sentimental value so that, ultimately, it may be priceless!

Fun photos by amateur photographers, including family members, make excellent decorations, and they have an added benefit — real sentiment that truly personalizes a room.

Art Do's and Don'ts

If you're going to hang art on your walls, choose what you love and can afford — regardless of what type of art it is. You may even decide to include fine, decorative, and fun art together in your home, in the same room, or even in a single wall grouping. From a decorating standpoint, you have every reason to do this. The only time you should not mix fine, decorative, and fun art is when it doesn't look good together. But, usually, that's just a matter of playing with an arrangement until it does look great (see "Hanging tips" later in this chapter for more information).

You want tips for selecting art? We got tips for selecting art:

✔ Don't buy a painting (or picture) you're not crazy about just because it's the right color to hang over your sofa. The odds are good that you'll never appreciate it and you'll have wasted an opportunity to hang something that makes you feel good every time you see it.

✔ Don't use art that bores you. If it bores you, it will probably also bore your friends and family. *Remember:* Art should evoke a specific mood, but boredom probably isn't the one you want!

✔ Don't hang fabulous artwork over furniture if it has no relationship to, or even fights with, the furniture beneath it. A great piece of art and your sofa both deserve the right setting.

✔ Do buy artwork that you enjoy looking at, that boasts colors that look smashing with your furnishings, and that grabs your attention each time you see it. With so much art available, all it takes is a little looking around until you find the right piece. So, what's the rush?

Where to Buy Art

Art, in the big, broad sense of objects you like to look at, is anywhere and everywhere. Finding art to complete your decorative scheme can be a fun and unexpected adventure. Don't neglect any possible source. In addition to the obvious places — art, antique, frame, museum, furniture, gift, and accessories shops — look at estate and garage sales, auctions, consignment shops, and flea markets. Treasures and bargains can be found in unlikely places — even in your mom's attic.

Looking for that perfect painting or pretty print requires either a very good color memory and quick judgment or a little planning and patience. For best results, bring along snapshots of your rooms or your sample boards and floor plans. They will help you decide whether a particular piece of artwork fits in with your room.

Fine art from fine sources

Buy fine art from a reputable dealer who knows the artist whose work he represents and who sells pieces at fair prices. Visit galleries. Ask questions. If you're not sure about which gallery to deal with, talk with museum curators and art professors. Ask them to recommend galleries. Read art journals and magazines to find the names of excellent galleries, the names of the artists they represent, and something of the value of these artists' work. Visit artists' studios when you have an opportunity. Talk with artists at openings. Check their biographies, which tell the names of celebrity clients, museums where their work is hung, awards won, and so on.

Decorative art from just about everywhere

Decorative art is available just about everywhere, including galleries. In addition to galleries, artists' studios, and designer showrooms, retail art shops and furniture stores are the easiest places to find this kind of art. Occasionally, you'll find pieces in consignment shops, flea markets, antique shops, and at auctions and estate sales. Personally, we've found some of our favorite pieces at thrift shops. As for knowing whether you're paying the right price for a particular piece, ultimately, *you* have to be the judge.

Not every piece by a great artist is great art. You may like a lesser, purely decorative piece and get a kick out of owning something by a big-name artist!

Fun art is where you find it

Most of the time, fun art is not bought. It's literally where you find it! It's something that only *you* would have framed, and usually for sentimental reasons. You can frame and hang almost anything. You can even place three-dimensional objects into a shadow box frame.

No matter what the object, if you think you'd like to see it hanging on your wall and need help with a frame choice, ask a framer to suggest a suitable frame and matting. Participating in this exciting, creative process in which you and the framer transform your treasure (which others may consider trash) into a visual delight is a lot of fun.

Relating Art to Other Stuff

Where should you hang that 24-x-48-inch oil painting of a herd of Holstein cows that was left to you by Uncle Willie? Although some people tell you to buy what you like and not to worry about matching your art to your sofa, decorating is about relating objects that look great together — often better together than each would look alone. So, making sure your art and sofa complement each other and don't clash is a good idea.

Which objects look right together? Professional decorators use a long list of traditional criteria. Of course, you're free to accept or reject tradition and experts' opinions. But it never hurts to consider the possibilities.

Mood and colors matter

If you happen to have a painting of black-and-white cows (an informal subject), think of hanging it in an informal area (a den or family room, for example). Relate the color — black-and white-cows — to a black leather or black-and-white tweed sofa that repeats the black in the art. Or, if the black-and-white cows are standing in a vast green meadow, you could hang the art above a predominantly green sofa. You get the picture.

When you hang a large, important picture, repeating some of the dominant colors in other accessories throughout the room is a good idea. Recently, a friend bought a painting with a lot of bright golden yellow and deep purples and pinks. We repeated the purple in a lounge chair across the room from the painting, and we added purple toss pillows to the off-white sofa beneath the painting. Relating the painting in this way to other objects in the room is a kind of bonding that emphasizes unity.

Subjects matter

No hard and fast rules have been written about which subjects can hang where, but some strong social conventions do exist. Following are a few no-nos:

- Some people consider nudes inappropriate subjects for living rooms and dining rooms. Beauties au naturel are considered naughty-but-nice for bedrooms and bathrooms.
- Traditionally, fruit or vegetable still life compositions are never for bedrooms. Save them, instead, for dining rooms and kitchens.
- Don't hang family photos in the living room. Opt for portraits instead.
- Never hang religious art in the bathroom; save it for the bedroom.
- Don't hang small landscape paintings near large still life fruits or vegetables. The disparate scales of the two paintings make both of them look ridiculous.
- Barnyard scenes are foul in a formal living room, but fair in the den.
- Don't hang blood-and-guts war scenes in the dining room.

Flowers, landscapes, and seascapes are welcome just about anywhere.

Gender and age bias

Floral subjects are considered feminine. Boats and seascapes are thought of as masculine. Whimsical themes are often considered childish. On the positive side, take advantage of this traditional thinking to make quick, easy, and uncontroversial choices. For example, floral subjects fit fine in feminine bedrooms. Boats and seascapes are naturals for men's dens or sporty family rooms. Who can argue with clowns for kids' rooms?

But, if you have an educated eye and a sense of adventure, you may want to go beyond traditional thinking. Ignore the biases, if you like. These are social conventions, not iron-clad laws. At least do some experimenting — most shops make that possible by permitting you to return and exchange art that didn't work out as you thought it would.

Discuss the possibility of exchanging your art at the time of purchase, keep your receipt, and return the art by the deadline (there usually is one) and in like-new condition.

Media and frame focus

By choosing a particular medium — oils, watercolors, woodcuts, etching, or lithograph — the artist has offered some direction for hanging the art. Each has a distinctive character that relates to other furnishings. A quick, effective way to find out about which art looks best where, is to look at how professionals — curators, interior designers, and others — hang various kinds of art. Visit museums, galleries, showcase houses, and furniture and department stores with room settings that include art. Browsing through decorating magazines is an inexpensive and time-effective alternative.

Past perfect solutions

A good starting point when finding the proper setting for your art is to look at what's worked well in the past. (Hey, why reinvent the wheel?) For example, each of the various graphic media — woodcuts, etchings, and lithographs — have particular characteristics that are compatible with certain decorating periods and styles. If you're concerned about which objects go well together, remember the old adage, "Birds of a feather flock together." Some examples follow:

- ✔ Woodcuts have a rustic, naïve quality that fits with Renaissance, Gothic, and even Early American decor. Some make a nice counterpoint to Contemporary furnishings. To read more about finding your decorating style, see Chapters 8, 9, and 10.

- ✔ Etchings are composed of finely-drawn lines that are elegant and get along well in dressy rooms.

- ✔ Lithographs are more painterly and colorful and take on a wide range of looks and styles, ranging from romantically Impressionistic to boldly modern.

A Contemporary choice

Happily, black-and-white photographs look fabulous with just about any period or style of furniture. They breathe a breath of fresh air into period rooms and sing the same tune as Contemporary style. Depending on subject matter (no nudes in the living room, please), black-and-white prints are handsomely at home in any room.

Modern methods

Modern interiors stress individual approaches to very personal rooms where just about anything goes — and the mix is magic. Call it *eclecticism* — the unexpected mix of unlike styles — if you like. Some eclectic ideas follow: (Note that the first two approaches are the yin and yang of eclecticism. The third involves an artful mix.)

- ✔ Create interest by contrasting a large, important, period-looking work of art with a crisp, modern background.

- ✔ Pit boldly colored, extremely geometric subjects against stark white walls in rooms furnished with wildly colored furniture.

- ✔ Create *art walls,* which mix a widely diverse group of works in interiors where all other furnishings are subdued and play second fiddle to the art.

None of these three techniques mixes a lot of disparate stuff together — that's called *hodgepodge.* These personal statements require a great deal of taste and a lot of confidence. The more you experiment, the better you'll become at mixing the best, eliminating the rest.

Backgrounds for Art

After you accumulate several pieces of art, you want to show it off in the best way possible. One way to accomplish this is to set an appropriate backdrop for your little jewels.

Although you're probably not going to design your whole house (or even one room) expressly for art, you may decide that a little fresh paint can help give your art a boost. Notice that the '70s and '80s trendy art gallery look, with light bleached floors and pure white walls, is giving way to rooms with more traditional color schemes designed to show off artwork just as well as, if not better than, the art gallery look. Some of the leading decorating magazines show a renewed interest in strongly colored walls, including dark greens, deep rusts, intense corals, passionate reds, and sunflower yellows.

If you're painting a wall to show off your art collection, choose a color that looks best with the dominant color in your collection. Test your choice by painting a portion of a wall and propping several large pieces against it.

On the flip side, if your room comes first and art is truly an accessory after the fact, you may find yourself choosing art to hang against a very busy background, perhaps wallpaper with cabbage roses. In cases like this, for best results, choose a substantial frame that contrasts strongly with the background. A slender pink frame the same color as the roses in your wallpaper will simply get lost against such a busy background. If your art has a mat, be sure that it, too, contrasts with the wallpaper. If your wall is a busy background, consider the subject, too. Obviously, pink roses against pink rose wallpaper will probably just disappear. Instead, a landscape or seascape will provide contrast and still maintain the romantic mood.

Placing Art Artfully

You can hang art effectively in many places. The most effective places are where the eye *expects* to see something (and feels a distinct sense of something missing when nothing is there).

The most obvious gaps often occur on the wall area above a piece of furniture. In such cases, artwork should relate in *scale* to the furniture you're placing it near.

- ✔ Art should be no wider than the furniture below.
- ✔ If the art is narrower, it should be at least half the length of the furniture.

  If a major piece of art is too narrow for the chosen spot, flank it with smaller pieces of framed or three-dimensional art that will fill the space and satisfy the eye.

- ✔ The bottom of the art should be close enough to relate to the furniture, but there should be breathing space (generally about 8 to 10 inches).

  If, for any reason, you need to leave as much as a foot between the furniture and bottom of the art, you can close the obvious gap with a floral arrangement or some other space-filling device.

Although certain spaces cry out for art, consider adding art to unexpected places, too. Art over a door or window pulls the eye up and makes the door or window look taller and more interesting. A tiny piece of art hung below the lampshade on a bedside table is a nice last thing to see as you turn off your light. Consider hanging a piece of art on that awkward blank wall area between the window sill and the floor. It may seem unusual, but boy, will it get noticed!

Be open to the idea of rearranging and even moving your art, hanging it in different places around the house from time to time. You'll discover new things in each of the pieces after they're hung in a different light, at a different angle (higher or lower than before), and with different furnishings, which will call attention (by contrast or similarity) to elements that were not highlighted earlier.

Grouping Art

Grouping art is a great way to decorate walls against which no furniture is or can be placed. In these cases (usually these walls are adjacent to a walkway, as in a hallway), art is an effective substitute for furniture. You can adopt an "all-over" approach and hang groupings higher and lower than expected, in order to cover more wall area.

Symmetry (or left-brained groupings)

Any grouping that can be halved down the middle and be the same on each side is symmetrical. *Absolute symmetry* occurs when exactly the same objects used on one side of the room are used on the other (see Figure 24-1). *Relative symmetry* creates a mirrored effect, but the objects on one side of the room are not identical to the ones on the other side of the room (see Figure 24-2).

Figure 24-1: Absolute symmetry, the most formal arrangement, creates mirror images using identical items on each side of a grouping.

Absolute Symmetry

Figure 24-2:
Relative
symmetry
strives to
create a
mirror
image
effect using
objects that
are similar
but not
identical.

An art grouping composed of similarly sized frames with each painting hung virtually equidistantly from each other is an example of a symmetrical arrangement. This approach to arrangement is often seen in Traditional room settings, where, for example, a dozen botanical prints are hung in rows and columns. A symmetrical wall grouping of paintings is easy to do when all the pictures are framed and matted identically. The effect is formal and serene. It's also considered Traditional, but this classic arrangement brings both surprise and tremendous stability to a Modern setting.

Asymmetry (or right-brained groupings)

An art grouping of variously sized framed pieces hung in a straight line, in rectangles, in triangles, or in other similar patterns, but placed so that they create an optically balanced arrangement, is *asymmetrical*. Asymmetrical arrangements achieve a sense of balance by carefully grouping items of unequal size, shape, and color (see Figure 24-3). When numerous paintings of various sizes and shapes are used, composition is trickier to achieve.

Figure 24-3:
In this asymmetrical arrangement, the dark rectangular mirror and the dark ball beneath it equal the impressive visual weight of a large dark pot.

Asymmetry

Usually, hanging the paintings to create masses that are similar and in close proximity makes them work much like a mural would. If you're working with several pieces of art in various sizes, shapes, and frame styles and colors, plan your grouping to form either a square or a rectangle by keeping either tops or bottoms of frames even or level. Doing so will create a greater sense of unity and order. You'll be making lemonade out of what may, at first, have looked like a bunch of lemons.

To compose a grouping of frames of various sizes and shapes, decide whether you're going to create a square or a rectangle, and whether the rectangle will be vertical or horizontal. Another option is to create a circular or oval arrangement. Using groupings of art in a range of frame sizes and mat choices, is dynamic and casual, the exact opposite of the traditional and static symmetrical composition.

A grouping of an even number of paintings is more dynamic than a grouping of an odd number of paintings (see Figure 24-4).

Figure 24-4:
The grouping on the right is more dynamic than the grouping on the left.

Avoid diagonal or stair-step arrangements where two or three paintings are hung so that the top of one frame is lined up with the bottom of the next, because this arrangement leads the eye off into infinity and creates a sense of chaos. (The only time stair-stepping pictures works well is in a stairway!)

If you follow these steps, you'll create a perfect grouping every time — without frustrating mistakes:

1. **Measure the wall space that you want to fill.**

2. **Outline that exact size on your floor using masking tape.**

3. **Arrange the art on the floor within the given area.**

   Doing so enables you to move pieces around until you arrive at the optimum arrangement.

4. **After you're pleased with the grouping, measure and hang.**

Be prepared for some surprises. You may need to shift pieces from spot to spot, because unusual factors can affect the sense of balance that you're striving for:

- **Generally, *heavier* pieces should go below *lighter* pieces.** Size alone doesn't make a picture seem heavier. You may discover that a large, delicate oil seems lighter than a smaller, darker, more rustic woodcut. And color has weight. So, a small dark red piece seems heavier than a much larger yellow piece. This "heavier versus lighter" thing can be a bit confusing. Ultimately, you'll just have to use your own judgment.

- **Leave several inches of breathing space around each piece of art.** Pieces hung too close together lose any sense of individuality; those hung too far apart don't look like a group and have no sense of unity.

Hanging tips

Be sure to use the correct hooks to hang your art. Check the package to make sure that the hooks you buy are designed to hold the weight of the art you're hanging. Using two hooks for larger works helps keep them hanging straight. And make sure that the hook you're using is the right one for your type of walls (plaster or plasterboard).

If you're nailing or screwing a hook into a plaster wall, put a crisscross of adhesive tape on the wall to keep the plaster in place and then drive the nail or screw through the tape. If you're hanging art on a slanted wall such as a *dormer* (slanted) ceiling, attach the artwork at the top and bottom of the frame. If you're creating a precise rectangular or square grouping, secure the pieces at the bottom, too, so that none will become crooked.

Whether you're creating a grouping or an entire art wall, be sure to arrange the art on the floor first. After you're satisfied with the arrangement and are ready to hang the art, start at the *center* of your wall and work on one side, then the other, maintaining balance as you go. In this way, you'll ensure that you don't find yourself with unattractive, off-balance, vacant space at just one end of the wall.

For added excitement, add three-dimensional objects such as mirrors, sconces, and brackets with sculpture. Add textural interest with tapestries and quilted, woven, or embroidered wall-hangings to these large groupings.

Off-the-Wall Display

We want to be sure to tell you that you can display your art in more than one way — you don't have to hang it. The following list gives you some of our favorite alternatives:

- Easels, large and small, have never gone out of style — just lean your art into one!

- It's also okay to set a large picture on the floor (if you don't have small children or rambunctious pets around), a small picture on the mantel, or a bunch of pictures atop a bookshelf, and just lean them against the wall (see Figure 24-5).

- The idea of a long, low, stained or painted wooden shelf for propping up a plethora of small artwork, including black-and-white photographs, is practical and pleasing (see Figure 24-6).

✔ Feel free to intersperse paintings with books in a bookshelf for an added tasteful touch.

✔ And an array of artfully framed miniatures inside a glass-topped display table, coffee table, or end table, or atop a big round table, is a fun idea.

Figure 24-5:
Art doesn't have to be hung on the wall but can be set on the floor or tabletop and leaned against the wall.

Figure 24-6:
An art shelf holds framed art that can easily be added to, rotated in and out, or regrouped without a nail hole in the wall.

Chapter 25

Accessories

. . . .

In This Chapter

▶ Personalizing your home with your accessories

▶ Using surprising accessories

▶ Accessorizing imaginatively on a budget

▶ Styling to create a look

▶ Finding beauty in unusual places

. . . .

After all the work you've put into preparing walls, floors, and ceilings and placing furniture in all the right places, don't be surprised to discover that your room still looks unfinished. It is. You need to add accessories — a myriad of small furnishings, including pictures for the walls, toss pillows for sofas and chairs, sculptures, and vases to decorate tabletops.

Accessories give rooms the lived-in-and-loved, *real* look that stylists and architectural photographers work hard to achieve for decorating magazines. Some of these items may serve a useful function; others may not. But the accessories you choose should make sense (no clutches of candlesticks on low coffee tables in houses with small children, for example). You don't want your accessories to look staged or out of place (like a tray with crystal decanters and champagne stemware on a family room ottoman). Your accessories should add interesting color, pattern, and texture to your room.

This chapter shows how you can accessorize every room in your house to show off your personal style. We take a look at where to find the right pieces, how to revive the life in the things you already have, and how to imaginatively use other tried-and-true secrets of professionals to create the look you want. Then we tackle several categories of accessories, giving you suggestions, tips, and tricks for making the most of finishing touches.

Make a Personal Statement

Accessories, like art, should reflect your personal interests. In doing so, they say emphatically that this is *your* home, and that it, like you, is special, unlike any other. Because accessories are personal statements, they only need to be decorative, and they certainly don't have to be museum quality. Accessories should be things that you love, even if they are lowly things like rocks, shells, leaves, and twigs.

Finding Accessories Is Part of the Fun

Take a fresh look at things you have around the house that may work as accessories. Find creative uses for objects you may have been hiding out of sight. Baskets, bird cages and bird houses (only someone with personal style would put a weathered birdhouse in a living room!), bits of antique lace, beautiful photographs — almost anything can be framed, mounted, or put on a stand and displayed. Look around for the unusual and unexpected to add just the right note of individual style.

Don't run out and buy a bunch of mass-produced things just to fill up space. What's the rush? Rome wasn't built in a day, and neither are most rooms. Give yourself time to discover objects of desire when and where you find them, or perhaps to craft your own. Our friend Norma saw a mosaic mirror that she liked, enrolled in a short course, and learned how to make her own. To her surprise, people who saw her mirrors wanted them. Now she's making and selling them at flea markets. Nothing adds personal style more than using accessories you designed and made yourself.

Become a <u>Quick-Change</u> Artist

Accessories don't have to be a part of your house forever. Change them as often as you like, just as you may change your jewelry. Accessories for your house serve the same purpose that jewelry does. Think of your room as a basic black dress and accessories, like jewelry, as something you can change frequently to have a different look for a new season, holiday, or special event. They're small and portable and can easily be moved in and out, around and about, for variety.

If you don't want to bring out a completely new group of accessories for a total makeover, occasionally move a few accessories to different spots in the room, or from one room to another. A vase or painting can look very differ-ent in a different setting. Gallery owners and retailers change their displays for this very reason — so people can discover in a new setting what they missed in the old.

Accessorizing Effectively

Accessories are like spices — they add zest to your decorating. Just as most dishes call for an array of seasonings, so does any room you're access-orizing. It's the layering effect produced by a pinch of *this,* a dollop of *that,* and a smidgen of the *other* that produces a complete effect. All the elements combine to create one perfectly executed room. A well accessorized room seems finished. Here are some tips and strategies from the pros:

✔ Use only a few accessories or a lot, depending on your personal style. Is your personal style minimal or maximal — do you like a lot or a little? See Chapter 10 for more details on discovering your style. In a nutshell, Contemporary style calls for only a few key accessories, as shown in Figure 25-1, while Traditional calls for many more accessories.

✔ If you decide that more is better when it comes to accessories, avoid a cluttered look by grouping similar or related items together.

✔ Accessories provide contrast to your overall scheme. But you can unify accessories themselves by choosing items in the same color or mate-rial. A dozen vases have more impact if they're all cobalt blue than if they're assorted colors.

Figure 25-1:
A few key accessories make a dramatic statement.

- If you're not sure which color to choose for pillows and other accessories, take a cue from the most important pattern in your room. Choose accessories in the dominant color in that pattern.

- Group accessories by material (such as porcelain, leaded glass, or antique silver), color, or subject (for example, sculptures of animals). The stronger the relationship among the objects, the stronger the personal style statement.

- To achieve unity, you can tie together accessories that are near one another, such as the toss pillows on a sofa and the lamp base and porcelain dish on the adjoining end table, by choosing the same color and pattern.

- If less is more your style, be sure that each accessory is up to the test of going solo. Choose pieces with dramatic shapes, exotic colors, heroic sizes, or provocative subjects.

- Have you ever wished your room looked like one in a magazine? Then view your room as though you were looking at a magazine page. It's easy to do. Just stand in each of the room's four corners and look through a camera lens. Is there a blank spot? Add a suitable accessory! Do a few accessories in a group look weak and unimportant? Add more. Is there too much clutter and confusion? Remove or reorganize until your new "camera eye" likes what it sees. Remember: Cameras don't lie!

Accessories One by One

A few accessories for any room are a must. But, just which ones do you really need? Is "less is more" better than "more is more"? Accessories sometimes do more than add visual interest. Oftentimes they have a function. For example, pillows can cushion and cradle as well as serve as an accessory. And a wall in your home office on which your hang your diplomas and awards lets your clients know how accomplished you are — and reminds you that you're a professional. Whatever the other roles accessories may play, make the most of their ability to add dimension to your room.

Pillow talk

Toss pillows were originally intended to add comfort and support where and when they were needed. But over the years, they've become a major decorating statement. You can find them covered in every conceivable fabric, color, pattern, and shape, to suit any decor. The more decorative (and expensive) ones are treated with trim that may add a masculine note (with welting, moss, or deep fringe, shown in Figure 25-2) or a feminine note (with ribbons, fringe, ruffles, or lace). Some toss pillows are reversible — a solid color on one side and a pattern on the other, two different colors, or two different patterns, as shown in Figure 25-3. Two choices make it easy to reverse the pillow for a new look.

Figure 25-2:
Decorative
pillows with
a masculine
touch.

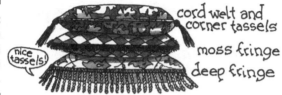

For easy cleaning, look for ready-made pillows with removable covers. Stuffing may be down feathers (which need plenty of plumping), cotton batting, or hypoallergenic synthetic fiberfill.

The current decorating strategy with pillows is to pile them several pillows deep on sofas and beds. Just be sure to leave enough room for sitting! We think it's best to leave sofas uncrowded and keep extra pillows handy in a basket.

You have oodles of options in arranging pillows. One easy arrangement alternates patterned and plain pillows in the same size and shape. You can also vary shapes so that you're mixing triangles, circles, rectangles, and squares, and pick sizes ranging from jumbo in the back to tiny in the front.

To successfully mix pillows in a variety of patterns and materials — such as chintz, needlepoint, suede, or embroidery — vary pattern sizes and scale and stick to a dominant unifying color.

Figure 25-3:
Patterned
pillows
contrast
boldly with
the white
slipcover
that
dresses a
wicker sofa
for indoors.

Mirror images

Nothing adds more decorating magic than mirrors. In addition to serving as a looking glass, they can double the pleasure of the view they reflect and add sparkle as they reflect and amplify light. Perhaps best of all, mirrors make spaces seem larger.

Place a mirror where you want to see your own reflection (an entry hall), reflect an interesting view (opposite a window), create a strong focal point (above a mantel), or light up a dark area (above a hall console or table in a corner). Regardless of where a mirror is placed, it should reflect something interesting. If the mirror doesn't reflect anything of interest, the effect is like hanging a frame without art. No matter how interesting the frame, the glass seems void and lifeless.

Frame-ups

Selecting framed mirrors in the same shape as a piece of furniture is always a safe bet. In a dining room with round- or shield-back chairs, for example, a round mirror above the mantel is a subtle and witty unifying element. Mirror frames come in every conceivable furniture style and period, including such favorites as Chippendale, Federal, Queen Ann, Empire, the Louises, Art Deco, and Modern, so matching mirror and furniture style is easy. But using a large modern mirror to add an eclectic note to a Traditional scheme, for example, is perfectly acceptable.

For variety, many frames that would look at home with fine art in them make fascinating mirror frames and look great in Traditional rooms. For the non-traditionalist, you can find many fabulous ethnic, whimsical, and purely creative styles.

Frame finishes range from traditional woods and wood tones to those gilded in a wide variety of bright to antique golds, as well as antique painted and decorated finishes in a diversity of periods and styles. You want a frame finish that's as formal or informal as your furniture. Choose one that con-trasts with the wall it's hung against: a dark frame to hang against a light wall or a light frame to contrast with a dark wall. The mirror frame should relate to the furniture below it in value (one shouldn't be too much lighter or darker than the other), if not in color.

Frame materials include finished wood, metal, bamboo, and stained glass. Newer, more eccentric designs may be ultra simple or heavily carved and embellished with natural-looking leaves and flowers as well as jewel stones, bits of marble, and colored glass. Contrast is important here, because the plainer the wall, the more elaborate the frame may be. The busier the wall, the plainer or simpler the frame.

Frame size is important. Like a work of art, a mirror should not be wider than the furniture below it nor less than two-thirds the width. If a mirror is too narrow to adequately fill the wall space, add paintings or sconces on either side. For more drama, hang a mirror vertically above a chest or console. Large mirrors can hang alone, without furniture beneath them. Medium-sized mirrors look more important if you group them with framed art, porcelain plates, or figurines and hang them above a dresser, chest, or table. A collection of tiny mirrors — especially those with inventive frames — can be grouped as would a collection of paintings.

Frameless fashion

Modern-style wall-hung mirrors may have no frame at all. Mirrors without frames, wall-to-wall mirrors, and do-it-yourself mirror tiles and panels can be found with plain or beveled edges. Beveled-edged mirrors are heavier, more substantial looking, and work well in Traditional interiors. Plain-edged mirrors look especially sleek and modern and get along well in Contemporary settings.

Colored and other glass

Clear glass is the norm for framed mirrors in Traditional styles. But more decorative glass includes mysterious, darkened, splotched-looking, antique glass (the real thing occurs when the mirror backing begins to deteriorate). A wide variety of colored glasses are available, ranging from a steel gray to various metallic colors, including copper and bronze. Another unusual glass is amber, a jewel-stone color.

Clear glass reflects only what's put in front of it, so it's acceptable in almost any setting. Antique glass is a natural with antique or traditional frames and furniture and can be a striking eclectic accent in a Contemporary room. Colored glass requires a greater understanding of color relationships and a deft hand, but it's generally at home in Modern or Contemporary situations.

Colored glass, popular in Victorian times, adds a great deal of excitement to table settings that use colored goblets and serving pieces. Venetian glass, blown in exciting color combinations and extraordinary shapes, looks beautiful in Traditional and Contemporary decor. Sandwich glass, made in Sandwich, Massachusetts in the 1800s, is interesting and a collectible, as is the iridescent glass developed by Louis Comfort Tiffany in the late 19th century. Distinctive 20th-century green glassware by Anchor Hocking is a recent collectible. Modern Swedish glass is distinctively bold and beautifully colored.

Stained glass

Old stained glass windows have been a favorite decorative accessory for years. If they're in good shape, these old windows can easily be hung from hooks inside an existing window. An architect we know installed one as an interior window between an entry hall and an adjoining family room. Another way to display a stained glass window is to put it inside a custom-made back-lit frame.

If the glass in an old window is loose and rattles in the frame, or if the lead channels sag so that there's space between the channel and the glass, take the window to a restoration shop for repair before hanging.

Ceramics

Ceramics is a general category name for fired clay decorative objects. Ceramics can be grouped in several subcategories. Of particular importance are china and porcelain. Texture, a distinguishing characteristic and quality, is an important part of your decision about which of the following materials to choose:

- *China* is the name given to ceramic products, especially dinnerware. Three major types of China exist: porcelain, bone china, and earthenware. Items made of these materials, along with colored glassware, are abundant for decorating. If you compiled a complete list of items made of china, you'd be writing for who knows how long. Just a few of the possibilities include vases, ashtrays, small boxes with and without lids, candy dishes, bowls, plates, sculpture, figurines, and photograph frames.

- *Porcelain,* the most expensive ceramic, is made from a particularly fine, pure white, kaolin clay that becomes glass-like when the *hard-paste* material is fired. When it's *vitreous* or glassy, porcelain is extremely hard and durable and does not absorb stains. Porcelain decorations are extremely fine and elegant, and they fit nicely in ritzy rooms. One great way to display porcelain plates is by hanging them in a decorative arch, as shown in Figure 25-4.

- *Bone china* or *porcelain* mixes bone ash to the porcelain mixture. It's not quite as hard as limoges porcelain, so it chips more easily. It's also not as white as porcelain.

- *Earthenware* pottery is quite porous, and it does absorb stains. The finishing glaze that gives it color and pattern is vulnerable to chipping. Earthenware is both inexpensive and popular. It's also rustic and right for Country-style rooms.

When you buy functional ceramic accessories, check to see whether you can clean them in your dishwasher.

Ceramic tiles

Decorated ceramic tiles are becoming popular as wall decor. Some tiles come self-framed; others are framed in wooden moldings. Subjects are often framed murals of rural scenes, floral bouquets, and Renaissance images made up of several tiles, with and without grout lines showing. Crackled glazes add an aged look. Individual tiles also can be displayed on a small easel, grouped for tabletop display, or used as coasters.

Add felt circles to the bottoms of ceramic tiles so that they don't scratch your table.

Flower power

Nothing is more decorative than flowers — fresh, of course, when they're available and advisable. The English way with flowers — straight from the garden and plopped into a big vase — is informal and fun. So is the idea of sticking a few stems into an old teapot, an interesting goblet, or a quaint tin can.

We once picked up a rusty, much-used paint pail from a rubbish heap, filled it with branches of green leaves and roadside tiger lilies, and placed it on a picnic table as a centerpiece for a photo shoot for *Home Mechanix Magazine*. "Whoa . . . pretty sophisticated," the photographer yelled. Actually, the rusted can with gray-blue and deep coral paint drips down its sides, filled with green leaves and orange tiger lilies, was pretty stunning. It was also handy (we were 25 miles from the nearest nursery) and cheap!

Arrangements by florists can look contrived and formal, but they don't have to. Just tell your florist what you're looking for. You may want to bring your vessel in so they can arrange your flowers just so.

At one time, silk or any kind of artificial flower was frowned on. Not anymore. Silk flowers not only look real, but they're also beautiful in their own right. Mixed with corkscrew vines and branches, they make dramatic focal points. They're the perfect solution if you travel a lot or want to stay within budget (you won't have to buy fresh flowers weekly!). Many silk arrangements are spectacular and well worth the having.

Save on silk flower arrangements by selecting stems and creating your own arrangement. They last forever without any care other than an occasional dusting.

Dried flowers and plants have also come into their own, now that folks have learned to appreciate their soft, faded beauty. You can air-dry plants by hanging them in bunches upside down in a dry, dark room that's well ventilated; air-drying takes about three weeks. Silica gel products are available in craft shops, and easy-to-follow directions for gathering, drying, and preserving make creating your own dried arrangements and wreaths of wild and cultivated flowers, weeds, and foliage an enjoyable pursuit. This process absorbs the moisture from the plant quickly so that it retains both form and bright color. (Check out a craft shop for instruction books and supplies.)

Show off silk and dried flowers in season. Change arrangements to fit the time of year. A bouquet of jonquils doesn't look nearly as convincing in December as it does in the springtime. Conversely, there's something unsettling about poinsettias in the spring. Nature knows best — have bouquets designed for different times of the year, and stay in sync with the growing calendar. Stay true to nature: Match flowers with the season, mix only flowers that bloom during the same season (no spring irises with fall mums, for example), and keep color schemes synched to both reality and your decorating scheme.

Don't forget trees and shrubbery as indoor decoration. Fake is fine, but don't use fake potted plants in illogical places. Trees, like flowers, need light, so placing them by a window or door makes sense. Everyone may know that your tree is a fake, but you'll suspend disbelief if you place it in a natural spot. Placing even a fake tree in a dark, unlighted hallway seems silly.

Collections

Collectors eager to show off their spoils have led the way in using collections of all sorts as decorations. Old toys, rusted iron farm objects, baskets, sculpture, thimbles, dolls, doll houses, miniature furniture, quilts, samplers, matchbooks, fans, antique evening purses, gelatin or chocolate molds — the list of possibilities is endless. Despite the number of china and curio cabinets and glass-topped display tables available, finding a way to adequately protect your collection while you show it off can present a challenge. Here's where you need ingenuity and perhaps the advice of professionals. Drapery shops can help you solve the problem of how to hang textiles best. Cabinetmakers can help you create a piece of furniture for displaying three-dimensional objects that are a challenge. Frame shops are also excellent sources of ideas for displaying collectibles on the wall.

Quilts

Collectible textiles in the form of quilts, tapestries, and handcrafted area rugs make impressive wall hangings. They're especially good for use in rooms with cathedral ceilings and in stairwells where large pieces are needed to fill two-story wall spaces. These wall hangings need special consideration. First, they should be carefully mounted so that the fibers aren't strained. Secondly, avoid hanging them in direct sunlight, which will fade and weaken the fibers.

Throws

Throws, afghans, and giant shawls, kept handy as cover-ups during a quick snooze on the sofa or to snuggle in while you watch TV, can serve many decorative roles. Fortunately, throws and afghans are readily available in a variety of fabrics, including wool, synthetics, and woven cotton. Afghans typically are knit or crocheted, but woven throws come in every conceivable color and pattern and in fabrics as plain as washable cotton and as fancy as cashmere. Shawls are readily available in department stores in challis wool (a very soft, finely woven wool) and synthetic fabrics. Antique silk and satin shawls and throws with rich, exotic trims may be more difficult to find, but they're worth the search. Of course, you can make your own silk or satin shawl, complete with fancy fringe.

Don't limit the many decorating roles of throws; instead, help yourself to ideas that make the most of these textile treasures, as shown in Figure 25-5:

- Fling a large fringed shawl over a grand piano, or use it to cover a round table — just like in old movies.

- If your sofa is dull and colorless, drape a beautifully colored or patterned throw across one end and toss pillows in the same colors at the other.

- Reduce the impact of a big, boring recliner by draping a throw across one side.

- Disguise a worn or boring footstool or ottoman by folding a throw and laying it across the top.

- Stack several colorful throws in a handsome basket and set it beside the hearth.

- Brighten up a boring wall by hanging a colorful throw on a low wooden curtain pole and brackets.

- In the bedroom, cover a rectangular table with a throw to serve as a dressing table or desk.

- Slipcover a small chair by tossing an eye-catching throw over it and tucking it in around the pillows. Secure it around the base with a rope or ribbon.

- Create an instant valance by draping a throw over the top of the window and securing it with high style hold-backs found in drapery stores.

Figure 25-5:
Cozy throws add a layer of interesting softness.

Screen tests

Movable screens have been around for about 3,000 years, and we haven't tired of them yet! They were probably invented for practical reasons — to conceal things, shield a door, serve as a dressing screen, create a wall, or block an unattractive view — but they're also very decorative. A screen makes a romantic frame for a sofa, introduces a sense of architecture (height and depth), holds favorite pinned-up snapshots, and provides gorgeous color, texture, and pattern that can be the focal point in a room.

Carved screens only partially conceal but let in light. Screens with *transoms* (see-through tops) provide privacy but look lighter than solid screens. Small, decorative, Oriental screens are often mounted on the wall, like art, above a sofa, a chest, or the headboard in a bedroom.

Style is important. Select a screen that is compatible with your furniture style and the mood of your room. An undulating screen with a sculptural Modern look, for example, doesn't mix well with Traditional furniture. And an iron screen with a *filigree pattern* (fancy, ornamental cut-outs) that looks ill at ease in a Modern setting is right at home in a garden room.

Screens intended for practical use are usually at least 6 feet high and have no fewer than three 2-foot wide panels. A screen that's 8 feet high is more dramatic but can be intimidating. A screen of four or more panels provides better coverage if it's to be used as a dressing screen or to conceal. Screens should be light enough to be easily moved, preferably by one person.

Check the hinges — they should be heavy-duty and double-action to allow the screen to bend in two directions for greatest flexibility. If your favorite screen style has feet, they should be sturdy and stable.

Hardware

Doorknobs, drawer pulls, curtain rods, and all kinds of interior hardware should also be chosen for their decorative value and should fit the rest of your decorating scheme.

Add a smashing bit of style with decorative hardware. Metals — wrought iron, antique and hammered bronze, brass, gold, silver, pewter, and aluminum — all have distinct character that lend themselves to designs of particular styles and periods. Be careful to select the ones that add to your plan.

Found objects

Imagination counts for a great deal in decorating. It's amazing what you can find right under your nose when you just stop to look. Countless times, we've said to clients and friends, "What you need on this coffee table is a big, round, white box or bowl. Do you have one?" More times than not, the answer is "Yes." Usually the big, round, white box or bowl is stashed away in some dark closet instead of out on the coffee table, earning its keep.

The first thing you should do when you need a decorative object to fill up space is check your cabinets and closets. Check your attics for old suitcases that you can stack and use as tables and trunks that double as a coffee table. The unexpected (and formerly useless) can make a statement, as in the stacked suitcases shown in Figure 25-6.

And don't forget the barn. Handsome leather saddles that linger after the horse has gone can do double-duty as a footstool! Of course, old yard and farm tools make unique accessories in Country-style or rustic rooms.

Beaches and backyards are good sources for interesting objects that cost nothing. Rocks and shells, washed and piled up on a beautiful plastic, glass, or silver tray can be totally captivating and fill up a blank spot on that table by the window. Driftwood makes great sculpture. So do birds' nests. Tree branches and bamboo poles are even showing up in homes as curtain rods.

Figure 25-6:
Old suitcases stacked up create an artsy end table.

Part VIII
The Part of Tens

The 5th Wave   By Rich Tennant

"When Harry decided to 'personalize' an area of the house, I had no idea he'd choose the kitchen."

In this part . . .

A part of every *...For Dummies* book, The Part of Tens provides quick, handy, and informative chapters covering some of the little extras in decorating you may not find anywhere else. These chapters cover everything from making old furniture work in a new place to updating an old lamp. Consider these chapters an extra treat. Enjoy!

Chapter 26

Top Ten Ways to Make Old Furnishings Work in a New Setting

- -

In This Chapter

▶ Painting to please

▶ Re-covering to renew

▶ Rearranging to revive

▶ Resizing to rejuvenate

▶ And more!

- -

*J*ust moved? Do your old furnishings, which looked so good in your last place, suddenly look out of place? Do you have too many pieces of furniture? Or too few? Is the color, style, or appearance just plain wrong? Want to keep the pieces rather than replace them? Follow these ten easy remedies designed to make ailing furniture fit into new surroundings.

Paint Play

Spread or spray a new color on old wood or metal furniture. A black, wrought iron, base table may seem too harsh and crude in a dusty-red room. The solution: Enamel it with Chinese red colored paint, and add finishing touches of gold to highlight decorative detailing. The wood of an inexpensive put-it-together-yourself (often referred to as knockdown [KD] or ready-to-assemble [RTA]) pine chest may have looked great in New York but appear awful in its new Florida setting. You can paint it sky blue and breathe new life into a once sorry-looking piece.

New Room, New Role

Find a new use for old furnishings. A chest of drawers was one too many pieces of furniture for the bedroom in a new home. Rather than give away the piece, the owner moved it into the dining room and used it as a buffet instead. Another person could find no space for her charming, antique-green, French Provincial vanity table. She placed it instead in her kitchen with its avocado green stove, where the vanity makes a great place to take phone calls, write notes, or add a dab of lipstick.

Slip On a New Cover

Upholstered sofas and chairs that don't work with the new location's carpeting or wall color deserve a cover-up. Slipcovers can be custom-made or ready-made. The variety of fabrics and styles is vast. A slipcover is out there to suit anyone's fancy and everybody's price range.

Reupholster

The permanent solution for upholstery that doesn't go with the new setting is to reupholster. Although this can be costly, if your furniture is well made, reupholstering may be less costly than buying new sofas and love seats of the same quality construction.

Artful Cover-ups

Don't bother repainting an old round or rectangular table that you want to use as a bedroom desk or dressing table — just drape a large, to-the-floor sheet, comforter, or dhurrie rug over it. (Consider topping it with cut-to-fit glass, for protection.)

Regroup and Recoup

If your room needs a specific kind of furniture that you don't have and perhaps cannot afford, consider grouping existing pieces that can serve the same function. We created a media center by flanking a china cabinet with glass doors on top and solid wood doors on the bottom with several inexpensive, ready-to-assemble (RTA) mahogany bookcases (in similar finishes).

The china cabinet holds the TV on the top shelves and stores tapes below. To add an interesting touch and make our new media center a focal point, we pulled the china cabinet forward about 10 inches to create a blockfront effect.

Hidden Treasures

You may move into a house and not be able to find a place for a certain piece of furniture. This problem is especially common for big pieces, such as triple dressers. We realize that some furniture just won't work with a new setting, no matter how hard you try. Does that mean you have to throw the piece out? Of course not! Use it in hidden spaces. For example, if you run out of wall space for a big dresser, bookshelf, or cabinet, place it inside large closets to store shoes, purses, and other necessities.

Faux Fun

Does your Queen Anne dining room furniture that looked so wonderful when you lived in an urban setting seem too fussy and formal in your new place? Gain a new casual look with a faux finish from a kit. You can choose among lots of options, including crackle, marble, and a new granite or stone look. Kits make it easy for anyone to transform furniture.

If you're really in an adventurous mood, you may opt to paint on freehand floral or geometric patterns. Or, you may want to try your hand at *trompe l'oeil* — a painting technique designed to fool the eye. Look in your local craft shop for books on faux painting that lead you step-by-step through the process of creating various fun finishes.

Go to New Heights

Need a tall piece of furniture to create drama in high places? Take a tip from a clever designer who stacked a small, plain chest of drawers atop a low, wide, sturdy table, and topped them off with a glass-doored cabinet. Because the pieces were made from different woods, she treated her new creation to a new, antique-white, crackled finish. The new piece is not only decorative but also a great storage place.

Don't hesitate to experiment. Regroup, restack, reconfigure — and let your eye be the judge!

When you stack furniture, be sure that it won't tip over. For safety's sake — especially in homes where small children are around — consider attaching to the wall all pieces of furniture that could tip over.

Cut It Down to Size

Another way to create harmony from discord, or gain a much-needed piece of furniture without going out and buying it, is to simply change the size of a piece of furniture. For example, create a coffee table from an old dining room table by sawing off the legs at the appropriate height, as shown in Figure 26-1. (If the table is especially nice, you may want to have this done by a carpenter.) For convenience, consider adding *casters* (small rollers or swivel devices) to the bottom of the legs.

Figure 26-1: Saw off the legs of an old dining table to make a coffee table.

Make Old Furniture Work!

Cut down the legs of an old table so it's coffee table height!

Chapter 27

Top Ten Tips to Update an Old Lamp

. . . .

In This Chapter

▶ Creating shades of glory

▶ Beautifying bases

. . . .

Some designers refuse to use lamps, they say, because lamps can date a room so quickly. Although most folks use lamps because they need them, we agree: Lamps can become tired and sadly out of date. Here are 10 ideas for updating old lamps that may be out of fashion, don't suit your current decorating style, or are flea market finds that deserve a new lease on life. These ideas are just that — viable ideas. For actual how-to information, check with your local craft shop for specific products and detailed instructions.

Off with the Old Shade and On with the New

One of the quickest ways to give your lamp a new look is to top it with a new shade. Take your lamp to the nearest shade shop and try on a few new shades until you find the one that's just right. For great-looking, inexpensive shades, try Target; Bed, Bath & Beyond; Home Place; and similar stores.

Infuse an Old Shade with Flower Power

Attach silk flowers with the proper adhesive (ask your craft shop maven) solidly over a faded white or ivory shade. We've seen a lampshade done up in rosebuds that was sheer magic! This suggestion is especially romantic for a bedroom.

Spatter On Paint

White ginger-jar lamps can be pretty boring and create no impact when silhouetted against a white wall. Add some pizzazz and real Country style by spatter painting the base and/or the shade. To spatter paint, use a toothbrush dipped into an appropriate paint (ask your craft shop expert to recommend a ceramic paint) in the color of your choice to fleck paint onto the base. Cover the base as lightly or heavily with flecked specks and spatters as you like.

Rope In Some New Style

Give the base enough rope — and a nautical look! Wrap the base in rope by winding it around and around, gluing it into place as you work.

Create a Mosaic Look

You can invigorate a ceramic-base lamp with mosaic. Crafts groups often do mosaic projects, using grout and crushed china plates. Perhaps you can find a group in your neighborhood or check your library for mosaic how-to books and adapt the directions to your lamp project.

Go for a Country Cottage Look

Make your lamp think it's in the country by hand-painting simple geometric shapes — circles, swirls, dashes, and dots — in a plethora of colors. Stick to either a primary or pastel color scheme and plot out your design before you start painting.

Decoupage Your Lamp

Experiment with decoupage, either on the lamp shade, base, or both. Decoupage kits make the whole process fairly simple, and the look is terrific. Determine your subject matter and then find the clippings that you want to glue on. Magazines, flower catalogues, and so on are excellent sources for clippings.

Age a Wooden Base in a Jiffy

An easy-to-use antique paint kit is your route to making an ordinary lamp base extraordinary. We've seen choices of crackle and glazed finishes that are very handsome.

Produce an Antique Finish

Give a carved wood or plaster base a patina. Shop the craft shops for a kit that can give your lamp an aged-bronze or copper look.

Add Sparkle

Glue faux jewels to the base and/or the shade, add beaded fringe to the bottom of the lamp shade (check out Figure 27-1 for an example), or attach gold braid and trim to the shade.

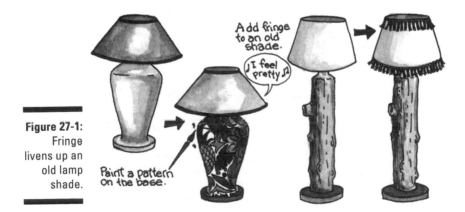

Figure 27-1:
Fringe livens up an old lamp shade.

Index

(continued)